THE WEXFORD RISING IN 1798

THE
WEXFORD
RISING
IN 1798
ITS CAUSES AND ITS COURSE

CHARLES DICKSON

WITH AN INTRODUCTION BY
MICHAEL NICHOLSON

CONSTABLE · LONDON

This edition published in Great Britain 1997
by Constable and Company Limited
3 The Lanchesters, 162 Fulham Palace Road, London W6 9ER
First published in Ireland by The Kerryman Ltd, 1955
Copyright © Charles Dickson 1955
Paperback edition 1998
ISBN 0 09 478390 X
Printed in Great Britain by
St Edmundsbury Press Ltd
Bury St Edmunds, Suffolk

A CIP catalogue record for this book
is available from the British Library

ACKNOWLEDGEMENT

I HAVE received willing and valuable help from many persons and among these I wish to express my gratitude especially to the following:
Professor Seamus O Duilearga,
Rev. Brother Luke, Ballaghaderreen,
The Staffs of the National Library,
The Library of Trinity College, Dublin,
The Royal Irish Academy
and various Departments of State.
Messrs. P. S. O'Hegarty,
Diarmuid Coffey,
Seamus Doyle of Enniscorthy,
Gerard Donovan of Rosbercon,
Lieut.-Colonel J. E. Nolan and
the late Thomas Fleming of Shillelagh.

By the rage of party, or the influence of power, has the truth of history in all ages been distorted, obscured, or lost in oblivion. . . .
—The Rev. James Gordon.

In plain truth every religion is good, every religion is true to him who in his conscience believes it . . . but the good religion may be, and often is corrupted by the wretched and wicked prejudices which admit a difference of opinion as a cause of hatred.
—Daniel O'Connell (speech in defence of John Magee).

CONTENTS

CONTENTS

Part III.

FOREWORD

IT MAY seem desirable to justify the appearance of yet another book about County Wexford in 1798.

Firstly, practically all publications on this subject are long out of print and the best of them are becoming difficult to obtain. Secondly, the contemporary writers, perhaps naturally enough, were nearly all violently partisan and from them a case could readily be made for either side by a judicious selection of material.

It is hardly open to question that the works of later writers, with two or three honourable exceptions, have been merely propagandist and often unworthily and disreputably so.

It is felt that there is a place for a balanced re-telling of this painful and tragic, but proud story, and it is told here without a trace of conscious bias, sectarian or otherwise.

Thirdly, by drawing on unpublished manuscript sources, it has been found possible to supply the solution of some hitherto unexplained problems of that time.

Fourthly, an attempt has been made to present the picture in its own setting and in this way to enable the reader to identify actual places with persons and events.

There are many signs in County Wexford, as elsewhere, that local knowledge and that proper pride which comes with such knowledge, are sadly lacking among the younger generation. They are thus in danger of losing contact with their own past.

I have written this book in the hope and belief that it will help to quicken and maintain a living interest in that beautiful and historic countryside.

GAYFIELD,
KILLINEY,
COUNTY DUBLIN.

Introduction

by Michael J. Nicholson

CHARLES DICKSON's *The Wexford Rising in 1798* is one of a trilogy of books by the author that cover the dramatic events at this period in Ireland. The other two in the trilogy were *The Life of Michael Dwyer* and *Revolt in the North*.

1798: 'THE YEAR OF LIBERTY', 'THE YEAR OF THE FRENCH' – those were names coined for a revolution that shook English control of Ireland to its core and left an indelible mark on Irish history for the next 200 years. Was Ireland ripe for revolution in 1798? Centuries of English rule with its suppression of religious and civil liberties had certainly prepared the way for revolt. The rising aspirations of the Irish middle and professional classes had found some expression in the 'Volunteer' movement of the 1770s, but when those were blocked a more militant outlook led to the formation in 1791 of the Society of United Irishmen. Such men as Arthur O'Connor, Thomas Addis Emmitt, Williams James McNevin and Wolfe Tone combined elements of classical republicanism, the ideas of the philosopher John Locke and the recent examples and ideologies of the French and American Revolutions to create a vocal and explosive challenge to English ascendancy rule in Ireland. The Society of United Irishmen included both Protestants and Catholics as its members and its non-sectarian approach won considerable support among a wide range of social groups and classes throughout Ireland. It has been a matter of considerable debate how far the Society of

United Irishmen had succeeded in organising and recruiting members in the County of Wexford where the Rising of 1798 was to begin. The absorbing issues for the mass of peasantry that composed such counties were overwhelmingly economic, rather than political or religious. Security of land tenure, the ability to regulate and pay rents and the nagging imposition of tithes payable to a Protestant ascendancy Church were the questions that occupied the minds of most of the people of Wexford. These grievances had found violent militant expression in the activities of rural groups such as the Whiteboys and Defenders, whose nightly attacks and depredations evoked near hysteria in the English Establishment. Indeed, as Charles Dickson illustrates, as early as July 1793 an attempt led by a young farmer, John Moore of Robinstown, to free several arrested Whiteboys from the gaol in Wexford town had led to a battle with the military in which several local men were killed and five others arrested and executed. This precursor to the events of 1798 had led to the manufacture of arms (notably pikes) and their concealment. The County of Wexford was thus, by the year 1798, already in a state of near insurgency and awaited only the spark that would light the conflagration.

The policy of the English Government and its agents in Ireland at this period has always been a subject of controversy and contradiction. The Government in London without doubt lived in fear of France and its Revolution. The possibility of the spread of French- or American-inspired revolutionary ideas in England occupied its attention and fuelled its fears. Ireland seemed particularly vulnerable to French influence, both in its susceptibility to and ripeness for revolutionary ideas and, more importantly, in its geographical and strategic position. The English Government, informed by its numerous spies and agents, was well aware of the organisation, aims and progress of the Society of United Irishmen, and was constantly badgered by its supporters in Ireland about the dangers of rural unrest as typified by the activity of groups like the Whiteboys and Defenders. Some of the English Government supporters had already taken independent action against such depredations by the formation of extra Yeomanry corps. A more virulent reaction was the formation of the militantly protestant Orange Society in September 1795 with the tacit or overt support of the English Government. The Orange Society from its inception mirrored the violent and provocative activities of its forerunner, the Peep of Day Boys, and intimidated both Catholics and Protestant dissenters, Presbyterians, Quakers and Methodists. As early as 1797 military commanders in Ireland were issuing warnings that such actions were driving large sections of the peasantry to desperation and possible insurrection. Such warnings went unheeded in a policy that seemed a deliberate attempt to provoke a rising in Ireland. Perhaps the English Government thought that such a rising, if provoked early and thus unprepared and starved of French aid, could be easily crushed by the available military forces. A failed rebellion and the ensuing repression would then give the English Government ample opportunity to enact a legislative Union of the two countries. The Irish problem, with its French dimension, would no longer exist. The only unknown factor in this equation was the scale and violence of the Rising that would ensue. If this was the English Government's plan, they gravely underestimated the strength, courage and determination of those they had provoked into rebellion.

By May 1798 the stage was set and Wexford was in a state of ferment and fear. The Yeomanry had been let loose upon the people by those magistrates determined to pacify the county. The peasantry were subjected to a ruthless campaign of terror and intimidation, a system later described by the Lord Lieutenant and Commander-in-Chief, Lord Cornwallis, as being 'universal rape and robbery throughout the whole country'. The tortures and murders, horrifying in themselves, were multiplied a hundredfold by rumour. Hysteria gripped both sides as the violence escalated. Yeomanry corps, in particular a notorious Welsh corps of fencible cavalry, the Ancient Britons and three corps of German dragoons were at 'free quarters' in the county. This was a punitive practice with units forcibly taking lodgings and supplies from the inhabitants, and many people slept out of doors at night in the fields and woods for fear of these and other gangs of marauding loyalists. The news from neighbouring County Wicklow of the mass murder of thirty-five prisoners at Dunlavin on 24 May and of twenty-four others at Carnew the next day made the Rising inevitable.

On Friday, 26 May 1798, in the Parish of Kilcormack a rebel party of Wexford men under the leadership of Father John Murphy accidentally encountered a patrol of the Enniscorthy Yeomanry commanded by Lt. Thomas Bookey. In the brief skirmish that followed, Bookey and his deputy officer were both killed and the Wexford men victorious. With news of this victory the Rising began and throughout Wexford men and women joined the rebel ranks.

It would take three long months before the Wexford Rising came to a close and the last surviving outlaw gang under an old rebel named James Corcoran were not hunted down and killed until the spring of 1804. The Rising, its prelude and bloody aftermath cost thousands of lives and the memory of 1798 has helped shape Irish culture and history for the past 200 years. Throughout Wexford are to be seen the memorials and statues dedicated to the events of 1798 and the brave men and women who died in that Year of Liberty. A wealth of songs, folk myths and legends have arisen from 1798, but nowhere is the true story of these stirring events told more accurately and lyrically than in the marvellous works of Charles Dickson.

Michael J. Nicholson
Manchester – January 1997

PART I

Retrospect

HISTORY, even local history, should not be a mere chronicle. It is the business of the honest historian to discover if he can, the motives of those who shaped the events of their time and to understand and endeavour to make others understand the influences which were at work upon friend and foe alike.

In applying this method to a restricted area like County Wexford in 1798, there are many difficulties. There is first and foremost the obstacle of *emotional resistance*. By this is meant that tendency which is inherent in us all, in varying degrees, to give less weight and credence to evidence which does not appear to favour our own preconceptions and predilections. It is an obstacle which I would ask all who may read the following pages to endeavour consciously to overcome. Propaganda at the time (and since) has been concerned to show either that the Rising was part of a popish plot for the extirpation of heretics, or that the Catholic population was to have been massacred by the Protestants who were erroneously given the general title of 'Orangemen'.

I am well aware how references to this subject are liable to be misconstrued, but on the other hand it is impossible to understand the actions of each side without a brief reference to the reasons why such propaganda was to a great extent successful.

I

In the first place, why was it so easy to persuade many Catholic members of the community that their lives were in jeopardy?

Ireland, partly owing to her geographical position, remained for a time undisturbed by the movement which convulsed the continent of Europe and of which Martin Luther was merely the rather vulgar mouthpiece. The quarrel between Church and King in England, however, began to be felt in this country after the fall of the House of Kildare (about 1535) when the abbeys were dissolved and their emoluments vested in the crown, while at the same time the Church was reformed 'on lines similar to that of England, that is Catholic in doctrine, but royal in government'.[1]

Henry VIII, whatever may be thought of his morals, was no reformer in matters of faith. He lived and died a Catholic and contented himself with being anti-clerical, like Erasmus. His despoiling of Church lands and goods was not an incident in the Protestant Reformation, as is so often supposed and he had received from Pope Leo X the title of Defender of the Faith for his treatise against Luther in 1521. He robbed the Church merely because he was an absolute monarch and in need of money.

The serious trouble for this country commenced at a later date, towards the end of the reign of his daughter Elizabeth. In this connection should be mentioned a matter which seems to be imperfectly understood on both sides of the Irish Sea and that is, that the greatest injury which England ever inflicted on the Irish people was to combine with her first great war of extermination at the end of the sixteenth century her zeal for the Protestant Reformation, thus ever since identifying in the minds of many of our people the idea of Irish nationality with the religious faith of the majority, since both were simultaneously assailed.

[1] E. Curtis: *History of Ireland*, p. 170.

Then came the Stuart period when Ireland suffered at the hands of both James I and Charles I. During the Cromwellian interlude she fought and bled in a quarrel not her own. When James II lost his throne in the Williamite revolution, she fought and bled again, not so much, perhaps, from any deep affection for the idea of monarchy as for a way of life and in defence of a religious faith.

Whatever may have been its results elsewhere the Williamite War inflicted a well-nigh mortal wound on a country struggling to recover from the Cromwellian barbarities then within living memory, in the course of which many places including the town of Wexford had felt the full weight of the policy of mass murder.

The Williamite War was followed by the violation of the Treaty of Limerick and the enactment of anti-Catholic penal laws which were only finally removed from the Statute Book in 1829! As a result of confiscation and penal enactments we have the sorry spectacle of a country governed for generations by a faction and in the sole interest of a minority, the people taxed to maintain a church establishment of that minority, the land alienated for the most part into the hands of that minority and the majority of the people forced to accept, *in their own country*, the position of unfranchised bondmen.

It should be remembered, however, that the penal laws in Ireland were not designed to extirpate Catholicism. They were concerned to ensure the retention in Protestant hands of Catholic lands and goods and as at least one Protestant writer has pointed out, had their effect been to convert the Catholic people, the whole scheme would have been defeated.[1]

Then came the revolt of the American colonies, the rise of the Volunteers, the Constitution of 1782, the meagre Catholic

[1] John Mitchel: *Jail Journal* (1854), p. 10.

Relief Act of 1793,[1] the constitutional agitation for Parliamentary reform and emancipation, the cynical preparations of Government to force a legislative Union as the only means of neutralising the effects of Emancipation which appeared to be inevitable and the fomenting of insurrection to terrify the propertied classes into agreeing to the destruction of even the partial liberty which, with so great labour, they had succeeded in achieving.

So much for the general background. The more immediate causes of fear will be referred to later.

There was, however, another side to the picture which in its turn was a cause of apprehension and suspicion among non-Catholics.

Ireland has suffered grievously in one important respect—she lies both too near and too far from her more powerful neighbour. Such events as the Protestant Reformation and Jacobitism, for example, vitally affected both countries, but in the course of time these upheavals ceased to be matters of cardinal national importance in Britain. In Ireland, however, the reaction to the religious side of Jacobitism continued very much alive and the events enshrined in the names of Derry, Aughrim and the Boyne are still, as it were, 'an impulse of yesterday'.

The Protestant community in Ireland found themselves in an anomalous position. Their strength lay in the fact that it was the policy of the British Government to maintain them with all its armed power; their weakness, that their land tenure rested ultimately on confiscation.

On the religious side they had heard of the zeal of Catherine de Medici and of the horrors recalled by the name of Saint Bartholomew, nor were they likely to forget the treatment of

---

[1]   This Act, whether by accident or design, appears to have had the effect of sowing dissension among those hitherto united—that is, between the Catholic aristocracy and Dissenters on the one hand and the Catholic masses on the other, these latter being the principal beneficiaries under the Act.

     This point is discussed by Philip Harwood: *History of the Irish Rebellion* (1848), p. 79, et seq.

the Protestant Huguenots in France, first by open persecution when 'Louvois' dragoons were quartered in their homes, and pillage, murder and rape became the price of continued loyalty to the faith of their fathers', and culminating in the revocation by Louis XIV of the Edict of Nantes (1685), 'prohibiting their worship, proscribing their ministers, destroying their churches, closing their schools and so driving some two hundred thousand of the best artificers of his kingdom into foreign lands'.[1] Many of them settled in Ireland and carried to this country the story of their unhappy experience.

Events nearer home at that time were in retrospect no more reassuring. It was easy to sympathise with the desire on the part of James II to procure some kind of equality for his co-religionists in that bigoted age, but it was remembered with deep misgiving that in pursuance of his designs he had declared that in such matters he regarded himself as above the laws of the land which he had sworn on his accession to maintain.

Protestant misgivings arising from historical retrospect were not relieved by the march of events since those more remote times and they genuinely feared the growth in political power of a church which laid claim to a monopoly of truth, a claim which they seem to have felt led logically to the enthronement of intolerance as a virtue.

Thus the preservation of what was then termed the 'Protestant ascendancy' took on a very definite *defensive* as well as an *offensive* character.

It is not surprising, therefore, that when the time was ripe to spread discord and suspicion the necessary material lay ready to the hands of the propagandists on both sides.[2]

[1] H. A. L. Fisher: *A History of Europe* (1936), p. 675, et. seq.
[2] The Government was fully aware of the possibilities of the situation. Thus, Pelham to Elliott (Military Under-Secretary) on June 3rd, 1798:
   '. . . it will be indubitably the object of the chiefs of the rebellion to fan the flames of religious dissension which the foolish and acrimonious conversation and conduct of the intemperate part of the Protestants will not tend to abate.'
   (Irish State Paper Office—hereinafter referred to by the initials I.S.P.O.)

Missionary zeal on behalf of the Reformation failed in Ireland. Coming as it did from England, it was too obviously identified with English policy and that policy to date had not succeeded in endearing itself to the Irish people. Such efforts thereafter were replaced by the more concrete measures of confiscation, plantation and penal law and in the course of time they were successful over large areas, particularly in the North.

The stage was thus set anew for the production of the old play of 'divide and conquer' which has had a phenomenally successful run from that day to this.[1]

In a 'humble petition to the King's Most Excellent Majesty', on 8th May, 1797, the Freeholders of the County of Antrim (the Hon. Chichester Skeffington in the chair), charged His Majesty's ministers with 'having laboured with the most remorseless perseverance to revive those senseless and barbarous religious antipathies, so fatal to morals and peace'.

'Power, Property and Church Establishment' [1]

IT WOULD, in my opinion, be no extravagance to describe power, property and church establishment, in the sense in which they were then understood, as the triple curse of Irish life in the eighteenth century and the determination to maintain them *at all costs* was, without any doubt, a root cause of the insurrection and of the miseries which preceded, accompanied and followed it.

The power referred to was that which, from causes already mentioned, was monopolised by a small ascendancy faction; the property was that possessed by this faction and acquired for the most part, by means known to every student of history, while church establishment was a system whereby Catholic and Dissenter were compelled to contribute to maintain the church of that minority faction who, as long as they possessed the power and the property, affected to despise Catholic and Dissenter alike upon whom they so largely depended for their support. The situation was fantastic.

At length, however, instead of two 'classes' only, there gradually emerged a third possessing neither power nor property except such as was derived from their mercantile activities and for the most part indifferent to church establishment.

[1] As early as 1792, Pitt and Westmorland, the Viceroy, had agreed on the desirability of an union on the grounds that 'admission of Catholics to a share of suffrage would not then be dangerous. The Protestant interest, in point of power, property and church establishment would be secure, because the decided majority of the supreme legislature would necessarily be Protestant.' See *Westmorland Correspondence*, I.S.P.O.

7

A natural result of the growth of this middle-class was the development of liberal opinion and resentment at the denial of the elementary rights of free men to the vast majority of their fellow citizens. This was the response in Ireland to the European ferment which was the cause of the decline of the idea of absolute monarchy and of the growth of parliamentary government.

The Northern Whig Club[1] was founded in Belfast in 1790 and a movement took shape, the objects of which were later described by Henry Grattan as 'a reform of parliament which should give a constitution to the people and the Catholic emancipation which should give a people to the Constitution'. The Society of United Irishmen, founded in Belfast in 1791, offered a means by which all men of goodwill could combine for the furtherance of their objects and the Society included persons of widely differing outlook. It was inevitable that such a Society would encounter many difficulties, some of which were well described in a letter written fifty years afterwards:

There were 3 Distinct Parties in this country, not cooperating, often contending . . . there were 1st 'actual Reformers', 2nd 'Emancipators', 3rd 'Revolutionists', all these cooperated, but on many occasions diverged—they were 3 instruments in a Concert, very good when in tune and sounding together harmoniously, but when the 2nd or 3rd fiddles absorbed the whole, it did not prosper, hence the Presbyterians, who were principally of the 1st and 3rd class and with whom the thing originated when Emancipation was a *secondary* object, would not move in unison with the Party to whom Emancipation was the primary object and so on— and according as the one or other motive preponderated, they often intersected each other, and this alone was the cause of their failure —I saw a great deal of their difficulty constantly arising from this Defect in their plan or system—a considerable Nọ of leading Reformers receded when the Oath was first propos'd and never

[1] The Madden MSS. in T.C.D. Library contain an autograph list (undated) of sixty names of its members, including all that was best of Protestant liberal opinion there, and strangely enough, we find in this list the names of both Theobald Wolfe Tone and Robert Stewart (afterwards Lord Castlereagh)!

returned—and yet this oath became afterwards the strongest bond of union among the rest. . . .[1]

Reform of the legislature and the redistribution of political power were more the concerns of the so-called middle and upper classes and such considerations hardly touched the bulk of the people. With property and church establishment it was far otherwise. There were no effective laws to regulate rent in accordance with the capacity of the tenant to pay, or to secure the latter in his tenancy, or the fruits of his labour. There was in addition the galling exaction of the tithe from his scanty earnings for the upkeep of a church not his own.

I have dwelt on the subjects of church establishment and sectarianism because, in my opinion, it was the questions of tithe payments and emancipation (especially the former) which chiefly exercised the minds of the people of County Wexford towards the end of the eighteenth century. This county had for years before 1798 been most active in the anti-tithe agitation and as early as July, 1793, this had led to the arrest of several Whiteboys or Defenders in the neighbourhood of Enniscorthy and their removal to the gaol in Wexford beside Stonebridge. A large crowd of men approached the town with the object of rescuing the prisoners. They had provided themselves with rude weapons, chiefly farm implements, but were apparently without firearms. The garrison turned out and the collision took place at the top of Hill Street as the party of Defenders endeavoured to enter the town from the direction of Taghmon.

The officer commanding the military party was killed early by the blow of a scythe, following which some *eighty of the would-be rescuers were shot down*, including their leader, a young farmer named John Moore of Robinstown. Taylor, the 'loyalist' historian, records that both Moore's legs were broken by the first volley 'but so very zealous was he in that cause that

[1] Dr. James McDonnell (Belfast) to Dr. R. R. Madden, 17th May, 1842. Madden MSS. T.C.D. Library.

he fought on his stumps . . . and was shot by the military'. He was buried at Carnagh, near New Ross. Five others were arrested and executed.

Such incidents as this would naturally lead to the manufacture and concealment of arms and I think it is highly probable that many of the pikes surrendered in the early months of 1798 had been for some years in the possession of their owners.

In County Wexford preparations appear to have been made more on the lines of the Defender organisation, than on that of the Society of United Irishmen and some support is given to this view by a correspondent who informed Father Patrick F. Kavanagh (the historian) that on his side of the county, 1798 was referred to as 'the second rebellion' and 1793 as the first. In addition, significantly enough, Lieutenant-Colonel Foote of the North Cork Militia, in a letter to Castlereagh, written in Wexford after his escape from Oulart Hill, refers to the force under Father John Murphy as Defenders.[1] The term Defender was still being used in government documents as late as 1800.[2]

The literature of this period, both public and private, is full of evidence that the 'middle class' was of such recent growth that the general bent of men's minds was still largely determined by social distinctions based on a property qualification. Those in power simply could not understand how men of property like Bagnal Harvey, Colclough, Cornelius Grogan, Fitzgerald, Perry and the rest, with no material benefit to expect from reform and emancipation, could actively sympathise with their less fortunate fellow-countrymen.

[1] I.S.P.O.
[2] See also letter from Lord Mount Norris to Elliott quoted on p. 22.

Yeomanry and Militia

THE YEOMEN OF 1798 were the successors of the Irish Volunteers of 1778-82, but with an important difference. The older body rose spontaneously in national defence and were self-supporting. They forced from the Government that instalment of political liberty enshrined in the constitution of 1782, but in an evil hour they were induced to disband. Militia were embodied in 1793 and later still (1796) it was decided to enrol the new yeomanry. To both these projects there was violent opposition attended by bloodshed. Lord Fitzwilliam, during his brief vice-royalty, had proposed the raising of yeomanry, but the Government had refused, partly, apparently, to prevent arms getting into the wrong hands and partly to avoid offending the militia who, it was thought, might not be easily convinced of the necessity for a new force in addition to their own. The eventual decision to enrol yeomanry seems to have been influenced by the suspicion of the militia which was felt by the gentry.

The chief difference, apart from origin, between the old Volunteers and the new yeomanry was that the commissions in the latter were from the Crown and as it was by design a project for 'arming the property of the country' it was naturally enough regarded as a means of arming Protestants against Catholics. In the north this was the case from the beginning; in the south, for example in County Wexford, such Catholics as had joined were for the most part got rid of in the early months of 1798, by the imposition of a new test oath.

The estimate first presented to Parliament mentioned 20,000 men for the whole country, but within six months this number had risen to 37,000 and later it increased again to 50,000. The later increase may have been due to the addition of what were known as 'supplementaries' hastily enrolled and armed after the capture of the Leinster Directory in March, 1798. These under the command of such 'active' magistrates in County Wexford as Hunter Gowan of Mount Nebo, and Hawtrey White of Peppard's Castle, came to be known as the 'black mob'. Lecky states that 'in great districts which were torn by furious factions it consisted exclusively of the partisans of one faction, recruited under circumstances well fitted to raise party animosity to fever heat. Such men with uniforms on their backs and arms in their hands and clothed with the authority of the Government, but with scarcely a tinge of discipline and under no strict martial law, were now let loose by night on innumerable cabins.'[1]

The Government used this weapon to force the people to take the field before a French landing and in this policy it must be admitted they were successful.

When actual hostilities commenced, as has been stated, these yeomen were almost entirely a Protestant force[2] and this in its turn served to fan the flames of sectarian hatred especially when for weeks before the rising actually took place, they were employed by the fanatical magistrates in north County Wexford to terrorise the people by whipping, house-burning and otherwise, and eventually to drive them from their homes in ever increasing numbers. This aspect of the business, though mentioned by some writers, has hardly received in detail the attention it deserves.

[1] *History*, Vol. IV, p. 39.
[2] Hay states that no Catholic was admitted even to the old Volunteers in County Wexford and that Wexford was the only county where this was the case.

In the case of the militia on the other hand, the officers were, for the most part, Protestant and the men Catholic (at least in the south) and were chiefly remarkable for the incompetence of the officers and the indiscipline of the rank and file. It is likely that had the tide of war flowed in favour of the insurgents, most of the militia would have changed sides. As it was there were considerable desertions on receipt of the news of Humbert's landing on the 22nd of August, 1798, and Joseph Holt has stated that he had with him deserters from thirteen different regiments!

The popular view of the cause of the outbreak receives confirmation from an unexpected quarter. General Lake's biographer expressed himself as follows: 'It appears unhappily clear that in Wexford at least, the misconduct of the militia and yeomanry and particularly that of a corps of German cavalry and of the Welsh corps known as the Ancient Britons, was largely to blame for the outbreak and . . . it can only be said that cruelty and oppression produced a yet more savage revenge.'[1]

As early as April, 1797, it had become so apparent that 'the Government had been deliberately propagating religious animosity and persecutions' especially in the north, that the Duke of Leinster resigned his command of the Kildare militia. Lord Bellamont retired from the Cavan militia and Henry Grattan withdrew from the yeomanry. Grattan, with perhaps excessive optimism in view of the rapidly changing state of the country, expressed himself anxious to see the old Volunteers of 1778 re-established, on the grounds that the mass of the people would look on them as friends, whereas they already regarded the yeomanry as enemies.

Brigadier-General (later Sir John) Moore stated that 'when the militia were first formed had pains been taken to select

[1] Col. Hugh Pearse. *Memoir of the Life and Military Services of Viscount Lake.* (1744-1808), p. 95.

proper officers and to introduce discipline, they might by this
time [16 February, 1798] have been respectable troops, but like
everything else in this country the giving of regiments was
made an instrument of influence with the colonels and they
made their appointments to serve electioneering purposes.
Every sort of abuse has been tolerated . . . the officers are, in
general, profligate and idle.'[1]

Lord Cornwallis, the Viceroy and Commander-in-Chief,
wrote a letter, marked 'private and confidential', to the Duke of
Portland on the 8th of July, 1798, in the following terms:

> The Irish Militia are totally without discipline, contemptible
> before the enemy when any serious resistance is made to them, but
> ferocious and cruel in the extreme when any poor wretches either
> with or without arms come within their power; in short murder
> appears to be their favourite pastime.[2]

There is ample confirmation of this terrible indictment.[3]

A recent writer mentions the strong probability that disaffection and indiscipline on the part of the Irish irregular
troops were, in retrospect, not altogether unwelcome to the
Government and especially Cornwallis who had been sent over
to consummate the Union and was in a position to use instances
of cowardly and rapacious conduct on the part of militia and
yeomen, to prove to the Irish gentry who opposed the Union
that they could rely on England alone to protect the country.[4]

---

[1] *Diary of Sir John Moore*, Vol. I, p. 273.
[2] Cornwallis: *Correspondence* (2nd Edition), Vol. II, p. 359.
[3] At the time when the 'loyalist' writers were showering praises on the conduct
of the troops, Brigadier-General John Moore was recording in the privacy
of his diary that the officers of the Militia were 'as ignorant and as much a
rabble as those who have hitherto opposed us. Our army is better armed
and provided with ammunition: that of the rebels has the advantage of zeal
and ardour. If the rebellion continues, or if the French effect a landing, even
in inconsiderable numbers, I shall consider the country as lost unless a
completely different system is adopted.'
[4] Sir Henry McAnally: *The Irish Militia* (1949).

The Catholic Church and the Rising

SIR RICHARD MUSGRAVE placed posterity in his debt by his industry, but his anxiety to prove that, especially in Wexford, the insurgent movement was a popish plot led him into extravagances of over-emphasis and of suppression which mar his work. He laboured to show that statements made by the Roman Catholic clergy and the actions of such men as Father John and Father Michael Murphy and others in protesting their loyalty and urging their people to surrender their arms were in reality merely examples of elaborate duplicity for the purpose of lulling the Government into a sense of security until the hour came to strike!

This I believe to be not only wholly false, but absurd as well. Apart from other considerations, I find it impossible to conceive that men actively preparing for war would insist on their followers surrendering their arms as part of that preparation.

It may be recalled that the Catholic Committee, with unbecoming humility, issued a 'Declaration of the Catholics of Ireland' as early as the 17th of March, 1792, composed of nine sections of which three are in the following terms:

Section 2: We abjure, condemn and detest as unChristian and impious the Principle that it is lawful to murder, destroy or anyways injure any Person whatsoever for and under the Pretence of their being Hereticks. . . .

Section 8: We do hereby solemnly disclaim and for ever renounce

15

all Interest in and Title to, all forfeited Lands resulting from any Rights, or supposed Rights of our Ancestors. . . .

Section 9: . . . if we shall be admitted into any share of the Constitution by our being restored to the Right of election Franchise, we are ready, in the most solemn Manner, to declare that we will not exercise that Privilege to disturb and weaken the Establishment of the Protestant Religion and Protestant Government of the Country.[1]

This declaration was signed by Edward Byrne (Chairman), and Richard McCormick (Secretary) and subscribed to by the Catholic Archbishop (Dr. Troy) and the other clergy of the Diocese of Dublin.

Three days after hostilities had broken out in Wexford—that is, on the 30th of May, 1798, the Lord Lieutenant was addressed in the following words:

We, the undersigned, his Majesty's most loyal subjects, the Roman Catholics of Ireland, think it necessary at this moment publicly to declare our firm attachment to his Majesty's royal person, and to the constitution under which we have the happiness to live. . . . We cannot avoid expressing to Your Excellency our regret at seeing, amid the general delusion, many, particularly of the lower orders, of our own religious persuasion engaged in unlawful associations and practices.

This loyal address was signed by Lord Fingall, Lord Gormanston, Lord Southwell and Lord Kenmare 'with seventy-two baronets, gentlemen of distinction and professors of divinity together with the Rev. Peter Hood, D.D., President of the Royal College of Maynooth, for himself and the professors and students of said College and above 2,000 whose names are too numerous to be inserted.'

Dr. Caulfield, the Roman Catholic Bishop of Ferns, boasted that only curates had taken part in the insurrection. He states:

Happy for those Popish priests of the County of Wexford that not one of them who had a flock, not one parish priest was implicated, or had any concern in fomenting, encouraging or aiding the rebellion. . . . I have good cause to know and to declare to the world that if the Popish, or parish priests had possessed that degree of authority

[1] This was embodied in the Catholic Relief Act of 1793, Section IX.

and influence attributed to them in this manner, there would have been no rebellion in that county; and if they retained, or obtained such influence after the rebellion broke out, their respective flocks would have laid down their arms and returned to their respective homes and to their allegiance to their King and Government.[1]

When General Lake entered the town of Wexford on the bloody day of Vinegar Hill, he 'acted with a brutal, stupid and undiscriminating severity that was admirably calculated to intensify and to prolong the conflagration'.[2] But Dr. Caulfield waited upon him and stated later: 'I know and shall ever gratefully acknowledge that he received me with politeness and, I must say, with kindness; for he gave me and the clergy of the town protections for our persons and properties, houses of worship and the exercise of our religious functions. God bless him and preserve him.'[3]

Dr. Caulfield, by a strange omission, makes no mention of the long list of sick and wounded stated to have been murdered in the hospital at Wexford after the arrival in the town of the same General Lake.[4]

I think it must be admitted from the quotations given above that the Catholic hierarchy and the parish priests may be acquitted of the charge of complicity in the Wexford insurrection.

At least eleven Catholic curates took an active part and of these three were executed, one was killed at Arklow and one died of wounds received during the retreat from Vinegar Hill. In addition, one (Father John Redmond of Camolin) was hanged, although almost certainly his only participation was an attempt to prevent looting at the house of his friend, Lord Mount Norris of Camolin Park.[5]

[1] *Reply of the Right Rev. Dr. Caulfield*, (1801), pp. 4 and 5.
[2] Lecky: *History*, Vol. IV, p. 46.
[3] *Reply of the Right Rev. Dr. Caulfield* . . . 1801, p. 11.
[4] Cloney: *Personal Narrative* (1832), p. 218.
[5] It may be added that in the counties of Antrim and Down, eighteen Presbyterian ministers were implicated, of whom two were hanged, six transported, three proclaimed and two imprisoned.

Miles Byrne denounced the Catholic clergy, not for having taken part in the war in Wexford, but for not having done so and he roundly declares that the 'priests saved the infamous English Government in Ireland from destruction'.[1]

The views of the hierarchy were largely determined by their abhorrence of 'French ideas' which were the inspiration of the United Irishmen. With the laity it was otherwise and they published a handbill on the 27th of March, 1798, containing these words:

> We are accused of a predilection for French principles—supposing the fact, who forced them on us? Men who have taken from us that which not enriches them, and makes us poor indeed.[2]

Of the curates who joined the ranks of the Wexford insurgents, a majority, if not all of them, were compelled to do so by the force of local circumstances, but I think Philip Roche and Moses (Mogue) Kearns required rather less compulsion than the others. They were both powerful men with some capacity for leadership and a taste for soldiering. In joining the priesthood they probably missed their true vocations.

Among the insurgent rank and file, in the course of the four frenzied weeks of active operations, heresy-hunting became widespread. There is a mass of evidence, reliable and beyond dispute, that large numbers of Protestants were compelled to conform, at least nominally and it is certain that in the town of Wexford during the insurgent occupation and in some other places, Protestants found it prudent to attend Mass as the only means of saving their lives.

Mrs. Brownrigg of Greenmound, states in her narrative that Dr. Caulfield came to see her while she was detained in Wexford. He 'was very kind and gave me an ample Protection, but like Harvey, declared he had no influence and added that he was cautioned in the street coming, to beware how he protected Protestants . . . the people could not be described, that in reality

[1] *Memoirs*: Vol. I, p. 39 (1906).
[2] *Report of Committee of Secrecy*, Appendix XXV.

the Devil was roaming at large amongst them . . . that they would make it a religious War which would ruin them.'[1]

The Rev. James Gordon, the most temperate of the 'loyalist' historians, states that 'no fact is more certain than that the common people of the Catholic persuasion in all parts at least of the County Wexford, whenever they had hopes of success in the rebellion uniformly declared that no other form of worship than their own must ever be permitted, and that God had never intended that any other should have place.'[2]

It has often been stated that the fanaticism of the insurgents was not directed against Protestants as such, but against Orangemen. Musgrave denies this on the ground that there were no Orangemen in County Wexford until the arrival of the North Cork Militia, on the 26th of April, 1798. It was widely held, however, that most of the insurgent rank and file made no distinction between them, or at least were readily convinced when they were told that all Protestants were Orangemen and that their aim was wholesale massacre of the Catholics. It is significant, nevertheless, that although there was no mistaking the Protestantism of the Quakers or Society of Friends, their immunity from personal violence was complete. The insurgents made free with their belongings, but refrained from injuring their persons. This was due to the fact that Quakers resolutely refused to take sides—they held themselves free to comfort and relieve, without distinction, all who sought their help.

In addition they were known to possess no offensive weapons and as a result their houses were safe from attack during those searches for arms which so often led to tragedy in the early days of the Rising.

One other matter may be mentioned in this connection. While, unquestionably, numbers of Protestants suffered death on account of their Protestantism, or their steadfast refusal to

[1] Wheeler and Broadley: *The War in Wexford.* p. 175.
[2] *History of the Rebellion* (1805), p. XIII.

conform at the bidding of the rabble, a large and now un-
identifiable proportion of these were yeomen or supplementaries
known, or believed to have been guilty of outrage, or oppression.
These were treated with as little mercy, especially during the
early days on Vinegar Hill, as the government forces treated
those known, or believed to be sympathisers, or participants
on the popular side.

Further references to this subject will be found in the
Chapters on Vinegar Hill and Wexford Bridge.

County Wexford
and the United Irishmen

IT HAS ALWAYS been a matter of uncertainty to what extent
the Society of United Irishmen had taken root in County
Wexford before the Rising. Francis Higgins, the informer,
wrote in October, 1797, that Wexford had then only enrolled
284 United Irishmen. An anonymous writer has stated that
when hostilities commenced, the number of sworn men in
the country did not exceed 360[1] Miles Byrne records that
the Society made great headway in his part of the county—
that is, in the vicinity of Monaseed—and he mentions that
Anthony Perry of Inch, 'was one of the first and most active of
the United class'. It is clear also that Byrne and his companions
were greatly influenced by Perry and held him in high esteem.
When we turn, however, to Perry's own account[2] and his
reference to the visits of the provincial organiser, William
Putnam McCabe,[3] we are left with the impression that although
meetings were held in his own neighbourhood, Perry had no

---

[1] *Irish Monthly Magazine*, Vol. II, May, 1883—an article entitled 'Fook's Mill'.
[2] See p. 45 et seq.
[3] The notorious Judkin Fitzgerald, Sheriff of Tipperary, in a letter to Lord
Castlereagh written from Clonmel on 15th June, 1798, refers to McCabe as
follows: '. . . the fellow within described was the right arm of Sedition in
the whole of this Province; if he was sent down to me by Yeoman expresses
I would make him enmesh the whole Province to me and then I would dispose
of him after—nothing would do more good to the cause here . . . .'

high opinion of the state of the organisation elsewhere in the county.

Miles Byrne explains the absence of information by reference to the fact that his relative, Robert Graham of Corcannon (a neighbour of Perry), who was county secretary, was late for the meeting of the provincial directory at Oliver Bond's house and that therefore, the nominal roll of sworn men from Wexford was not known to Government. It may be mentioned, however, that a press report giving a list of persons arrested 'at 11 o'clock on 12 March at Oliver Bond's' or later the same day, included one Peter Brennan designated 'delegate for Wexford'.[1]

I have been unable to obtain any further information about this man except that his name appears on the Banishment List and as Madden refers to him as coming from Portarlington, the press report is probably wrong.

After hostilities had commenced it became the practice to impose the oath of the United Irishmen, or some similar oath on every person who voluntarily or otherwise joined the insurgent forces, but this practice does not appear to have been seriously undertaken, at least in the town of Wexford, until the 14th of June.

Some interesting local information is contained in a letter dated 5th October, 1797, from Lord Mount Norris of Camolin Park to William Elliott, Dublin Castle:[2]

> . . . you have, of course, heard of the two barrels of gun-powder that were stolen out of a car at Newtown Barry, alias Bunclody—If my information is right the Theft may as well be imputed to collusion as to the Roguery of the neighbourhood of Clonegal and N.T.B., where, I understand, the United Irishmen have made many proselites! [sic] But Colonel Maxwell will assuredly prevent the

---

[1] *Freeman's Journal*—15th March, 1798. In the Register of Kilmainham Prison there is an admission on 13th March of a prisoner named Peter Bannan and as his name appears with those similarly charged with High Treason, it clearly refers to the same person.

[2] Military Under-Secretary—I.S.P.O.

future Progress of this growing Evil—! This strange fanaticism
is spreading rapidly in the county owing to the great supineness of
many gentlemen. One of my Corps made a Discovery of the
Progress of this horrid evil and I sent him to a Tennant of mine,
Mr. Hawtrey White, who has raised a troop of my Tennantry
principally—! Some of these cruelly deluded People have in
consequence thereof been Committed —! The Seat of these Defenders
is from beyond Newtown Barry, along by Slieve Buy, Slegower,
Little Limerick and Arklow, round by Lord Courtown's.—If a
troop was to be quartered at little Limerick under the command of
Mr. Hunter Gowan, of Mt. Nebo, a most active Loyal Magistrate,
things would soon be returned to good order—In case cavalry
cannot be spared, a company of infantry would be of great use.

Four days later Elliott replied: '. . . I am truly concerned
to hear that the spirit of disaffection has endeavoured to seduce
the loyal County of Wexford and directions shall be given for
sending troops into that Country'.

Madden, referring to William Putnam McCabe and his
attempt to organise County Wexford, states that the Wexford
people were apathetic and that the organisation made no way
in that county.

The position there, as I see it, was briefly as follows. The
lay leaders—that is, those who found themselves thrust into a
position of nominal leadership—most if not all of them against
their wills—were, practically without exception, well-disposed,
liberal-minded men, Protestant and Catholic alike, anxious to see
all Irishmen in a position of political equality by means of
Parliamentary reform and emancipation. That minority of them
who had taken the oath as United Irishmen, did so with these
constitutional objects alone in view. There was nothing of the
Jacobin about them. This certainly applies to Bagnal Harvey,
Edward Fitzgerald of Newpark, Dr. John Henry Colclough of
Ballyteigue, Matthew Keogh, Cornelius Grogan of Johnstown,
John Hay, Thomas Cloney and probably also, Anthony Perry
of Inch.

The *clerical* leaders, all of them curates and five of them destined to suffer death for their participation[1] may have been actuated by various motives. As I have stated elsewhere I am convinced that Father John Murphy of Boleyvogue and Father Michael Murphy of Ballycanew, were swept into the field on a wave of warm sympathy with their persecuted parishioners —a sympathy strong enough to constrain them to defy even episcopal censure. Father Philip Roche, Father Moses (Mogue) Kearns and Father Thomas Clinch were, I feel, in a different category. Big-bodied and big-hearted as they were, they seemed more designed by nature for the field and the camp than for the more usual exercise of their vocation.

The rank and file in Wexford were on the whole in the succession of the Defenders and as such the rapid declension of many of them in the later stages of the hostilities to stark fanaticism was more intelligible than it would have been had their inspiration derived solely from the principles of the United Irishmen.[2]

---

[1] I do not include Father John Redmond of Camolin, who was murdered. He took no part at all.

[2] In the north the Defenders became practically wholly absorbed in the Society of United Irishmen. In Wexford this took place in my opinion, to a minor extent only.

Although James Anthony Froude, in his references to County Wexford, relied chiefly on Musgrave, he was constrained to express himself as follows:

'Of all the counties of Ireland, Wexford had the fewest grounds for taking arms . . . with a fertile soil, a gentry and clergy generally resident, its towns thriving and a population made universally denser by the more advanced civilization of its inhabitants, it had escaped contact by its situation with the revolutionary elements at work in the rest of the island.'

See *The English in Ireland* (1874), Vol. III, p. 375.

County Wexford
and the Orange Institution

THE CATHOLIC RELIEF ACTS OF 1782 and 1793, coupled with
the rise of the Society of United Irishmen (founded in 1791),
one of whose objects was complete Catholic Emancipation,
raised in the minds of Irishmen the hope, or the fear, that in the
normal course of evolution the Irish Parliament was bound to
extend such measures until they reached their logical conclusion.
As this would mean a local legislature in which the majority of
members would be Catholic, it would naturally bring to an
end Protestant ascendancy and the rule of the majority by the
minority. The reaction was twofold—firstly determination on
the part of the British Government to encompass a legislative
Union, following which emancipation would be politically
harmless with Catholics in a permanent minority in the united
Parliament at Westminster; and secondly, an equally determined
resolve on the part of an active section of Protestants in the
north, (commencing in County Armagh) to take the law
into their own hands and to establish a local predominance by
terrorising their Catholic neighbours. This Protestant faction
was known as the Peep-of-Day Boys and their victims as
Defenders. The former enjoyed an obvious advantage in
having the actual, or implied support of the magistracy.

It is, I think, significant (although the coincidence appears to have escaped the notice of historians) that in 1784, two years after the first great step forward, the activities of the Peep-of-Day Boys began to attract public attention and, in 1795, two years after the second advance embodied in the Catholic Relief Act, they reached the summit of their power and on September 21st, the day of the 'Battle of the Diamond', they adopted the name of Orangemen.[1]

Once these sectarian feuds began they developed rapidly, and in the counties where Protestants were in a majority, the Catholics were ruthlessly oppressed. When, however, the movement spread to other counties where Catholics predominated, the opposite was the case and there, in addition, the agitation became strongly agrarian in character.

There is, however, in my opinion, no reasonable doubt that in its origin, this sectarian disorder was a Protestant reaction in defence of their threatened ascendancy.

Although a wealth of evidence could be adduced in support of the foregoing statements, perhaps it will suffice if the following extracts are given from a letter to Government from a magistrate named Henry Clements, Forthenry, Co. Cavan, dated 7th March, 1798:

> I think it necessary to acquaint you that there was [sic] some time ago Notices put up on the Doores of some Papists in the town and neighbourhood of Drum in the county of Monaghan, deseiring [sic] the Inhabitants to leave their Houses or that they and everything belonging to them would be Destroyed . . . there is an Association formed between Drum and Clones in the same County under the Title of Orange Boys, that they already amount to some hundreds. . . . I have, since I began this letter, Received some notices put on the Doores of Papists last night in this county Desiring the Inhabitants to quit their Houses before the 11th of this month or they would suffer for it. These Papers are signed Oliver Cromwell. . . . I am

---

[1] Lord Gosford in an address on 21st December, 1795, lamented the 'ferocious cruelty' which had been perpetrated on unoffending Roman Catholics and declared that they had been, and were, at the mercy of 'lawless banditti'.
   See Stanhope: Life of William Pitt. (1862), Vol. III. The date of the address is important.

sorry to think this Business may again Disturb the Peace of this County which has long beene in a Perfect state of Tranquillity.[1]

On the 15th of October, 1797, Lord Courtown transmitted to the Executive, a document containing the statement that 'the partiality of Government to the Orangemen (in the neighbourhood of Belfast) and the cruelty exercised against the Defenders, are loudly complained of'.[2]

While the Orange Society and its forerunner were always predominantly Episcopalian, there were many individual Presbyterians associated with them in those northern counties where sectarian bitterness was sufficiently acute to overcome the natural antipathy of Dissenters to political association with those who denied them, as well as the Catholics, equality of citizenship. It should be noted that at the end of the eighteenth century and often since, the term *Protestant* has been regarded as synonymous with *Episcopalian*. Thus in the so-called 'Fabricated Rules and Regulations of the Orangemen', published as Appendix XXVI to the report of the Government Committee of Secrecy (1798), the third resolution is that 'no member is to introduce a Papist, or Presbyterian, Quaker, or Methodist, or any persuasion but a Protestant'.

Brigadier-General John Moore in his camp at Skibbereen, on the 17th March, 1798, noted in his diary:

I reprobated some meetings of *Orange boys* (Protestants) . . . which, as I heard, had taken place . . . if it was to create a distinctive and separate interest from the Catholics, it was wicked and must be punished . . . for a man to boast or be proud of his religion was absurd. It was a circumstance in which he had no merit; he was the one or the other because his parents were so before him and it was determined for him before he had a choice. Any man might fairly pride himself upon being just and honest, but not on his religion. If they followed the doctrine of the one or the other, they would be good and upright.[3]

[1]   I.S.P.O.
[2]   Courtown to Pelham, I.S.P.O.
[3]   *Diary*: Vol. I, p. 279.

The practice of pitch-capping, scourging and half-strangling as a means of extorting information, came into County Wexford, or at least was intensified there, with the arrival of the North Cork Militia in April, 1798, and they have always been popularly credited with introducing the Orange system into that county. The Chief Secretary, writing to the Military Under-Secretary as early as the 3rd June, 1798, and referring to north County Wexford, expressed himself as follows:

> The war in that part of the country has certainly assumed a strong religious spirit and I cannot help suspecting that the Orange associations which you will recollect were formed and promoted by Colonel Rochfort and some other gentlemen in the counties of Wexford and Carlow operated very mischievously.[1]

It was inevitable that the barbarous practices referred to, should, rightly or wrongly, be associated with that system and that the people who were the victims of these practices should turn with fury upon those they believed to be their persecutors.

As one writer has well expressed it: 'The admitted policy of Lord Castlereagh was to accelerate the explosion of the insurrection in order to confound the plans of its leaders. For this purpose it was necessary to drive the people mad with terror; and the subordinate agents of this policy were allowed to take their own ways of accomplishing the Minister's designs.'[2]

[1] I.S.P.O.
[2] R. R. Madden: *The United Irishmen*, (1842), Vol. I, p. 345.

Insurgent Arms and Tactics

WHEN THE WEXFORDMEN were forced into the field, they suffered from the severe handicap of being almost entirely unprepared. Pikes and other weapons had been surrendered in large numbers during the preceding weeks in order to procure 'protections'. Accordingly, when fighting commenced they seized such farm implements as lay to their hands and hence we hear of a curiously varied equipment—'scythes, hay-knives, scrapers, currying-knives and old rusty bayonets fixed on poles'. A fresh supply came from the defeated North Cork Militia at Oulart—more than one hundred muskets and bayonets, together with practically all the ammunition the soldiers carried as they had only time to fire three or four rounds each before the pikemen reached them. The capture of Camolin Park on the 28th of May, provided Father John Murphy's rapidly growing force not only with quantities of previously surrendered pikes which had been stored there, but also carbines and sabres which had been delivered, but had not been distributed.

Smiths worked day and night to add to the supply until they were rounded up, with the exception of those few who accompanied the fighting men.

While, therefore, the types of arms were many and various, the chief weapon was the pike, a form of halberd. The handle of the halberd seldom exceeded six feet, but in Wexford the pike staff was usually at least ten feet in length and frequently several feet more.[1] The hook on many pike heads had often a cutting edge for severing the reins of cavalry and so rendering the horses unmanageable. It was also useful for dragging a horseman from the saddle.

Firearms were relatively small in number and as they varied greatly in type and as suitable ammunition was scanty, the effective number was smaller still. Except for the Shelmalier men few of those who carried firearms were expert in their use and many a man provided with a gun went into battle using it as a club.

Cloney relates a melancholy incident which happened on the roadside at Carnagh during the march from Slievecoiltia to Lacken, on the 10th of June:

> . . . as they sat down to rest on the green sod, one of them unguardedly placed his firelock between his thighs crossways, and having accidentally touched the trigger it exploded, the contents passing through the body of one young man who sat next him and breaking the thigh of another; the first died immediately and the second was brought to an infirmary at Enniscorthy, where he was burned in the military hospital with about seventy other wounded men on the return of the King's troops to that town, lest the bad precedent of Scullabogue should want a faithful copy.[2]

There was hardly any effective artillery—a few one pounders, a six pounder or two, an odd mortar, or howitzer captured from the enemy and some ship swivels, but little ammunition and except for Esmond Kyan, practically no one with any knowledge of gunnery. Some gunners had been captured at the Three Rocks on the 30th of May, but these, particularly at the Battle of Arklow, deliberately misused their guns and did little damage. At Vinegar Hill such guns as still remained in insurgent hands were silenced after firing a few rounds.

The method of offence adopted in view of the absence of training and tactical cohesion was, of necessity, the tumultuous

---

[1] The English weapon known as the bill was like a scythe blade with the cutting edge on the concave side and mounted on a long handle.
[2] *Personal Narrative*, p. 47, (1832).

rush, similar to that employed in warfare in the Scottish Highlands in the seventeenth and eighteenth centuries. The design was to receive the fire of artillery and musketry, relying on numbers and momentum to carry the pikemen to close quarters and finish the business as they invariably did when they succeeded in reaching their objective.

The absence of effective drill and field training precluded the possibility of rapid switching of the main attack when a hold-up occurred in the course of a battle, though occasionally deployment of those in reserve to one or both flanks was carried out, for example, during the attack on the Duffrey Gate at Enniscorthy on the 28th of May.

It was also, I feel sure, the lack of tactical cohesion which decided the leaders against employing the night attack. This measure, in other circumstances, would appear to have been the operation of choice after the failure at Arklow and before the Battle of Vinegar Hill.

The Number of Insurgents in
County Wexford

ANYONE WHO HAS READ the various accounts of the Insurrection
in Wexford, must have been struck by the enormous number of
combatants mentioned as having taken part in various engagements in the insurgent ranks. As practically all these references
are from hostile sources there would be a very obvious inclination
to exaggerate the numbers either in order to enhance the credit
of victory, or to extenuate defeat. It is desirable, therefore, to
ascertain as far as is possible, the man power available at that
time.

· There was no official enumeration, or census of population
in Ireland until 1821 and therefore all estimates at an earlier
date were largely guess-work, but there are nevertheless, some
rough guides.

There is no agreement, even approximately, among such
writers as Young, Beaufort, Duigenan and others. Early
estimates were based on the Hearth Money Rolls and the
number of houses having been in this way ascertained as far as
possible, that figure multiplied by the average number of
persons in each house (taken as six) represented the population.[1]

[1] Towards the end of the 18th century the estimated population of Ireland,
in comparison with that of Britain was sufficiently large to cause apprehension
in the latter country, in view of the possibility of French alliance with Ireland
during the Napoleonic War. After 1800 the growth of industrialism in Britain
and later, famine and its results in Ireland altered the ratio out of all proportion.

The first actual enumeration in 1821, gave the population of
County Wexford as 170,806, distributed among the eight
baronies as follows:

Ballaghkeen	..	..	..	26,620
Bantry	..	..	..	28,088
Bargy	..	..	..	11,212
Forth	..	..	..	20,891
Gorey	..	..	..	20,107
Scarawalsh	..	..	..	28,016
Shelburne ..	..	..	..	17,963
Shelmalier	..	..	..	17,909
				170,806

In every barony there was a preponderance of females over
males. There is general agreement that during the years
preceding 1821, there had been a yearly increase of population
and the problem is thus narrowed down to estimating what
figure short of 170,806 in 1821 would represent the population
twenty-three years earlier.

There is no known method, I am informed, by which such an
estimate can be accurately made in reverse. An anonymous
writer[1] guessed that the figure for 1798 was about 132,000.
He possibly followed the estimate of Bushe[2] based on the
number of houses and allowing six to each house. Fraser[3]
calculating from particulars relating to 1800, gives the population
of the combined baronies of Forth and Bargy as 24,462, and
the fact that the figure for these two baronies in 1821 was
32,103 is a point in support.

I propose, therefore, to take the figure of 132,000 as a basis
and a leading authority[4] informs me that this 'seems plausible',
but in order to avoid the possibility of an under-estimate of
the number of insurgents, I shall increase it to 135,000.

[1] See *Irish Monthly Magazine of Politics and Literature*, Vol. II, May, 1833.
[2] Bushe: *Transactions of Royal Irish Academy*, 1789.
[3] Robert Fraser: *Statistical Survey of the County Wexford*, (1807).
[4] K. H. Connell: Author of *The Population of Ireland*, 1750-1845, (1950)

Of this number more than half were women, if, as is likely, the sex distribution was the same in 1798 as we know it was in 1821. This would give approximately 67,500 males. Although there is evidence that some men of seventy years of age were killed in the insurgent ranks, I shall ignore all under fifteen and over sixty-five. The remainder (between fifteen and sixty-five) are usually taken as comprising about sixty-five per cent of the total. The number of effective males would, therefore, be reduced to 43,875. County Wexford had an exceptionally large 'loyalist' population and it is regarded as probable that one quarter of the total would not be an over-estimate under this head.

We are, therefore, left with a gross figure of 32,906, say 33,000. From this further deductions must be made. Even if the other six baronies put every effective into the field (which is doubtful) we know that the baronies of Forth and Bargy certainly did not supply their full quota.[1] I think, therefore, that at no time is it likely that the number of combatants reached 30,000 for the whole county of Wexford and if we allow for division of forces, for garrisoning of camps, for non-effectives in such places as the towns of Wexford, Enniscorthy and New Ross and for periodic desertions which undoubtedly took place, the number was probably much less.

I feel justified therefore in concluding that there is much exaggeration in the numbers commonly mentioned and that substantial correction must be made accordingly.

I do not think that the Wicklow contingent under Garrett Byrne of Ballymanus exceeded 1,000 at any time when fighting in County Wexford, while Carlow and Kildare men came there in small numbers only.

---

[1] Gordon states that no floggings took place in the town of Wexford, or in the Baronies of Forth and Bargy, and that in those Baronies no atrocities were committed before or since the rebellion. This, no doubt, had the effect of limiting recruitment to the ranks of the insurgents as was the case in south County Wicklow. See p. 41. (Note).

On The Eve

IT IS NOW NECESSARY to describe the state of the county during the period immediately preceding the outbreak.

There had been unquestionably large numbers of weapons in the hands of the people as was shown by those surrendered to Lord Mount Norris and other magistrates during the early spring of 1798. Without doubt, many men had supplied themselves with pikes as participants in the Defender movement long previously and others in the later months of 1797. As time passed feverish manufacture was carried on by the local smiths following the proclamation of the county towards the end of March, 1798, after the raid on Oliver Bond's house in Dublin.

The yeomen were now let loose at the instance of such 'active' magistrates as Hunter Gowan and Hawtrey White and whipping to extort confessions and informations, house-burning, picketing and other abominations were carried out with complete immunity to the perpetrators who were aware that they had the power of the Executive behind them and that no means existed at that time by which the outrages on their victims could be made public. It is significant that the first outbreak took place in the north of the county, in the district centred on Gorey, where these magistrates operated.

However, while such methods were perhaps most notorious in that part of the county, they were actively applied elsewhere also. To take only one example: a resident in New Ross and a prominent 'loyalist' records in his *Narrative* that 'about the middle of 1797 . . . gentlemen's houses were robbed by people who otherwise conducted themselves very peaceably'.[1] He mentions that at the close of 1797 and the beginning of 1798, 'car loads of rebels, sometimes twelve or fifteen loads together often came into this town (Ross) to Duncannon fort, or a prison ship near it for the purpose of serving in the fleet or abroad'. He also states: 'I now hear of many punishments of suspected persons both by flogging and strangulation being put in execution in the barrack yard to extort confessions of guilt . . . it is most certain that the severities in general served to accelerate the rebellion.'

I have little doubt that even without the help of such men and such methods County Wexford would have caught fire and joined a general rising if the French had made a timely landing, but from such knowledge of the period as I possess, I cannot avoid the conclusion that without a French landing and without the compulsion applied by the magistrates and their agents, especially in the north of the county, there would have been no Wexford rising at all.

The Government, however, were well supplied with information from their agents at home and abroad. They were aware that a French landing was an essential part of the plans of the United Irishmen. They even knew that the harbour of Wexford, both on account of its geographical position and the expectations of the United Irishmen's headquarters itself, was a likely place for such a landing. Accordingly, it was plain commonsense *from the Government standpoint* to force the people into the field before their supposed preparations were completed and before the arrival of the French. It so happened that owing to its general unpreparedness and otherwise, County Wexford was the chief sufferer in the application of this policy.

[1] James Alexander: *A Succinct Narrative . . . of the Rebellion in the County of Wexford.* (Dedicated to General Johnson), 1800. The 'robberies' mentioned were the early raids for arms.

With a blank cheque given to every government supporter, real or professing, a golden opportunity presented itself for wiping off old scores, personal, political, or sectarian and it is little wonder that respectable 'loyalists' viewed such deeds with horror which they plainly saw must have the effect of confirming in the minds of the people what the propagandists had been whispering among them. This is reflected later in courtmartial evidence by the frequency of such statements as: 'The only object was to procure arms to defend the Catholicks from the Orangemen', and 'the Catholicks were apprehensive of being murdered by Orangemen'. See also references in Appendix XIV.

Most 'loyalist' commentators are silent on this period, but one, more candid, or more honest than the rest admits that the Government, confronted by a formidable and secret organisation were 'forced by the magnitude of the threatened evils into a temporary violation of the political constitution'.[1]

The stage was now set. By a system of terror much information had been obtained and with the encouragement of the clergy in the north of the county[2], quantities of arms were surrendered and 'protections' issued. As, however, no 'protection' was given unless a pike was handed in, the possession of a 'protection' was little more than a proof that the possessor had once been the owner of an offensive weapon!

One Peter Foley, who fought through most of the Wexford campaign, told Luke Cullen many years later, that some of his companions refused to surrender their arms, saying: 'a protection in our hands is only a death warrant. It will be an evidence of our disaffection and a Government that never kept faith with us will not be converted easily, especially whilst they receive

[1] Gordon: p. 29.
[2] Including the following, John Murphy, Michael Murphy, Nicholas Redmond, John Redmond, Nicholas Synnott, Francis Kavanagh, Michael Lacy, David Cullen and Nicholas Stafford. They all took the oath of allegiance in April, 1798, and several of them presented loyal addresses to the Lord Lieutenant.

their information from such upstarts as Gowan, Boyd, White and Jacob.'[1]

Attention has been drawn to the fact that many who later took up arms were found to be in possession of 'protections' and this and the protestations of loyalty until almost the day of the outbreak, have been put forward as proofs of duplicity. I do not think this charge can be sustained. Engagements of this kind are two-sided and surrender of arms should be followed by effective protection. The authorities, however, on whose behalf Lord Mount Norris acted, were more concerned with disarming the people than with affording them protection when disarmed. As it happened, the surrender of arms was followed by intensification of the system of terror against the now practically defenceless people. In addition to the yeomanry, the Ancient Britons (a Welsh corps of fencible cavalry) and three corps of German dragoons[2] (who came to be known as 'Hessians') were let loose at free quarters—a system later described by the Lord Lieutenant and Commander-in-Chief (Lord Cornwallis) as comprehending 'universal rape and robbery throughout the whole country'.

On the 23rd of May, when Kildare, Carlow and Wicklow took the field and bodies of practically leaderless men with no concerted plans, drifted about their respective neighbourhoods, County Wexford made no move.

Then came the news of the mass murder of thirty-five prisoners at Dunlavin on the 24th and of twenty-four others on the following day in the ball alley at Carnew. Men took their wives and children at night into the fields and ditches. Here are two accounts of the state of north Wexford at that time, each taken down from an eye-witness:

[1] Luke Cullen MS., T.C.D. Library.
[2] As early as August, 1796, it was arranged to send to Ireland 'three Foreign Corps of Lowenstein, Hompesch and Waldstein', originally intended for service in the West Indies. (Wheeler and Broadley). Hompesch Dragoons (presumably reinforcements) landed at Cove on 21st April, 1798.

A publican named Wm. Lacy, residing then two miles beyond
Oulard, told me that in the night of the 27th of May, '98, and on the
nights immediately before it, his wife and children lay out in the
hedges, as did also the generality of the people in that locality.
Himself stopped within lest some evil-minded persons might make
too free with his stock of drink. In the dead of night he heard a
horseman going in the direction of Wexford. He arose to meet
him. He passed on still crying out, 'get up, get up and fight, or
you will be burned or butchered in your beds. The country is
in a blaze all round you'.[1]

The second account is from the townland of Kiltilly in the
parish of Kilrush, about four miles east of Bunclody:

On that Sunday morning (27th May), several persons from this
townland with their whole families, had been sleeping out in the
hedges. In the morning light the men fled towards the elevated
ground of Slieve Buide (Slieveboy), from the fury of the mounted
yeomen who had been riding madly through the country all the
preceding night. In fact they had been doing the same every other
place from the time that the people had surrendered their arms for
protections. These were followed to the place[2] and Nichls. Jackman
was shot. Darby Doyle . . . was severely wounded and for a considerable time they had to change him from hedge to hedge.

. . . Js. Doyle shot, same place. Patk. Doyle taken prisoner coming
from Dublin, sent to Carnew to see if he could get a protection.
Brought to the Castle yard and shot. Nicholas Kinshela of Knockna-
lour, the adjoining townland and Js. Doyle and one cousin were
also shot.[3]

The 'loyalist' historian, Taylor, puts his own gloss on such
proceedings in the following words: '. . . the yeomanry Corps
were ordered upon permanent duty and constantly patroled
[sic] the roads during the night. They were also, by order of
the magistrates under the disagreeable necessity of flogging
several of the prisoners to compel them to acknowledge where
their murderous weapons were concealed. By this means,
though painful to humane men, many pikes were taken up

[1] Luke Cullen MS. I have an uneasy feeling that this mysterious night rider
may have been what is now known as an *agent provocateur*.
[2] This refers to Kilthomas Hill—see p. 67.
[3] Luke Cullen MS.

through the county and many individuals who had been informed against, fled from their habitations.'[1]

Gordon's thinly veiled censure is significant: 'I shall not suppose that any magistrate could have pretended to receive information which he had not received, for the indulgence of his private spite against any individuals; but some gentlemen invested with these new powers were led into grievous errors by false informers whose names notwithstanding, have never been divulged'.[2]

The responsible minister, (Lord Castlereagh) maintained in the House of Commons the cynical pretence that no such terrorising measures had been adopted, while at the same time it could be pointed out that albeit the methods were rough, they were successful and that without them the situation would have got out of hand.

The root cause was *fear* and throughout history fear has been the motive for the worst of the cruelties recorded there. But such brutalities as we are now considering, must be viewed in the setting of their time and though we may recall outbursts of even greater horrors in more recent days in various parts of the world, it must, I think, be admitted that in the course of the last century and a half (as shown, for example, by the changes in the penal code) man's inhumanity to man has, on the whole, demonstrably lessened.

If, apart from its obvious unpreparedness, further proof were required that County Wexford was forced into the war, it would be found in what I believe to be a fact beyond question, namely that it would be difficult to point with certainty to a single entirely willing insurgent in the whole county. I feel convinced that had an honourable alternative presented itself, no rising would have taken place there. The outbreak of hostilities was mainly the end result of a deliberate 'forcing out' process

[1] Taylor: p. 25.
[2] Gordon: p. 71.

designed to cow the people into submission before a French
landing took place.[1]

The reaction to such a policy of terrorism far exceeded
expectations. It is easy to trace in the correspondence at
ministerial level during those weeks an undercurrent of strained
anxiety—a feeling that something had gone wrong with the
arrangements and that somehow the plans in County Wexford
were not working according to schedule.[2] It had seemed so
simple to give covert sanction to a policy of house-burning,
flogging, rape, robbery and murder with the comfortable
knowledge that, aided by a completely controlled press, the
good work could proceed with both secrecy and safety. Then
when at last the survivors would have submitted with becoming
humility, it would be time enough to explain away the whole
business by reference to 'excessive zeal' and by the cynical use of
such expressions as 'prevention is better than cure'.

A comparison between the reactions of two counties, say
Tipperary and Wexford, is instructive. I hold no brief for one
county against another, but the truth of history compels me to
record that in the first-named, the measures adopted (particularly
the scourge) were completely successful. Tipperary was flogged
into abject submission and disclosure before a shot was fired.

County Wexford, certainly less prepared and in some ways
less favourably circumstanced for resistance, met the same
challenge to its manhood, not by submission, but by such a
formidable counter-challenge that utterly untrained, practically
leaderless and miserably armed as they were, an army of more

[1] The Rector of Arklow (Rev. Henry Lambert Bayly) refers to the very
small numbers who joined the insurgents from the neighbourhood of Arklow
and the district further north and attributes this to the fact that 'no instance of
provoked or aggravated oppression or torture was practised or authorised
by the officers of the army before or during the rebellion'. W. Shaw Mason:
Statistical Account and Parochial Survey of Ireland, Vol. II, (1816).
[2] Thus Castlereagh to Pelham on the 13th of June: 'The rebellion in Wexford
has disappointed all my speculations. I had not a conception that insurgents
could remain together and act in such numbers'. (I.S.P.O.).

than 20,000 men was required to beat them down.[1]
It is this which stands to the eternal credit of County Wexford.

---

[1] If the resistance in any county can be measured by the aggregates of amounts claimed by 'suffering loyalists', then the following figures speak for themselves: County Tipperary, £1,366; County Wexford, £311,341. (See Appendix, House of Commons Journals, 1800).

It can be said for Munster, however, that the situation there was confused on account of old traditions of Jacobite and Royalist loyalties from the time of the Wild Geese.

Anthony Perry of Inch

IN THE MIDST of these scenes of terror and confusion, the Government made an arrest which had more far-reaching results than any other single act in the war in Wexford. Anthony Perry of Perrymount, half-a-mile south of Inch cross-roads, was a first lieutenant in the Coolgreany corps of yeoman cavalry. A man of liberal principles he viewed with detestation the outrages committed on the people and some time in the latter half of May, he quitted the corps in protest while actually on parade in the grounds of Charles Dawson of Fortchester, a mile from his own house. Thereafter he was, of course, a marked man and on either the 23rd or 24th of May (it is uncertain which), he was seized by a party of the North Cork Militia and brought to Gorey. There during the next forty-eight hours he was subjected to torture at the hands of a North Cork sergeant whose sadistic performances earned for him the title of *Tom the Devil*. In Perry's case the hair of his head was first treated with an inflammable mixture containing gunpowder and then fired. It is not known how long this process continued before his resolution faltered and gave way and an 'information' was extorted from him. Let no man dare lightly to condemn his action until he has himself withstood the same agonies.

Miles Byrne refers to Perry's subsequent appearance as follows: '. . . though he had got out of prison a few days before, he was suffering so much from the cruel treatment he

43

had received there . . . which raised all the skin of his head and part of his face, that he was miserably low spirited and weak'.[1]

Perry's information, dated the 26th of May, is given here in its entirety and it has not been printed before. It supplies the key to the arrest (by order of Government) of Bagnal Harvey at Bargy Castle at 11 p.m. the same day and of Edward Fitzgerald of Newpark, at daybreak on the 27th and of John Henry Colclough, at Ballyteigue, later that day.[2] Also of Matthew Dowling who was imprisoned in Fort George until 1803.[3] No doubt all those others mentioned were immediately arrested also, though I am unaware of their fate, which is perhaps better imagined than described.

Accounts vary as to Perry's movements during the subsequent few days. According to George Taylor, who lived at Bally-walter, two miles and a half south of Gorey, when the garrison of that town heard the news of Oulart Hill and of the arrival of the insurgent army at Camolin and Ferns, they marched hastily away to Arklow on the 28th of May, leaving several prisoners in the gaol and guardroom and Perry who was confined in a private house.[4] They shot a few of their prisoners in the street before they left. Perry on being liberated placed himself at the head of the remaining prisoners and joined the main body of the insurgents. Miles Byrne mentioned that Perry was present at the battle of Tubberneering on the 4th of June though unable, owing to his condition, to take an active

[1] *Memoirs*, Vol. I, p. 77, (1906).
[2] It should be mentioned, however, that Mrs. Jane Adams of Summerseat (now Somerset), three miles south of Wexford town, states in her narrative that on Whit Sunday (27th of May), on her way to church she 'met the Wexford Cavalry escorting Mr. Colclough . . . and Mr. Bagnal Harvey to jail . . . what a task for Captain Boyd! Both men at whose houses he was in habits of intimacy'.
[3] Matthew Dowling was the Dublin solicitor who instructed John Philpot Curran in the court exposure of the infamous Government agent in Wexford —Cooper, alias Morgan. He fought a duel at Holyhead with Borough of the Chief Secretary's staff. Hamilton Rowan was his second.
[4] Gordon, however, states that he returned to his own house four miles from Gorey where he was followed by some yeomen from whom he escaped.

part. Luke Cullen states that Perry was not liberated until the insurgents reached Gorey after that battle, but I think on this occasion Cullen was either misinformed, or what is more likely, confused the two retreats from Gorey, which were a full week apart.

The following is the complete text of the document:

County of Wexford ⎧ The examinations of Anthony Perry of
        to witt   ⎨ Inch in sd. county Esqr. taken before us
                     ⎪ at a session held in the town of Gorey in
                     ⎩ sd. county the 26th day of May, 1798.

Who being duly sworn and examined deposeth and saith that some time in summer in the year 1797 seven this examinant went to the house of Mr. Mathew Dowling, attorney, No. 4 Longford Street sd. Dowling swore examinant the United Irishman's oath and took him to a meeting at John Forman Kennedy's in Mercer Street where sd. Dowling acted as Secretary, sd. examinant Perry saith he never swore any Person also saith he went to the House of Moses Kehoe at Castletown where at a meeting he saw several Secretary's, viz. John Brien of or about Ballinacree, Peter Bolger of Tomnahely, Philip Riely Pedlar, Laurence Donnelly of Ballinacree who put their names in a hat and drew for their numbers; next seditious meeting was in his sd. Perry's own Barn, and Edward Byrne, carpenter presided there, John Kinnshela of Inch was there, also Edward Byrne of Boolabreda—examt. saith he was at another meeting at Mr. Robert Graham's Coolgreany, Simon Crean of Knockgrenay and Michl. McDermot a smith, was there also, also Joseph Byrnes of Coolgreany and James Doyle, Publican, in Coolgreany; they warned against tumult, least it might create suspicion. Next meeting was at Thomas Howlet's Miller in Inch in his mill,[1] where Mathew Doyle of the County of Wicklow . . . proposed to organize the County of Wexford in the same manner as the County of Wicklow; there was present at sd. meeting James Doyle of Coolgreany, John Redmond the Elder of Kilcavan, Edward Byrne

[1] Gordon states that to his knowledge a man named Howlet was flogged in Gorey to extort information. The result, if any, is not known.

Carpenter, and sd. Thomas Howlet. They proceeded to organize the parishes of Kilcavan, Inch and Kilmorgan and Kilnenor . . . saith Howlet told examinator he was a Baronial member and Pat Darcy of Tomcoyle was another, afterwards Inch, Kilcavan and Kilnenor formed Baronial Committee; Thomas Howlet was sent to the Barony of Ballaghkeen and sd. Howlet said he organized said Barony. Patrick Darcy was sent to the Barony of Scarawalsh but sd. Barony would not be organised, the reason Howlet and Darcy were sent to sd. Barony was to form a County Committee to elect a member, but the whole county has as examt. believes since been organized but never sent in a Member. Examnt. further saith that Mr. Robert Graham of Coolgreany went to the house of Mr. Edward Fitzgerald of New Park and when he came back he informed Perry that Mr. Ed. Fitzgerald he believed was an United Irishman but would not step forward, Robt. Graham also said to examinant that Mr. John Colclough, called Doctor Colclough, would step forward, he also told examt. that Mr. Beauchamp Bagnal Harvey was not at that time an United Irishman,[1] but would become so, and the persons that were to be elected to represent the County in the Provincial Committee was [sic] examnt. Anthony Perry, B. B. Harvey, and sd. John Colclough, but examnt. saith they were not elected. Robt. Graham went a second time as examnt. saith to Mr. Fitzgerald of New Park and brought word that the County Committee would meet and that sd. B. B. Harvey was to be Treasurer, sd. John Colclough was to be Secretary and examt. Perry was to be Delegate and Representative, when examt. came from Dublin to County Wexford, he was to have been assisted by one McCabe[2] to re-organize the County and after sd. McCabe left examt. he went to the house of Mr. Ed. Fitzgerald and examt. was informed and believes McCabe went to New Park to know whether the Barony was organized or not, Ed. Fitzgerald did not tell examt. whether the Barony was organized but brought one Adams who told examt. it was and said to the best of his opinion the Barony was Arm'd, the said Adams also informed this examt. that said McCabe would call at examt.'s house in coming back from the County of Waterford or else that sd. Adams would call to inform examt. the time and place where the County would meet, in order to send in provincial Delegates, but examt. saith the proceeding stopt.

[1] Harvey stated at his trial that he became a United Irishman three years before.
[2] William Putnam McCabe. He was a member of Lord Edward Fitzgerald's bodyguard.

Sworn before us the 26th day of May, 1798
Examinant acknowledges   Courtown
himself bound to prosecute   Thos. Grogan Knox
at the next . . . Assizes   Annesley Brownrigg,
for said County in two   J. Beauman,
Hundred Pounds Sterg.   Hawtrey White,
                                  Jas. White,
        a true copy   Peter Browne,
                                  Edd. D'Arcy.

Interleaved with the foregoing is the following original document:

To his Excellency John Jeffreys, Earl Camden, Lord Lieutenant and General Governor of Ireland, etc., etc., etc.

The Memorial of the undersigned Magistrates for the County of Wexford met at a Sessions at Gorey, 26th of May, 1798——

That in consideration of the candid acknowledgment and very useful Information given to sd. Magistrates by Anthony Perry of Inch in said County Esqr.—said Magistrates beg leave to recommend to Your Excellency said Mr. Perry as an object deserving of Your Excellency's clemency, he being ready to come forward to substantiate the evidence produced by his Information—and your Memorialist's will pray—

	Annesley Brownrigg,	Courtown,
Peter Browne	J. Beauman,	Thos. Grogan Knox,
	Hawtrey J. White,	Edwd. D'Arcy.
	Jas. J. White.	[1]

---

[1] I.S.P.O.

Little wonder, with this on his conscience, that Perry should have been noticed by his companions to be 'miserably low spirited'. Musgrave and Gordon were both aware that he had given information, but apparently neither realised its full significance.

For further information about Perry see Appendix I.

PART II.

The Harrow [1]

'EARLY ON FRIDAY the 25th of May, 1798, the people of the parish of Kilcormack were but too well acquainted with the inhuman acts of that little runaway coward Archy Jacob, in all the county around him, particularly at Enniscorthy and the village of Ballaghkeen, about five miles from the former place. On that day the neighbours had assembled as was their usual custom to cut turf for the priest for his winter fuel. They were at their work in the bog not far distant from the road and about eleven o'clock, a troop of the local cavalry came dashing at a furious rate along the road, their swords drawn. . . . Father John Murphy, of Boolavogue, was standing on the turf bank where his men were working . . . they drew up their horses and faced them round in the direction of the working men and after a minute or two they wheeled round and dashed on at their former speed. . . . After a short time they returned and drew up again in a menacing position before Father Murphy and his workmen. . . . A Mr. Thomas Donovan was on the turf bank with the men and when the party rode off, he and the Revd. Mr. Murphy expressed it to be their opinion that it was not safe for them to remain any longer at work. . . . The

---

[1] I give the account of the Harrow and the events immediately preceding it in the words of Luke Cullen's informant who was himself a participant. It is a valuable record with a wealth of detail and it bears all the signs of authenticity.

men washed themselves and returned home to dinner, each man forming his opinion of the gathering storm.

'On that night the greater portion of the people slept out in hedges and many spent the night hiding what things they had of any value. On Saturday morning [the 26th] early [came] the intelligence of the awful butchery of the ball alley at the Castle of Carnew [on the 25th] and the still more bloody news of the wholesale slaughter at Dunlavin [on the 24th] both places in County Wicklow.[1] Some had now regretted that they had surrendered their arms and yet a number of persons were going in and taking out protections. In Oulard on that day a large concourse of people who had collected to surrender their arms and to take out protections, were addressed by the Right Revd. Dr. Caulfield, the Catholic Bishop of Ferns, at Mr. McAuley's Hotel, where he had just arrived on his return from Dublin. He exhorted the people to relinquish their wild notions of insurrection, to live in peace and charity with each other and threatened the disobedient to the laws with the heaviest of God's chastisements.[2]

'On the 23rd of May, a proclamation was issued by the magistrates of the county allowing fourteen days for the surrender of arms, but on that very night some of the magistrates with their corps were out through the county dragging to prison, flogging and otherwise cruelly torturing the inhabitants. They saw now plainly that neither proclamations nor a written protection availed, for Hawtrey White was torturing in the east, Hunter Gowan in the north was letting some of the people escape for equivalents in cash and Archy Jacob in the west

[1]   Dr. Caulfield stated in his famous Reply, that fifty-four were murdered at Carnew—twenty-eight on the Friday before the Rising and the remainder on the following Monday.

[2]   It is impossible to reconcile with this statement Taylor's story of the 'rebel captain' instructing Dr. Caulfield to stop the massacre in Wexford on the 20th of June and meeting with the reply that 'the people must be gratified'. Luke Cullen's record of this incident in Oulart is confirmed by Dr. Caulfield's own statement—see his Reply. . . . (1801).

was training a regular set of executioners in all the varieties of their calling such as the picket, the triangle with half and whole hanging and the Boyds of Wexford in the south were picking up the higher game such as Messrs. Ed. Fitzgerald and Colclough.

'A portion of the men in this district had now become spiritless. They saw that a proclamation issued with all the formality and apparent binding of an Act of Parliament was despised and made no account of by the very men who issued it and had their names appended to it. Their arms in a great measure surrendered they became silent, sullen and resolved to meet their fate with such arms as they were in possession of; but such thoughts were only individually entertained and I only speak now of the Parish of Kilcormack, or rather a small portion of it. . . .

'Several of the farmers had gone in the course of the day to Father Murphy to solicit his advice as to what was the best to be done. . . . I never could hear what counsel he gave them, but he was in the neighbourhood of the little village called the Harrow about eight or nine o'clock that evening. . . . "I know," said he, "that they have me marked out; look to the inhuman slaughter in Carnew, about nine miles from you, and if the report of the butchery in Dunlavin be true, it is worse. Our jails are full of the best and most beloved of our inhabitants and it may be our own lot to be in company with them before tomorrow night."

'Some two or three of the few he then addressed said that they would stay with him and abide the consequences of an attack from the cavalry as they expected nothing else. It was now up to ten o'clock at night. . . .

'A farmer named John Boyne lived about three furlongs to the west of the Harrow.[1] Father Murphy called on them for a few minutes, it was the last house that he called into on that night. On leaving it they proceeded in the direction of the

[1] See note at the end of this chapter.

Harrow. About midway between Boyne's house and the Harrow there is a sudden bend or curve in the road. The Camolin cavalry had just passed on from the direction of Boolavogue chapel which had been set on fire[1] and some say that it was a party of the Enniscorthy cavalry that done [sic] it before the others came up (note—certainly by the Enniscorthy cavalry). However, the Camolin cavalry and the little party with Father Murphy entered the bend in the road, from opposite directions, at the same moment.

'The cavalry [were] about twenty in number, every one . . . armed to the teeth and mounted on an excellent steed, whilst the other party consisting of about thirty men (and between ten and eleven o'clock) had but a few weapons that were anyway formidable with the exception of two guns; and one of their popular songs of that time says—

' "And with two gunsmen we did begin."

'The meeting was quite unexpected on either side, but the fight commenced that moment by the cavalry firing a volley. Some of the people crossed the road fence and Father John told them to take to the stones. Lieutenant Bookey, of Rockspring, who had the command of the corps that night, and a young gentleman named Donovan, a private and nephew to the before-mentioned Thos. Donovan, pressed their horses forward through their opponents and reached Boyne's house which they instantly set fire to. The rest of the corps was stunned at such unexpected resistance, fell back in dismay and galloped with all their speed through the Harrow.[2]

'Lieutenant Bookey and Mr. Donovan were not long in

[1] Boulavogue Chapel was not burned until the following day, see p. 189. The reference here may be to Father Murphy's *house* which was probably burned that night. His lodging is believed to have been in Tomnaboley.

But see also Appendix XV, which contains the statement that 'the first house that was burned in the rebellion of 1798 by the King's army was that of priest Murphy in Tincurry; it was done as a reprisal for the murder of Lieut. Bookey near the Harrow'.

[2] See Detail Book of Camolin Yeoman Cavalry (Wheeler & Broadley).

firing the house of Boyne. The weather was dry and the house was thatched. . . . Not finding the corps to follow their leaders they hastened back to join them and scarcely had ten minutes elapsed when they were returning to the spot where the rencontre took place. Mr. Donovan fell by a shot from his uncle.[1] Bookey received a stab of a pike on the side of the neck. It was not mortal. He fell to his horse's mane, but the next plunge passed through his body and a third entered his horse's flank and the agonised animal plunged with such fury that he dragged the pike out of the man's hand and had reached the little village of the Harrow ere it fell from its body.

'The first blow of the insurrection in the County of Wexford was now struck and they immediately proceeded to rouse their neighbours—a thing easily done, as scarcely any of them had slept in their houses on that, or the preceding night.'

Note

Neither from the Tithe Applotment Books (1825), nor from any other document has it been found possible to identify Boyne's farm. If Luke Cullen's informant is correct in his statement, it seems probable that Boyne was evicted before 1825. There is no traditional information connecting that surname with a holding in the place designated. If the Boynes were evicted they might well have drifted into Enniscorthy, where the name is still to be found, or to the townland of Coolatore, between the Harrow and Ferns, where Boynes lived sixty or seventy years ago.

It is unfortunate that Cullen is not more explicit on the point. He mentions that Boyne's house lay west of the Harrow, but there is no road running due west—one leads to Ferns

[1] But see note on p. 64.

(north-west) and the other towards Tinnacross crossroads (south-west).

As the surviving yeomen escaped through the Harrow and along the Ferns road, (assuming that Luke Cullen is correct in his account), I think it may be regarded as certain that the fight took place on the Tinnacross road; this would agree with the existing tradition which describes as 'Bookey's Stream', a small water-course a short distance from the Harrow along that road.

Bookey's body was left there and when picked up the following morning by his fellow-yeomen, his pockets contained 'seventy-five guineas in gold, a guinea bank note and a gold watch'. (Taylor). That night Rockspring, Bookey's house, was burned.

The Attack on Kyle Glebe

DURING THE NIGHT of the 26th of May and the day following, there was a good deal of indiscriminate house-burning, especially in the parish of Kilcormick—the yeomen firing the homesteads of those they chose to regard as 'disaffected', most of whom had fled to the woods and fields, while these latter in their turn did likewise, especially to the houses of yeomen and supplementaries.

At daybreak on the 27th, a large party accompanied by Father John Murphy, appeared at Kyle Glebe, then, as now, standing half-a-mile north-east of Oulart Church. For some reason the occupier, the Rev. Robert Burrowes, Rector of Kilmuckridge, had supplied himself with a considerable stock of firearms and garrisoned his house with a force of nine or ten yeomen. The intention of the attacking party was probably to obtain possession of badly needed arms. A contemporary described the incident as follows:

> As soon as the Kilcormack men entered the village of Oulard they were told that Mr. Burrowes' house was prepared for defence and a strong party well-armed and well provided with ammunition was securely posted within. This was told to them as caution against approaching so strong a party, but they resolved on demanding a surrender of the arms. On entering the premises of Mr. Burrowes they were not bent on any hostility towards him further than taking the arms and ammunition . . . but on entering the place they were unexpectedly saluted with a volley from the upper windows. It

appears that Mr. Burrowes did not command this firing for as that
irregular volley ceased he came out to the men and was commencing
a parley with them. A few more shots were fired that instant and a
man named Redmond was wounded in the cheek and the blood
gushed copiously from the wound. His brother turned around and
perceiving him covered with blood thought that the wound was
mortal; . . . and in his consternation and without reflection he rushed
on Mr. Burrowes who ran along a square of the little lawn that
scarcely contains a rood of ground. He overtook him before any
other person could come up and unfortunately the good and harmless
gentleman fell, for such was the character I often heard of him.
One thing is certain he was not a tyrant. . . .

The house was immediately surrounded and set fire to. All the
inmates were let off safe, but such men as were brought there for
the defence and who had fired out on the people. These were put
to death with the exception of one or two that got off in the confusion
of the moment. Mrs. Burrowes and her children were brought to
Mr. McGawley's Hotel where everything that could be done to
alleviate their sorrows and misfortunes was done.[1]

Mr. Burrowes' eldest son was wounded and his wound was
dressed in McAuley's hotel.

This account is to an extent borne out by the fact that James
Redmond was hanged on 30th July, 1801, for the murder of
Mr. Burrowes and his body handed over to the surgeons
for dissection.[2]

On the 12th of July, 1798, the eldest son, T. C. Burrowes, aged
fifteen years, swore an affidavit before Judge Downes in which he
stated that a man named Murphy had warned them the night
before that an attack would be made and that, having arms
and ammunition sufficient for eight or nine persons, they
resolved to defend the house. He stated further that there
appeared to be three or four hundred men in the attacking
party and that several of these were killed or wounded as they
approached the house. He said that after the house had been
set on fire, he and his father came out having been promised

1   Luke Cullen MS.—T.C.D. Library.
2   Hay.

protection by 'one Murphy, a priest who headed said party', on condition of surrenderng arms; that he and his father gave up their firearms following which his father 'was attacked and murdered by several men and this deponent himself was severely wounded by a stab of a pike through the body' and left by the side of his father, apparently dead and that seven of the nine men armed by his father were murdered.

He admitted that later in the day he was carried on a door to the hotel in Oulart village where his 'mother, brothers and sisters had been received' and that two days later they 'were escorted by a party of said rebels to Castle Annesley, five miles off, where they remained until Wexford was retaken on 21st June'.[1]

It will be observed that the two accounts, given above, agree very closely making some allowance for the natural feelings of a young boy who had seen his father piked to death and who had himself suffered a severe wound, from the effects of which he is stated to have died two years later.

I have been informed by a very old man living on Oulart Hill, who had worked at Kyle Glebe for forty years, that opinion in the neighbourhood had always emphatically been that the death of Mr. Burrowes was unpremeditated, that the visit was a raid for arms and that his death was greatly regretted.

Mary Burrowes, the widow, claimed £1,285 compensation and was allowed £725.

[1] See Musgrave, Appendix XVIII. 4.

The Battle of Oulart

AFTER THE BURNING of Kyle Glebe, Father John Murphy and his party marched three miles south to the Church at Castle Ellis. 'They halted at this church for a little time where they received some accession to their numbers . . . we now could muster about four hundred and we went about a mile further to the village of Ballynamonabeg.' Here they learned that Edward Fitzgerald of Newpark (whom they may have expected to join them) had been arrested early that morning.

'We halted on the rising ground over that village. Mr. Morgan Byrne of Kilnamanagh near Oulard was with us there, dressed in his regimentals; he was then a member of one of the yeomanry corps of cavalry, I think Shelmalier, and Mr. Ed. Roach of Garrylough also in his regimentals with five or six of his corps (the above was afterwards called General Ed. Roach).'

At this juncture Hawtrey White appeared at the head of two hundred yeoman cavalry from Gorey, comprising corps from Gorey, Ballaghkeen, Camolin, Castletown and Coolgreany. 'Our position was an excellent one . . . the fields were small with good hedges well covered by furze and the land rose high immediately over the road.' Probably under the direction of Edward Roche a movement was made to outflank the approaching cavalry, but when this intention became clear the yeomen, showing a decided preference for discretion rather than valour, retreated hastily in the direction of Gorey, contenting

60

themselves with shooting twenty defenceless people on the way.

Towards one o'clock in the afternoon, the numbers of insurgents had increased to about one thousand, a considerable proportion of whom were mere fugitives from the fury of the yeomen and unprovided with a weapon of any kind.

'We directed our steps now to Oulard Hill . . . where we arrived between two and three o'clock and very shortly after, the detachment of the North Cork Militia . . . appeared in sight on an elevated part of the road crossing Boleyboy Hill, a few perches more than a mile from the little field where we were stationed. They were supported by the Shelmalier local cavalry commanded by le Hunte. At this place the officers seemed to hold a short consultation.[1] The Royal troops and the people had now a perfect view of each other. The movements and numbers of each were quite visible. The battlefield on which the people were encamped inclined to the south whilst the road on which the army were descending inclined to the north. . . . Colonel Foot considered our position a good one and, as we were afterwards informed, was unwilling to attack us, but was pressed to it by Major Lombard and some of the junior officers. . . .

'About three o'clock in the evening they entered the nearest part of the village of Oulard, which is composed of two small villages nearly one quarter-of-a-mile asunder. At this place a road branched off to their left and turned around the height. . . . At this turn of the road they halted for a few minutes; all their movements at this moment seemed to be governed by caution and our party stood in breathless anxiety on the hill. There were many there that day that had never seen a red coat. . . . Mr. Ed. Turner of Newfort was a magistrate and sergeant in the

[1] Hay states that the mounted yeomen rode from Wexford through Castlebridge, while the North Cork Militia took the road to the east ('the low road'). The two forces joined at Ballyfarnoge cross-roads beside Newfort, the house of the magistrate, Edward Turner, who is stated to have ridden that morning to Wexford announcing that his house had been attacked and a large number of surrendered pikes taken.

Shelmalier cavalry. It was now proposed to burn some houses and unhappily for Mr. Turner he volunteered for the service and actually burned two or three cabins for the purpose of distracting us,[1] thinking that we would rush down on them for retaliation, break our lines and abandon our position. Not a soul of us stirred. They were well aware that Hawtrey White at the head of two or three corps of cavalry had been scouring the country to the north and south of Oulard on that morning and should now be in our rear.

'The Shelmalier cavalry were now getting round to our right, the infantry advancing in front of us and had every facility to take us on the left. Some of the youths, the timorous and badly armed began now to retreat. Some of them had crossed a couple of fields when they unexpectedly perceived White's divisions of cavalry slowly approaching them. . . . A safe retreat appeared impossible and they kept their ground; some returned to us. . . . But this appearance of White's cavalry at that critical moment, in a great measure contributed to the complete victory over the royal force on that day. At this time of their partial retreat we were about one thousand strong, but when the fighting commenced we were not more than five hundred. Our gunsmen were about forty or fifty. None of our guns were good and only a few of them deserved the name of middling. Our little band of gunsmen were on the right of our main body. The ditch at our rear was about eight or ten perches from us. . . . As the royal troops advanced to within about thirty perches of us they commenced firing. . . . the balls whistled by us and over us. We, the gunsmen, resolved to stand together and not to fire until our enemy would be quite close to us and then to fire and rush in amongst them. The Revd. John Murphy, a Catholic curate of Boolavogue, was our principal leader and indeed to do the gentleman justice,

---

[1] It is believed that this act of Turner was the reason for his murder on the bridge of Wexford on the 20th of June.

at this time he was but little use to us. We were all novices
in the art of war. Even Mr. Ed. Roach, a man of education
and of courage, and so far as the discipline of the local cavalry
went, he was qualified to command, but he and a few others
were engaged in council and preventing desertion.[1] I may say
we had no commander but we were all determined to stand
together. . . .

'They advanced to within about twenty yards of us. We had
not lost one drop of blood at the time. The line of the enemy
was something extended to our left . . . and that portion of it
made a charge to pass over the ditch in our rear where they
saw our pike men concealed. A man from that part of the
country called Macamores, stood beside me. He had a stone
in each hand—he had no other arms and a man with a brass
barrelled blunderbuss was on the other side of me. They were
now not more than fifteen yards from us. The man armed
with the stones fired one of his bullets and instantly sent the
other after it. The first told with such effect on the arm of one
of our assailants that it caused him to drop his musket. I can't
tell if his second round told for on that instant the man on
my other side fired his blunderbuss and I my musket and *pop pop*
. . . went a shot from every gun.

'While this action was in progress on the centre front, the
pikemen were working round on both flanks in the shelter of
the parallel earthen fences (called 'hedges'). At this opportune
moment they leapt over and bore down all opposition.

'The conflict had now become general. Few of us attempted
to re-load. We dashed in amongst them and in a summary
way we used both breech and barrel of our guns. . . . The

---

[1] Edward Roche of Garrylough had been permanent sergeant in le Hunte's
corps of Shelmalier cavalry and he is referred to in the information of Robert
Edwards as follows:
  'The cavalry did not engage, but Lieutenant Cavanagh of Le Hunte's corps
made a cut at a person named Roach who commanded the Rebels and one
whom Cavanagh had been particular in making a good soldier while he
was in the Corps.' (I.S.P.O.).

soldiers running down the hill kept looking over their shoulders, the insurgents in amongst them knocking them down with their various weapons, numbers of them with stones of which the hill offered a plentiful supply.

'The most of the troops were dispatched with pikes and many of them calling out for mercy and presenting Catholic prayer books. . . . (Note) I saw one of these prayer books (a Catholic one) with a rich farmer named Synnot who said he would keep it . . . and although the son of a wealthy farmer he was unarmed on that day except with stones which it is said he used with dexterity. They done [sic] us no injury by their irregular firing as they advanced, nor could they have done anything better to cool down and steady our mind than to set fire to the houses in the village. But few of us had before the preceding night, ever witnessed a house on fire. . . . The persons who fell on our side were Thomas Donovan of the Harrow (the man who fired the first shot from our party on the night before, when his nephew[1] and Lieutenant Bookey fell), Humphrey Crowley of Kilpierce, John Dunphy of Monavouling (Mona-willing)—Sommers of Finchoge and a weaver from Courtclough whose name I forget. These five fell by our enemies. A young man named Murphy, from Kilcotty, was also wounded and fell on his face. He was a very poor young man and in his poverty was under the necessity of wearing for a waistcoat, a round red jacket of a horse soldier. . . . He had thrown off his coat at the commencement of the battle and as he lay on his face among the fallen he was not recognised by his companions and one of them drove a pike through him. . . . The six are interred together in the churchyard of Oulard. . . .

'In the retreat some of the fugitives crossed the road to the south of the Chapel near to the burning cabins. They gained a bog, but here the pikemen came up with them and about ten

[1] Seamus Doyle of Enniscorthy informs me that Thomas Donovan was his great-great-grandfather and that John Donovan of Tubergall, killed at the Harrow, was Thomas Donovan's cousin and not his nephew.

of them fell there. Five more of them made a desperate and gallant race up a rising ground for the distance of one hundred perches to the house of a farmer named Synnot, three of them were overtaken before they reached the house. . . . The other two continued on their route for another mile. They were running parallel to the road and in the next field to it and were now almost two miles from the battlefield when they perceived two men closing on them—Thos. Cullen and Js. Reily, two powerful men. . . . The two soldiers were running side by side when overtaken at a ditch by their pursuers, their lives and retreat were ended in a moment.

'Cullen and Reily went on to Gaby's Cross, about a quarter-of-a-mile further where they fell in with a drummer that got drunk in Ballynamonabeg. . . . These two men gave up any further pursuit after killing the drummer and Colonel Foote, a sergeant and a private or two made a good retreat to Wexford.'[1]

. . . .

One important result of this encounter was the acquisition by the insurgents of more than a hundred muskets and a considerable supply of ammunition as the militia had only fired three or four rounds and they are stated to have been served out with sixty rounds each.[2]

---

[1] The long quotations in the above account are from that portion of the Luke Cullen MS. which is among the Madden Papers in the Library of Trinity College, Dublin. Cullen took down the particulars from one Peter Foley who was an actual participant in the battle.

[2] See also Appendix II.

Carrigrew,
Kilthomas Hill and Ballyorril Hill

AFTER THE VICTORY at Oulart the insurgents moved to Carrigrew Hill, five miles to the north. Here they established a camp and spent the night. This hill is four miles due east of Ferns and two miles south-east of Camolin. It was, therefore, a convenient rallying point for hundreds of homeless men. On that same day (27th May), according to the Detail Book of the Camolin yeomanry[1], that corps marched from Ferns to the Harrow where they found the bodies of Bookey and Donovan and 'joined by the Enniscorthy and Healthfield Yeoman Cavalry they took a circuit thro' the country, killed a great number of the Insurgents who seemed as if collecting in a body and burnt upwards of 170 houses belonging to Rebels whose inhabitants had fled, and also the Popish chapel of Boulavogue'. The latter entry is important as suggesting that the burning of this chapel took place *the day after the Harrow*. The depositions of John Rossiter of Grange, and Peter Crawley of Glandaw [Clondaw] both state that the houses of John and Robert Webster of Garrybrit in their neighbourhood were fired some hours before the Enniscorthy cavalry burned Father John's *house*.[2]

---

[1] See Wheeler and Broadley: *The War in Wexford* (1910).
[2] See Musgrave, Appendix XVIII. 3. There is a rather suspicious resemblance between these two depositions.

While these happenings were taking place towards the east of the county, similar scenes of terror were witnessed towards the west. Reference has already been made to the events in the townland of Kiltilly in the parish of Kilrush.[1] Fugitives from a wide area gathered on the rising ground known as Kilthomas Hill, two miles north of Ferns. The 'loyalist' historian, Gordon, refers to this gathering as 'a confused multitude of both sexes and all ages'. They were in all probability practically unarmed. They were attacked by two or three hundred yeoman cavalry and infantry from Carnew, five miles to the north, and dispersed with the loss of one hundred and fifty cut down in the pursuit.[1] One yeoman is reported to have been wounded! It was, of course, a pure and simple massacre, following which 'two Romish chapels and about a hundred cabins and farmhouses of Romanists' were set on fire.[2]

Father Michael Murphy, of Ballycanew, was present and succeeded in collecting a number of the survivors with whom he marched across the bridge at Scarawalsh, to join the victors of Oulart on Ballyorril Hill, on their way to Enniscorthy.

On this day of outrage and counter-outrage, the house of Charles Dawson of Charlesfort, three miles north-west of Ferns, was looted and its owner wounded, while at Ballingale, in the same neighbourhood, the rectory of the Rev. Francis Turner, a magistrate, was attacked and burned and its owner shot. The attacking party set out from the house of William Carthy of Ballycarney, and was headed by James Maher and Denis Carthy.[3]

Father John Murphy's force, now greatly augmented, had left

[1] Page 39.
[2] Musgrave and Gordon.
[3] Gordon.
   The latter's aunt, Mrs. Cambia Carthy appeared as a witness against both at their trial. (Musgrave).
   The Rev. Francis Turner leased fifty acres of the lands of Ballingale on 30th April, 1787, from Matthew Derenzy of Clohamon. See Registry of Deeds, Book 391, No. 257098. See also Appendix XIV.

camp at Carrigrew Hill early in the morning of the 28th of May and marched to Camolin. They found the village deserted by its yeoman garrison and its 'loyalist' inhabitants, all of whom had fled to Gorey. In Camolin Park, the residence of Lord Mount Norris, the insurgents possessed themselves of large quantities of pikes and other arms which had been stored there since their surrender during the previous weeks. From Camolin they proceeded to Ferns, where the house of the Protestant Bishop (Dr. Cleaver) was looted of its contents, but not burned. Their arrival in Ferns is thus graphically described by a Quaker merchant in that town:[1]

> . . . we remained in doubtful suspense until the town and neighbourhood filled with an undisciplined and ungovernable crowd consisting of many thousands of the United Irishmen, following the steps of the Army to Enniscorthy and demolishing the houses of those called loyalists, Orangemen, etc., (the inhabitants having fled). My house was soon filled when to our astonishment and humble admiration instead of the massacre which we dreaded, we were met by caresses and marks of friendship, declaring they intended us no injury, but would fight for us and protect us . . . adding that they required nothing from us but some provisions. They seemed to be in extreme want of something to eat and the victuals which were prepared for those they called enemies were now ready for them, which having eaten they proceeded on their rout to Enniscorthy, where in a little time after we could see the columns of smoke arising from the burning houses six miles distant.
>
> The next day a man with a malicious countenance came to me with a long spit in his hand and threatened to kill me for some offence which he said I had given him. 'I have killed Turner', said he, 'and burned him in his own house' . . . by the persuasion of a neighbour, he was prevailed upon to be quiet and at length parted in friendship.

From Ferns the march was continued across the Slaney at Scarawalsh Bridge to the summit of Ballyorril Hill, a mile to the south-west. This hill, though not of great elevation (270 feet at its highest point), commands an extensive view and

[1] Joseph Haughton: *Narrative of Event during the Irish Rebellion of* 1798.

was a suitable halting ground for resting the men who had been marching from early morning; and since four roads meet near its summit it was in addition an admirable place of assembly.

Miles Byrne states that this move of Father John Murphy afforded 'a better opportunity to the brave and unfortunate country people to escape from their hiding places and come to join his standard' and that 'he was joined by crowds, and amongst them many of those splendid young men who so much distinguished themselves in every action afterwards against the enemies of their country, such as Ned Fennell, John Doyle of Ballyellis, Nick Murphy of Monaseed, Michael Redmond and Murt Murnagh from Little Limerick. Thomas Synnot of Kilbride, though not so young as many of the others, surpassed them in activity.'[1]

[1] *Memoirs.* Vol. I, p. 38, (1906).

The Battle of Enniscorthy

FROM THE ASSEMBLY POINT on Ballyorril Hill, Enniscorthy may be approached by several roads. Mrs. Newton Lett mentions in her narrative[1] that she and her family fled from their house at Killaligan on being told that 'a great body of armed rebels' were assembled near them. Killaligan House (now in ruins) is situated at the end of a long and now grass-grown avenue off the road from Ballyorril Hill to Milehouse[2] and less than a mile north of the latter cross-roads. The road from Milehouse enters Enniscorthy at the Duffrey gate. As the Lett family fled to the town on Sunday morning, the 27th of May, it would appear that the people were already gathering on Ballyorril Hill before the arrival of the contingent from the north late on the morning of the 28th.

About one p.m. on the latter day the insurgent forces had reached the outskirts of the town. One account refers to an immense column on the Newtownbarry road extending a mile in length and 'so thick as to fill up the road'. It seems probable that use was also made of the road past Moyne House[3] and although by both these roads an approach could be made

[1] National Library, Dublin; also published in *The Past*, No. 5, 1949.
[2] Newton Lett claimed £614 compensation, but his claim was disallowed. This was probably on account of the friendship shown by his father, Joshua Lett to Thomas Cloney (see the latter's *Personal Narrative*).
[3] Then the residence of George Hore.

to the Duffrey gate, it is also likely that a contingent came off Ballyorril Hill through Milehouse. Some support is given to the latter suggestion by the fact that the advance posts of the garrison on the western approaches were placed four hundred yards from the Duffrey gate.

Captain Snowe, who commanded the garrison of Enniscorthy, stated later that if the insurgents had had anyone of military knowledge they would have divided their forces at Scarawalsh bridge and advanced on the town in two columns, one on each side of the river and made simultaneous attacks on the Duffrey Gate and Templeshannon. The insurgent force at this time has been estimated as between five and seven thousand, probably an exaggeration. To oppose them the garrison is officially stated to have comprised thirteen officers and three hundred and eighteen men, drawn from North Cork Militia, Enniscorthy yeoman infantry and supplementaries, Scarawalsh infantry and Enniscorthy cavalry.

Captain Snowe of the North Cork Militia, as commander, took post at the bridge connecting the main part of the town with the suburbs of Templeshannon and Drumgold. Captain Pounden of Daphne, with the Enniscorthy infantry formed the advance guard at and beyond the Duffrey Gate. Captain Cornock and the Scarawalsh infantry were at first in reserve on Castle Hill, but as the attack on the Duffrey Gate developed they were moved forward to assist in the defence there. Guards were stationed in the Market House and the Castle and reserves in the streets nearest the river on the west bank.

Father John Murphy and Edward Roche of Garrylough, shared the chief command of the attackers. The main thrust came from the west. Miles Byrne mentions an early and gallant sortie from the Duffrey region by the Enniscorthy cavalry which was repulsed. Other authorities mention this cavalry charge as taking place later in the battle. The first movement about which there is general agreement is the detaching of strong parties of insurgents in an outflanking movement to right and left, with the intention of entering the town at several points at once and so cutting out the strongpoint at the Duffrey Gate. Following the initiating of this movement, a herd of thirty or forty young cattle were driven in on the defenders, breaking up their positions and forcing them into the streets of the town. Here a hot fire was directed on the attackers from the houses and heavy casualties were inflicted. Captain Pounden was killed and Lieutenant Hunt mortally wounded at the Duffrey Gate. Captain Isaac Cornock and a detachment of the Scarawalsh infantry, were now diverted to oppose a heavy attack which developed from Irish Street, but they were driven into the Market Square where they met the survivors of Captain Pounden's men retreating from the Duffrey Gate. Their position in the Square was covered by fire from the Market House, which was held by Sergeant Bennett and a party of Enniscorthy infantry. In the later stage an approach towards the bridge by a party of insurgents led to some hand-to-hand fighting near Lett's brewery. Thatched houses in the upper part of the town had been set on fire and the conflagration spread. The position of the garrison was now hopeless and at this critical time a strong body of pikemen, led by Thomas Synnott of Kilbride, after an unsuccessful attempt to ford the river opposite the island above the town, succeeded in crossing higher up opposite Blackstoops, the river being low after an exceptionally long spell of dry weather. From there they advanced on Templeshannon. A last despairing attempt to defeat this most serious threat led to some hard fighting in the laneways on that side of the river. A letter referring to this party of insurgents states that 'a small number of them only had firearms, but the pikemen, wonderfully tall, stout, able fellows, fought with their pikes in the most furious and desperate manner'.[1]

[1] Jones: *Impartial Narrative*, p. 106.

On the failure of this defensive effort Captain Snowe, to avoid encirclement, was compelled to order withdrawal to Wexford and this took place along the road on the west side of the river. Numbers of the inhabitants sought sanctuary in the woods of St. John, or Ringwood.[1]

The captured and burning town became the scene of murder and pillage at the hands of the rabble. Men armed with pikes or other lethal weapons, ranged the streets and broke into the houses in search of plunder. It is remarkable that during such an orgy of uncontrollable violence, women, though sometimes threatened, suffered no physical injury, but men professing the Protestant religion, who had not fled with the garrison, were murdered in considerable numbers. The worst of these wanton acts was the piking to death of the Rev. Samuel Heydon, the old and inoffensive rector of Ferns, in the presence of his wife, by a butcher named Beaghan.

Nevertheless, these deeds of blood were, to some extent, redeemed by many acts of kindness and of mercy. Thus Mrs. Newton Lett and others were protected for a prolonged period by a local insurgent leader named Williams, who concealed them from the fury of the mob in his own house, thereby exposing himself to the gravest risk. Mrs. Lett acknowledges that she was treated with much consideration by Williams, Barker and others. There are also incidents on record which show that homicidal violence was not entirely indiscriminate. Mrs. Lett states that 'Mrs. Johnson's trusty maid servant sought her out and came to induce her to return to her lodgings which were undisturbed; her abode was at a Quaker's in Slaney Street; these quiet people were not injured by the rebel party'. She also mentions that 'Mrs. Williams suggested that our better plan would be to send for the priest. She said if we were christened by him they would no longer look upon us as heretics. . . . I shall not omit to mention the kind and humane conduct

[1] William Snowe: *Statement of Transactions at Enniscorthy, etc.* (1801).

of Father Doyle who obligingly said he was ready to perform any office that might contribute to our safety. He supposed we were actuated by fear to make the proposal to him.'

Vinegar Hill—The Camp

LEAVING A FORCE in the burning town to restore and maintain some semblance of order, the insurgent leaders led the remainder to Vinegar Hill, and there established a camp which continued in being until the 21st of June. Gradually from this time onwards neutrality ceased for all except Quakers. Men who did not declare themselves on one side were assumed to be on the other and dealt with accordingly.[1] Parties were dispatched from the camp on the morning of the 29th to round up the waverers in the surrounding country. In addition, the news of victory brought in many who were merely waiting for a definite point of assembly. John Kelly of Killann led a party from his side of the county and Thomas Cloney of Moneyhore arrived —a reluctant volunteer. John Hay of Newcastle was also brought in—a most unwilling participant with, however, some military experience acquired in the service of France.

While success brought hundreds of strong and willing fighting men to the camp as well as many others, both Protestant and Catholic, who attended merely because the alternative was death, it brought also a multitude of fugitives, female as well as male, from the unprotected countryside, many of them crying out for retribution on those who had desolated their homes and driven them into the fields and woods. It was

[1] This did not apply with equal force then or thereafter to the baronies of Forth and Bargy.

inevitable also that there were some who came more intent on private feud and on the prospect of plunder, than with any resolve to risk their lives in any cause.

Careful lists have been prepared and published[1] showing the names of those 'loyalists' who suffered death on Vinegar Hill, at Scullabogue and on Wexford Bridge. On the other hand, I have not discovered, nor will it ever be known, how many hundreds of men, women and even children were butchered on the roads, at their doors or in the fields, or burned in houses where they lay wounded as in New Ross on the 5th of June and in Enniscorthy on the 21st of June,[2] apart from those killed in battle, mostly without firearms and mown down by artillery and musketry.

Thomas Cloney has left a record of his impressions as he arrived in the camp: 'On the hill were assembled some thousands of people, inhabitants of that part of the county, north and north-east of Enniscorthy, many of whom bore evident marks of the dangers they had encountered in the two preceding days—some recounted the actions they had performed against the enemy, and showed wounds that proved them not destitute of courage; others mourned their children, brothers, relations and friends who fell in the late engagements, or who had suffered death previously by torture. More exclaimed that they were left without a house or home, their houses and property having been consumed by the Orange yeomanry.'[3]

Many cried out for punitive expeditions into their own localities,[4] others with shrewder appreciation of the military

---

[1] See Musgrave.

[2] Cloney made some attempt to compile such a list, but most of the murdered died obscurely and unrecorded.

[3] *Personal Narrative*, p. 17. See also the evidence of witnesses at his courtmartial.

[4] Lecky states: 'One man pointed to his forehead scorched and branded by the pitched cap; another showed with burning anger his lacerated back; others told how their cottages had been burnt, how their little properties had been plundered or destroyed, how their wives and daughters had been insulted by the yeomen and implored that a force might be sent to protect their families from massacre by the Orangemen, or to avenge the grievances they had suffered.' See *History*, Vol. IV, p. 362.

requirements of the situation, urged immediate advance against New Ross and Bunclody (Newtownbarry) to the west and Gorey and Arklow to the north. Had this latter counsel been followed, the course of the campaign would have changed vitally and the fatal encirclement of the County Wexford would have been forestalled.

Almost immediately a long series of executions commenced, and these continued throughout the twenty-three days during which the camp was occupied.[1] It has, so far as I am aware, never been ascertained what proportion of those who suffered (estimated at between three and four hundred) were yeomen or supplementaries, but there is no doubt whatever that most, if not all of them, were Protestants and it may be taken as certain that if their association with the yeomanry were proved their chance of survival was slight. There seems to have been here, as elsewhere, a confusion between Protestants and Orangemen. The 'loyalist' historian, Taylor, records that Luke Byrne of Oulartard, who owned a brewery in Enniscorthy and who was much implicated in these trials and executions, enquired on one occasion at least, how many persons were condemned and on being told 'twenty-seven' he answered: 'If anyone can vouch for any of the prisoners not being Orangemen, I have no objection they should be discharged'. Apparently Quakers, though unmistakably Protestant, were readily absolved from the charge of being 'Orangemen' since, although a number of them were arrested, taken to the camp on the hill and underwent trial there, they were all set at liberty.

Those brought in as prisoners by the parties of men who ranged for miles in every direction during the first night and later, were confined in Beale's Barn. This was situated beside

[1] Musgrave states that thirty-two were put to death on Tuesday, the 29th of May, including two Protestant clergymen—John Pentland of Killann and Thomas Troke of Templeshannon, Enniscorthy. No claim for compensation is recorded in the case of Pentland. Sarah Troke, a widow, claimed £254 and was paid in full.

Beale's brewery, a mile from the town on the road to Darby's Gap and across the road from the present Bell Grove House.[1] From this prison there was easy access to the summit of the hill. The small circular windmill was used as headquarters, and there such trial as was vouchsafed, was carried out. On conviction the prisoners were taken outside and piked or shot.[2] Even allowing for some exaggeration on the part of the relatives of those who met their end here, there is no doubt whatever, that it was a very bloody business and that many of those condemned suffered unnecessarily painful deaths. Those who have had experience of war, or even of serious rioting, will not need to be reminded how near men in the mass can become to the primeval savage, how credulous they are and how cruel they may be when frenzied by hatred, or by fear. The fact must be faced, regrettable though it may be, that in such circumstances men are apt to have recourse to the oldest arbitrament in the world—*blood for blood*.

As the days passed, something resembling order was established with a kind of local Committee of Public Safety set up in Enniscorthy, of which William Barker was a prominent member, together with a shuttle service of guards between the camp and the town. But at the beginning all was disorder and confusion to such an extent that, as Cloney expressed it, 'a few hours was likely to end this local Insurrection, which never had been matured by previous organisation, or settled plan, but had its origin in the great principle of self-preservation'.[3]

However, into this camp of many counsels there arrived

---

[1] George Beale, Drumgold, later claimed £1,501 compensation and was awarded £1,051.

[2] One of the deaths most to be regretted which took place on this blood-stained hill, was that of Stephen Reynolds of Monart, a brother-in-law of Matthew Keogh. He was done to death on the 12th of June. His body was brought home by his widow and buried at Monart in the corner of a field beside the road. The memorial slab is now broken across owing to subsidence of the supporting walls. Catherine Reynolds, his widow, claimed £100 and was paid £95 for loss of clothes, cattle, etc.

[3] *Personal Narrative*, p. 18.

at four p.m. on Tuesday, the 29th of May, two envoys from the British garrison in Wexford town, namely, Edward Fitzgerald of Newpark and Dr. John Henry Colclough of Ballyteigue. They had been arrested in circumstances referred to on page 44 and they were released in the hope that they might, by their personal influence, induce the people to lay down their arms and return to their homes. In all the circumstances those at the head of affairs in Wexford showed by their action an incredible lack of understanding of the true position[1] and, as might have been expected, the result was the opposite of that which it may be supposed they anticipated. All major discussion came to an end and agreement was reached to march south with the object of attacking and occupying the town of Wexford. Colclough from the extreme south of Bargy, was unknown to most, if not all, in the camp and he was allowed to return to announce the failure of his mission. Fitzgerald remained and was given a command in the insurgent forces, but whether his failure to return was voluntary or not, has never been and cannot now be determined. My own opinion is that he was detained against his will. He was held in high regard by the people and his presence among them was looked upon as a very definite asset.

Leaving a garrison in Enniscorthy and a strong holding party in the camp on Vinegar Hill, the main force marched later the same evening by Ferrycarrig to Three Rocks on the high ground three miles due west of Wexford town.

---

[1] Miles Byrne's comment is as follows: 'The absurdity of telling a victorious army to disperse and go to their homes and there wait until they might be shot in detail, showed how panic struck the cowardly garrison of Wexford was and how easy it would have been to have captured them . . . had there been a rapid march made on the town instead of by the circuitous one to the Three Rock mountain.'

The Camp at Three Rocks

THIS POSITION was chosen with excellent judgment. Situated on a ridge of high ground at the junction of five roads, it was well suited for ease of assembly from any direction, for observation from the peaks in the vicinity and for rapid movement either in attack or defence. One of these roads led due east through Colestown to Wexford town, one across the high ground to the south and the other three reached the Taghmon-Wexford road at different points. The camp spread over the fields surrounding the three tall outcrops of natural rock, which give their names to the locality.

While the insurgents were thus busily engaged, plans to reinforce the garrison in Wexford town were being pushed forward. General Fawcett had gathered a force at Duncannon Fort, but for some unexplained reason he sallied out unattended on the evening of the 29th and arriving at Taghmon after dark, decided to spend the remainder of the night there. An advance party of eighty-eight men of the Wexford Militia under Captain Adams and a half battery of gunners with two howitzers under Lieutenant Birch followed later and passed through Taghmon, apparently unaware of the presence of General Fawcett there. They had proceeded some four miles further on the road to Wexford when disaster overtook them in the early morning light. As Hay describes it: 'They had already ascended the road along the sides of the mountain of Forth[1] when perceived by the outposts of the insurgents who poured down upon them with such rapidity that they were in a few minutes cut off, except Ensign Wade and sixteen privates who were taken prisoners.'

The story of this engagement is told modestly and briefly by Thomas Cloney who, on learning in the camp at Three Rocks of the approach of the hostile party, applied for instructions to several persons who appeared to be in a position of command —including Edward Roche, John Hay and Edward Fitzgerald— but all disclaimed the necessary authority. Eventually, impelled by pressure from men of his own neighbourhood, Cloney collected a party which included John Kelly of Killan, Robert Carty of Birchgrove[2] and Michael Furlong of Templescoby.

We suffered them to advance very close to our position—we rushed on them with more of irresistible impetuosity than military skill. The contest held but ten or fifteen minutes, for after firing a few rounds they were overpowered, the entire party being either killed, wounded, or taken prisoners, with the exception, as I afterwards learned, of one officer and four or five privates, who retreated to Duncannon Fort.

Birch, the gunner, was the surviving officer and in an official report he stated that 'after the first fire the militia betook themselves to flight having thrown down most of their arms'.[3]

It was doubtless these survivors who carried the news to General Fawcett, whereupon that officer returned to Duncannon with the additional troops who had by that time joined him.[4]

---

[1] The direct line from Taghmon to Wexford was then the upper road which skirts the Shelmalier Commons and passes close below the Three Rocks. The road link from Taghmon joining the main New Ross-Wexford road at Knockeen is not marked on contemporary maps.

[2] Five miles south of Enniscorthy on the right bank of the river.

[3] Quoted by Musgrave.

[4] There is a tradition (recorded in The Past, No. 2, p. 146), that those who were killed were buried in a field known as the Church Meadow in the townland of Ballyhine. The site of the church is marked by a cluster of thorn bushes north of the main road from Ross to Wexford and a few hundred yards west of Larkin's crossroads.

General Fawcett reported the incident in a dispatch to General Eustace the following day. It is likely that it was in order to to justify his rather dubious conduct that he included these words: '. . . any attempt that was not next to a certainty of succeeding in against them should never again be attempted. Believe me they are no longer to [be] despised as common armed Peasantry—they are organised and have persons of skil [sic] and enterprize among them. . . .'.[1]

The garrison in Wexford, aware of the original intention of General Fawcett and alarmed by the appearance of large numbers of people at the Ferrybank end of the bridge, decided to attack the camp from the east, while, as they hoped, they would have the co-operation of the troops advancing from the west. The garrison's force was commanded by Colonel Maxwell who had arrived in the town the previous morning with two hundred men of the Donegal militia and encamped on Windmill Hill. The infantry were supported by five detachments of yeomen cavalry. The latter were accompanied by a retired officer named Lieutenant-Colonel Jonas Watson who served as a volunteer with the rank of sergeant in the Shelmalier Cavalry. They halted on the road opposite Belmont House and Colonel Watson rode forward to reconnoitre the insurgent position. I think he probably turned up the hill road which branches off to the camp about half-a-mile beyond Belmont. Here he was shot from an insurgent outpost and the whole garrison force, in the absence of any news of the expected reinforcement from General Fawcett, retreated behind the defences of the town.[2]

They then decided to dispatch envoys to the insurgents, and Bagnal Harvey, who was under open arrest, was first approached.

[1]   I.S.P.O.
[2]   Cloney states that one round was fired from a captured howitzer and this may have assisted the yeomen in reaching the decision to retire. Colonel Watson was buried in the neighbouring churchyard. See note at the end of this chapter.

He declined for the reason that he was unknown to those in the camp who were chiefly from the northern half of the county. He, however, consented to write a letter stating that he and the other prisoners had been set at liberty and pleading with the insurgents to avoid massacre and the destruction of property. Eventually Loftus Richards, a Wexford apothecary and his brother, Counsellor Richards, two brave men, set out on this hazardous mission. It is not certain whether the garrison were more concerned for the safety of the town and its inhabitants, or for gaining time in order to permit of their own escape either by sea, or by road to Duncannon through the southern baronies of Forth, Bargy and Shelburne.

It is probable that they had both objects in view, but that the latter was uppermost in their minds is shown by the fact that the withdrawal commenced immediately after the envoys had departed on their mission.

When the brothers Richards delivered their plea for the sparing of life and property, the terms were accepted on condition that the garrison surrendered their arms and ammunition. There was considerable delay, however, as the envoys were compelled to ride with Edward Fitzgerald to within a mile of Taghmon in order to confirm that the remainder of the relief force had, in fact, retreated to Duncannon.

The reply was brought back by Counsellor Richards who was accompanied by Edward Fitzgerald, Loftus Richards being detained in camp as a hostage.[1]

Three hours further unaccountable delay now occurred, during which time fires were observed on the low ground several miles south of the camp. These, in fact, were caused by the burning chapel and houses in Moyglass, and showed how far the fleeing garrison had already proceeded on their

[1] Musgrave prints what he states is Loftus Richards' description of his visit to the camp. Portion of this I have given as Appendix III. Cloney stated that Loftus Richards remained under his care, but the latter makes no mention of Cloney.

way to Duncannon. It is not easy to understand why the garrison's retreat by this route was not anticipated and provided against. The soldiers were in complete panic and many of them had thrown away their arms. A comparatively small force, properly led, could have rounded them up without difficulty.[1]

As hour followed hour, murmurs arose in the camp and charges of bad faith were heard against both Fitzgerald and the brothers Richards. At last the hostage, with a good deal of sense, suggested that the matter could best be decided in Wexford itself.

Thus, late in the evening of this eventful 30th of May, the insurgent army marched without opposition into the abandoned town.

---

[1] Cloney records that John Hay (who had had military experience), proposed the sending of a detachment to intercept the fugitives before they reached the Scar at Barrystown, but he was not supported!

Note

The following inscription is still decipherable in Carrick churchyard:

LIEUTENANT COLONEL JONAS WATSON

Had been actively employed for thirty years in the service of His Country. During which period his life had often been Preserved amidst the shock of Battle.

But it pleased the Almighty that He alone should fall whilst Gallantly leading on the Yeomanry of this County to attack the Rebel force which was posted on the Three Rocks on the (30th) day of May, 1798.

The consequence of His fall was the immediate evacuation of Wexford by the Loyalists.

This disposes of the statement of Musgrave that there were other casualties on this occasion. See also the deposition of Robert Edwards (Appendix II) which may have been the source of Musgrave's statement.

See also Appendix IIIA for Colonel Maxwell's account of the evacuation of Wexford.

The Occupation of Wexford and After

IN 1798 the walls of Wexford town were still almost intact, although the various gateways had long been demolished.[1] The latter were, however, strongly barricaded and as the insurgents appeared on Three Rocks and the town was directly threatened, thatch was stripped from the houses within the walls in order to avert a repetition of the fires which had so embarrassed the defenders of Enniscorthy. The armed garrison, with ample munitions and supplies and comprising militia, yeomen and supplementaries, numbered twelve hundred. A single gun suitably mounted would with ease have secured the town from assault across the wooden bridge, even if it had been left passable otherwise, while the strong defences and ample armament, it may be thought, should have compensated for the numerically larger force of the undisciplined and poorly armed insurgents and presented a successful defence of the town as a reasonable proposition.

Following the failure of the sortie, however, panic spread among them and two hundred men composed of Scarawalsh yeoman infantry (Captain Isaac Cornock), a detachment of the North Cork Militia haunted perhaps by what they had heard of the pikemen at Oulart Hill, together with a party of armed civilians broke out of the town and headed south-west for Duncannon. They met John Henry Colclough (on his

[1] Hay.

86

way to Wexford to replace Bagnal Harvey in prison there in accordance with an honourable agreement) and compelled him to accompany the party as far as the Pass of Scar at Barrystown. As the tide was in and no boats were available, the long detour by Foulke's Mill became necessary, since Wellington Bridge had not then been built.

As this detachment approached the Owenduff river, they were attacked in the darkness by a party of mounted insurgents under John Murphy of Loughnageer[1] and driven on to Taylorstown bridge where they came under heavy fire from the rising ground nearby. 'About fifty of the North Cork and the Yeomanry were taken prisoner, a good many were killed'[2] and the rest dispersed. Captain William Snowe, who had been in nominal command of the party, arrived at Duncannon Fort exhausted and alone at seven o'clock in the morning.[3]

An hour after the flight of the first party the remainder of the Wexford garrison set out, headed by Colonel Maxwell. One officer and a few men of the Wexford yeoman infantry were left behind, not having been made aware of the intention to retreat. Colonel Maxwell's party followed the route Moyglass (which, with its chapel, they burned), Bridgetown, Baldwinstown, Duncormack to the Pass of Scar at Barrystown and thence by Foulke's Mill to Duncannon which was reached after a journey of eighteen hours, including a halt at the Scar.[4]

Four magistrates were particularly obnoxious to the people on account of their brutal misconduct during the preceding weeks. They were Archibald Hamilton Jacob of Templeshannon, Enniscorthy, James Boyd of Wexford, Hunter Gowan of Mount Nebo, and Hawtrey White of Peppard's Castle. Two

---

[1] Later in charge of the guard over the prisoners at Scullabogue.
[2] Musgrave.
[3] Captain Snowe claimed £192 for personal losses, but no award is recorded.
[4] Hay states that the retreat of these detachments was attended by wanton murder of the country people along the route and burning of their houses. Gordon agrees, but blames the North Cork Militia. See Appendix IIIA

of these, Jacob and Boyd, were in Wexford when the insurgent army reached Three Rocks. Jacob accompanied the sortie from the town and clearly foreseeing the likelihood of his meeting the fate he deserved if he fell into insurgent hands, he slipped away from his companions and escaped across country to New Ross, thence to Waterford and England.

Captain James Boyd of the Wexford yeoman cavalry, after failing in an attempt to escape by sea, rode hastily to the house of his friend King, at Barrystown, where he was fortunate, with a few companions, in obtaining a boat to cross the Pass of Scar and so reach Duncannon.[1]

While these unworthy transactions were in progress, the occupation of the town proceeded and the insurgents became aware of the extent to which they had been duped on discovering that practically all the arms and warlike stores had been either removed or destroyed. It is, therefore, hardly surprising that the insurgent leaders should have found themselves powerless to prevent looting and some destruction of property. It may be regarded as creditable in all the circumstances that the unfortunate envoys were not made to pay with their lives the penalty for the garrison's successful *ruse de guerre*.

Those who had sought safety in the various vessels lying in the harbour were brought ashore and some of them lodged in the town gaol and other buildings, along with all those known to be associated with the various corps of yeomen, or their supplementaries.

Immediate search was made for James Boyd and Archibald Jacob and when this failed, the house of the former, halfway down the north side of George's Street, was plundered and destroyed and his brother, John Boyd, was piked on the quay side and left to die.

On the 4th of June an Enniscorthy yeoman named George Sparrow, was recognised and killed in the Bull Ring. Both of

[1] Both James Boyd and Archibald Jacob returned to Wexford on the 21st of June.

these were Protestants. Two Catholics were executed as informers, Francis Murphy on the 3rd, and Joseph Murphy on the 14th,[1] and Protestant prisoners were forced to act on each occasion as executioners.[2]

After an uneasy night and a still more uneasy morning following, sufficient control was regained to establish a camp outside the town on Windmill Hill. Matthew Keogh was installed as Governor with William Kearney, a citizen of good repute, as his assistant and they exercised their authority in extraordinarily difficult conditions with some success. Except for the four cases mentioned, although there were several narrow escapes, no more lives were lost in the town until the final holocaust on the 20th of June.

The chief function of the governor, apart from restoring and maintaining some degree of order, was the organisation of supply. The town administration was by means of a committee and the flow of provisions and their equitable distribution were at once instituted and maintained, while the care of the sick and later of the wounded also, was placed under the control of Dr. Ebenezer Jacob.

On the 31st, Bagnal Harvey, who had been nominated commander-in-chief, moved camp from Windmill Hill to Three Rocks and there serious consideration was given to the general strategic situation. The fact had to be faced that the government was now fully alive to the dangers which confronted them and could be relied upon to take the necessary counter-measures. Precious time had already been wasted by the insurgents. William Barker had urged an attack on New Ross immediately after Enniscorthy—an obviously wise move as

[1] The first of these was gardener to Edwards of Ballyhire. He had informed against a Father Dixon of Castlebridge (see page 265).
[2] This barbarous practice was resorted to by both sides. Keogh, a prisoner in the hands of Colonel Longfield at Rathangan on 28th May was compelled to kill his fellow prisoners. (See Musgrave.)

that key town was then practically undefended.[1] The lure of Wexford town had been, however, too strong and the decision to move there was assuredly a prime cause of the ultimate failure. This, with the hopeless mismanagement at Bunclody (Newtownbarry) and the repulse at Arklow ensured the encirclement of the county and made final defeat inevitable.

Eventually it was decided to divide the forces into three. The first of them under Bagnal Harvey to march west against New Ross in order to open the road to Kilkenny and Waterford. This column was composed chiefly of Bantry and Shelmalier men, with the addition of newcomers from Forth and Bargy, the latter stung into activity by the depredations of the fleeing garrison. The second and third columns to return to Vinegar Hill and then divide—one under Father Moses (Mogue) Kearns to attack Bunclody and break through to Carlow and the other under Anthony Perry, Father John Murphy and Father Michael Murphy, to Gorey and Arklow and so to form a junction with the Wicklowmen for an advance on the capital. As these operations were carried out independently, they will be separately considered.

. . . .

The removal of the fighting men from the vicinity of Wexford town greatly increased the difficulties of the 'controlling' authorities and it is of the first importance for a just appreciation of the events of this time that we should actively resist the prevailing tendency to ignore what is distasteful to us. Accordingly it is necessary, having already referred to the bitter anti-Catholic laws and administration, to present also another side of the picture.

A situation was in the course of development over which Matthew Keogh as a Protestant, could exercise neither influence

---

[1] Gordon states that John Hay also advised the immediate advance on New Ross, but partly on personal grounds and partly in order to effect the release of the prisoners in Wexford, this was opposed by Edward Fitzgerald.

nor effective control and caused as it was by a frenzy of sectarian hatred, it became infinitely worse when, with the withdrawal of the pikemen, the rabble found themselves in the position of masters. There is no room for doubt that force, or the threat of force was employed to compel Protestants to abjure their faith; the evidence is overwhelming. Thus, Elizabeth Richards, a daughter of Thomas Richards of Rathaspick, was in Wexford from the 26th of May until the 22nd of June. She kept a diary in which she refers repeatedly to attempts made to force conversion. She herself, was detained for some days with this object in view, though she admits she was not harshly treated. She states: '. . . It is not, I think, possible that the rebels, although they may for a time be victorious, should ultimately obtain possession of Ireland . . . they will not long suffer hereticks to infect the air. . . .'[1]

Mrs. Brownrigg of Greenmound is equally emphatic in her Journal under the date 'June 2nd': 'Mrs. Lehaste [Lehunte] and many others went to the Chapel, renounced their Religion, were *Christened* (for it seems we are not Christians) and were marched in Procession through the town'.[2] Mrs. Brownrigg was detained from the 28th of May until the 21st of June and it must be stated that she herself, did not by any means 'lack gall to make oppression bitter' as is shown in the following entry in her Journal: 'Ask one of these Holy Men to save a Friend's life; they were all benevolence, but alas! had no Power. Their influence had long ceased over the minds of the People.'[3]

[1] *Orpen Papers*—Ainsworth Transcriptions, National Library, Dublin.
[2] Published in *The War in Wexford* by Wheeler and Broadley (1910). Charles Jackson, who was there, also records the same particulars about the Lehunte family and adds that Colonel Lehunte's life was saved later by the exertions of Father Broe.
[3] Edward Hay, the leading Catholic historian of the Rising, was also in Wexford during that time and he expresses himself in no uncertain terms as follows:
'Now that the insurrection in Wexford was at its height, there existed no kind of subordination or control; individuals assumed the privilege of indulging their own dispositions and of gratifying private malice. The populace were

continued at foot of next page

Although I do not feel satisfied that the sworn depositions of adversaries must necessarily be regarded as literally true and although I think the circumstances in which many of them were produced are open to the gravest suspicion, nevertheless, the evidence that the ignorant people murdered many persons at Scullabogue and elsewhere who refused to be baptised in the Roman manner is far too strong to be ignored and also that priests such as Father Doyle of Fethard and others, saved the lives of many persons by making a pretence of baptising them. In Wexford the threat of force, or the menace of death, appears to have been sufficient to induce many to go through the gestures of conforming and it was only towards the end of the occupation that events took a sudden and more dreadful turn. By that time, however, other causes besides sectarian rancour had arisen and these will be referred to later.

furious and ungovernable, and many of this description remained in Wexford after the great body of the insurgents had retired from the town; they seized upon and lodged in the gaol many persons from all parts of the surrounding country who had fled for protection and were now endeavouring to conceal themselves in the different houses of their friends to escape popular resentment.'
Page 137, (1942 ed.).

The Battle of Bunclody (Newtownbarry)

THE FIRST DAY of June was marked by greatly increased activity of various kinds. On that date Cooke, the under-secretary, wrote to Admiral Kingsmill that 'a Rebel Force has taken possession of the Town of Wexford and that there is Reason from private Information, to believe that a French succour of Frigates is expected there'. He directed him to 'send a force to prevent any assistance from France on that coast and I am to suggest that Gun Boats are calculated particularly for that Harbour'.[1] On the same date Captain Hill was directed by Cooke to turn his attention to the harbour of Wexford with the gunboats under his command in Waterford.[2]

On the previous evening the insurgents, already in possession of the whole of South Wexford except the fort of Duncannon and the town of New Ross, moved away from their base at Three Rocks. Father Moses (Mogue) Kearns was accompanied by Miles Byrne and the latter states that the column which attacked Bunclody did not exceed 2,500 men. This seems much more probable than the estimates by the defenders which vary from ten thousand to fifteen thousand![3]

[1] I.S.P.O. The Government were no doubt, well aware that in the plans of the United Irishmen, Wexford had been mentioned as the harbour of choice for a French landing.

[2] I.S.P.O.

[3] Robert Edwards (see Appendix II), was apparently informed at Vinegar Hill that the force dispatched to Bunclody was reinforced by a party of five hundred from the camp.

Hay suggests that Bunclody was attacked as an independent diversion originating with Father Kearns himself and Miles Byrne's account is consistent with this view, but there is, I think, little doubt that it was part of a larger strategic plan for breaking out of the County Wexford.

Taylor states that the attackers came from Vinegar Hill and he supplies the most detailed account of the battle. The garrison was under the command of Colonel Henry Peisley L'Estrange of the King's County Militia and comprised some four hundred men, including militia and yeoman infantry, with a number of volunteers and detachments of the 4th Dragoons and the Newtownbarry and Carlow yeoman cavalry. There were also two battalion guns.

About mid-day the insurgents approached on both sides of the river from the direction of Ballycarney. They brought with them 'a brass six pounder, a howitzer[1] and some ship swivels'. Taking up a position on high ground above the slate quarry, they fired a few rounds and immediately afterwards rushed into the town. Colonel L'Estrange, fearing encirclement, hastily withdrew his infantry without offering any serious resistance and retreated, screened by the cavalry, for a distance of at least a mile up the Carlow road.

Taylor's account continues as follows:

> The rebels entering the town, set the suburbs on fire, plundered the army's baggage, burst open the cellars and drank the spirits in such abundance that becoming intoxicated they ranged thro' the town, shouting and hallooing without any order. This confusion was much increased by the loyalists firing from several of the houses against which they soon bent all their fury. The yeomen . . . entreated Colonel L'Estrange to return and attack them with his cannon, alledging that as they were quite intoxicated, void of any order and not expecting danger, they would soon be overpowered.

A well-timed counter-attack headed by Lieutenant-Colonel Westenra, a volunteer officer named Major Marley and Captain Kerr and preceded by a few rounds from the two

[1] Probably one of the two captured at Three Rocks two days before.

guns which raked the main street and square, drove the insurgents from the town with considerable loss. Miles Byrne hotly disputes the statement that the defeat was due to 'drunkenness and pillage' but his account is not convincing, nor is his statement credible that 'the number of killed and wounded was nearly equal on each side'. The official admission of loss by the garrison was one killed and one wounded, while they claim to have inflicted two hundred and fifty casualties on the insurgents in the counter-attack and pursuit. Between such widely dissimilar claims it is impossible to form any accurate estimate of the loss on either side.

This engagement has an added interest on account of a small incident which occurred immediately before the attack. Young Miles Byrne of Monaseed, not yet twenty, ventured to approach Father Kearns with the suggestion, as I understand it, that the exits of the town should be secured before the frontal attack was made. The reply of Father Kearns to so eminently sensible a proposal and one which in all probability would have meant victory instead of ignominious defeat, must, for pure fatuousness, be regarded as almost a record in military history. 'Tell all those you have any control over,' he said, 'to fear nothing so long as they see this whip in my hand.'

The dispersed insurgents made their way in scattered groups to Vinegar Hill and on the 3rd of June they joined their companions on Carrigrew Hill.

. . . .

Colonel L'Estrange was regarded by his brother officers as having been guilty of pusillanimous conduct in abandoning the town without a fight and he gave added offence by taking the credit for organising the counter-attack to himself and to the volunteer Major Marley, whereas in fact the officer chiefly responsible was Lieutenant-Colonel Westenra (afterwards Lord Rossmore) and he was given no credit. This together with later charges of nepotism in the appointment of officers to his regiment appear to have made Colonel L'Estrange unpopular and eventually the various grievances became the subject of a court of enquiry held at Limerick in August–September, 1801. The result was a mild remonstrance and a direction that in future he was to pursue a more equitable system of promotion.[1]

One question and answer during this enquiry are, however, of historical interest. It will be recalled that the infamous Captain J. W. Armstrong, the informer, was an officer in the King's County Militia. Referring to that officer a witness, Lieutenant Thomas Warburton was asked: 'Don't you believe he was directed by Colonel L'Estrange in the most important transaction of his life?' The reply was: 'If he means the prosecution of the Sheares, I believe he acted with the approbation of Colonel L'Estrange'.

[1]   *Minutes of Proceedings, etc.*, printed in Dublin, 1802.

The Skirmish near Ballyminaun Hill

THE BATTLE of Oulart on the 27th of May, had two immediate results. It spread alarm and despondency among the 'loyalist' inhabitants which was not lessened when the insurgents marched north after the battle to Carrigrew Hill. Refugees crowded into Gorey, the nearest garrisoned town, where they no doubt felt secure under the protection of the various corps of yeomanry and militia concentrated there. The other result was an intensification of the activity of the yeoman cavalry who scoured the surrounding country now left more defenceless than ever by the departure of most of the able-bodied men to join the insurgent camp. Hay refers to their 'falling on the defenceless and unoffending populace, of whom they slew some hundreds'. Hay was in Wexford town at the time and relied on hearsay in this matter. It is probable, therefore, that there is some exaggeration in his account of the numbers killed. Lecky alludes to what he calls the 'atrocious accusations against the yeomen about Gorey' and cites Gordon's silence about the whole business in support of his own disbelief.

For two reasons I think murders by the yeomen on this occasion were widespread, albeit unrecorded. Firstly Gordon, who at that time lived in the vicinity[1] was himself under arms and two of his sons were yeomen. His reticence in the circumstances is therefore understandable. Secondly, I do not believe

[1] At Marlfield, a mile from Gorey, on the Courtown road.

that two individuals of the known character of Hawtrey White
and Hunter Gowan would have hesitated to add to their
already long list of cold-blooded murders in conditions so
favourable and so free from danger.

On the 28th of May, it will be remembered, the insurgent
army had moved from Carrigrew Hill at break of day, on their
way to Camolin, Ferns and Enniscorthy. The rumour apparently
reached Gorey that the town was threatened, with the result that,
at five o'clock in the morning, the entire garrison fled to
Arklow, followed by a terror-stricken multitude of the towns-
folk. This haste was so great that about a hundred prisoners
were abandoned uninjured in the gaol, but a number of men
were shot dead in the street, or wounded and left to die.

For nearly three days the town remained unoccupied by either
side, but on the 30th and 31st, civilian fugitives commenced to
filter back from Arklow where they had been treated with much
churlishness by the garrison there who refused to allow them to
pass the barricades. At the same time the militia and yeomen
resumed their stations in Gorey and recommenced their
customary activities in the neighbourhood.

On the 1st of June the insurgent concentration on Carrigrew
Hill was completed and as a preliminary to the contemplated
drive against Arklow it was decided to attack Gorey. With this
object a force under Father Michael Murphy, probably not
exceeding a thousand men, some of whom were mounted,
proceeded first to the village of Ballycanew in the course of
the evening with the intention of occupying Ballyminaun Hill
and linking up with a force from Carrigrew Hill in a combined
attack on the town the following morning.

The description of the subsequent events here given is
derived from three sources—George Taylor, who lived at
Ballywalter not more than a mile away, James Gordon who
was, to some extent, an eye witness and the relevant entry in

the Detail Book of the Camolin Yeoman Cavalry[1] then in Gorey.

During the 1st of June a patrol, probing in the direction of Carrigrew, reached the Crosses of Ballymore and there they observed large numbers of insurgents on the hill and some parties burning Mount Howard house and between that and Ballycanew, others 'burning Protestants' houses in Tomagaddy'. This latter party nearly succeeded in intercepting the patrol on its way back to Gorey via Ballycanew.

On receipt of the patrol's report that a large body of men was approaching from Carrigrew, the garrison, stated to comprise ninety infantry and one hundred and twenty-eight cavalry, moved out to meet them. They apparently crossed Ballyminaun Hill by the old road which traverses its shoulder to the west of the summit. From this elevated position they could see the insurgents marching down the opposite slope at Ballinamona, towards the low ground in the vicinity of Essex bridge. It was somewhere in the latter region that the engagement took place. Presumably the horses were sheltered behind the fences on both sides of the road, but the insurgents committed the grave error of carrying on a sustained musketry duel. The advantage thus lay heavily with the better trained and better armed yeomen and militia and after persisting in this folly for an hour 'the rebels began to be dismayed at seeing so many of their men fall and perceiving the army still approach in slow and regular order without the loss of a man, they broke and fled in all directions; the cavalry charged and cut them down without taking any prisoners.—There fell about one hundred and fifty in this action[2] and several of the wounded lay in the cornfields, ditches and meadows, being unable to go farther, where they expired; and the dogs of the country after some time carried their arms and legs from ditch to ditch and from field to field. After the action, the army entered Bally-

[1] See Wheeler and Broadley: *The War in Wexford*, (1910).
[2] Gordon mentions 'probably sixty'.

canew, where they destroyed and burnt many houses belonging to the rebels. This little victorious army returned into Gorey, with about one hundred horses taken from the enemy, some guns, pikes and two green standards, without the loss of a man'.[1]

The Rev. James Gordon, after describing the engagement in general agreement with Taylor, adds the following commentary:

> The hardiness and agility of the labouring classes of the Irish people were on this and other occasions in the course of the rebellion, very remarkable. Their swiftness of foot, and activity in passing over brooks and ditches, were such that they could not always in crossing the fields be overtaken by horsemen; and with so much strength of constitution were they found to be endued, that to kill them was difficult, many after a multitude of stabs not expiring until their necks were cut across.[2]

The effect of this repulse was the loss of three precious days during which time large reinforcements were poured into Gorey.

[1] Taylor, (1800): pp. 68-9.
[2] Gordon: 1803 ed., p. 136.

The Battle of Tubberneering

WHILE THE INSURGENTS based on Carrigrew Hill were completing their interrupted plans for the attack on Gorey, Miles Byrne, who was there, states that those who had any knowledge of drill from having been associated with the various corps of yeomanry, laboured to impart their knowledge to as many as possible and to teach the use of the musket. He points out that having no drummers, it was customary for the standard bearers of each corps to summon men to their units by calling out the names of their baronies or districts. He laments the lack of any distinguishing badge of rank in the case of the officers and hints at serious embarrassments having arisen from this obvious defect.

On the 3rd of June, Major General Loftus reached Gorey at the head of a mixed force of fifteen hundred men and five guns. By express he ordered Lord Ancram to march from Bunclody to Scarawalsh Bridge with the King's County Militia and a detachment of dragoons in order to keep Vinegar Hill under observation. In addition, part of the garrison at Carnew was posted to Camolin.

At nine o'clock in the morning of the 4th of June, most of the troops in Gorey were marched out of the town by the west end as far as the fork in the road, a few hundred yards to the south. Here Colonel Lambert Theodore Walpole continued along the line of the present main road to Clough, where he turned off to the left in the direction of Ballymore. General Loftus and his second-in-command, Colonel Scott, forked left along the Ballycanew road.[1] At the cross-road immediately south of Ballyminaun Hill a party of one hundred Antrim Militia under Captain MacManus were stationed as a rear guard for General Loftus' column and at the same time with a ready access to Clough as a reinforcement to Colonel Walpole should the occasion arise.

Colonel Walpole had not penetrated far beyond Clough when insurgent scouts were sighted and his officers suggested to him the advisability of an advance guard and flanking parties in such close country 'where the road was deep and narrow and the clay banks on each side, with deep trenches and bushes on top, were very high'. [2] Colonel Walpole, who appears to have been given his command more on account of Castle influence than military capacity, recognised no offensive significance in the presence of the insurgent scouts and refused to adopt the elementary precautions suggested. The result was that at some point between Tubberneering Rock and Balloughter cross-roads, he blundered into a hastily prepared, but well contrived ambush. Rounding a corner he was suddenly confronted with a gun planted in the middle of the road and fire was opened on his column from the concealed attackers.

The battle was raging for some time with very great impetuosity on both sides. Colonel Walpole rode a grey horse . . . and in every respect was very conspicuous. He dashed furiously from side to side ordering and encouraging his men. There was but little advantage on either side at this time when a man named Patrick O'Brien of Courtclough, parish of Castle Ellis . . . retired a short distance to an eminence. As he reached the desired spot another man named Hatter reached the same spot . . . O'Brien took very deliberate aim and fired. Hatter fired at the same instant and scarcely had O'Brien

[1]   There were approximately five hundred men in each party.
    See letter from Castlereagh to Pelham (6th June, 1798), I.S.P.O.
[2]   Musgrave.

lowered his gun from his eye when he perceived Walpole to tumble from his saddle.

Note: I had the above from a very worthy man who fought there and who was speaking to O'Brien as he was charging his gun for the above purpose and saw him fire and saw Walpole falling.[1]

Another account, purporting to be that of an eyewitness in Walpole's force, is in general agreement with the above; in addition it includes an interesting topographical reference:

We came to a beautiful situation by nature; the quicksets were very high on either hand; as also a woody country through which we were to proceed. . . . They secreted their force behind hedges, to allure us into the ambuscade—which unfortunately answered their hellish design. Our cannon consisting of two six pounders and a small field piece of the Ancient British Fencibles were ordered to the front—the road became narrow which prevented the great guns from acting agreeably to our wish; they began a heavy fire of musquetry from each side of the road and from behind the hedges on our army . . . the cannon ceased, owing to the narrow pass, as also the horses being killed in the traces . . . Colonel Walpole received a ball in the thigh and in a moment after, another through the head . . . a ball went through Colonel Cope's horse's ear which grazed his cheek and passed through his hat. . . . In a little time their line broke, which we took for an omen of their defeat; but this was only to deceive us for their two wings set up the *war-hoop* and made for Gorey to cut off our retreat which had been ordered to be made. . . . It was truly painful as we passed along, to behold our cannon on the roads useless to us . . . —also the groans of the wounded whose bodies, torn and pierced by pikes, while yet living, rendered the scene altogether very awful! . . . we fought and loaded while running and endeavouring to avoid the fire of our own cannon which were turned upon us by the rebels. We passed by Tubberneerneen Rock, [sic] where their green flag was displayed, and killed one of their chieftains on horseback; also a number who pressed after us.[2]

This account shows that the action commenced on the Ballymore side of Tubberneering Rock, a conspicuous land

[1]. Luke Cullen MS.—Madden Papers, Library, T.C.D.

[2] John Jones: *An Impartial Narrative*; letter signed W.H.G. 4th edition, pp. 121-3.
    This correspondent states that during the pursuit, many soldiers were killed and some prisoners taken who were found uninjured on Vinegar Hill seventeen days later.

mark a short distance to the west of the road.

Miles Byrne who was a member of the insurgent advance guard on this occasion differs from all other narrators in stating that Colonel Walpole was killed during the pursuit at the village of Clough, when he had rallied his troops after being joined by the reinforcement in reserve of one hundred men of the Antrim Militia from the post at the Ballyminaun cross-roads. Gordon states that this reinforcement was intercepted and decimated on the way across. I think Miles Byrne is mistaken and that his mistake arises from a confusion with the very spirited delaying action for which Colonel Cope was responsible.[1]

Luke Cullen states that Walpole is buried 'on the lands of Clough, near the road and on the right-hand side of it as you proceed from Ballymore to Gorey'.

The survivors of Colonel Walpole's division fled through Gorey to Arklow, and eventually reached the town of Wicklow ! The insurgents followed hard on their heels and occupied Gorey without further opposition, establishing their camp on Gorey Hill, half-a-mile west of the town.

General Loftus, as he approached Ballycanew, heard the firing less than three miles away across country, but seems to have over-confidently assumed that Colonel Walpole was driving the insurgents before him. He, therefore, pushed on through Ballycanew, round Carrigrew Hill and then doubled back along the road towards Clough, apparently with the object of cutting off their retreat. He was doubtless surprised to find that the flow of battle had taken the contrary direction and advancing cautiously, he traversed the road over and beside which the battle had been fought.

Approaching the camp at Gorey Hill and finding it strongly held, he considered it advisable to retrace his steps to Clough, and, guided by Brownrigg of Barnadown, he followed the bye-road to Carnew. 'Thinking Carnew an unsafe post, though the

[1] Castlereagh in his letter to Pelham, stated that Walpole fell early in the action.

gentlemen of that neighbourhood thought and still think quite otherwise, as he was there at the head of twelve hundred effective men, he abandoned that part of the country to the rebels, and retreated nine miles farther, to the town of Tullow, in the county of Carlow'.[1]

Note

Lecky, following Gordon, states that Father Philip Roche was present at Tubberneering, and Miles Byrne that he was with the division at Gorey on the 7th of June when he was appointed to succeed Bagnal Harvey. This appears to be altogether improbable. Musgrave mentions definitely that Father Roche accompanied Harvey to Carrickbyrne on the way to New Ross, and it is likely that, having been recently stationed at Pollpeasty near Killann, he would elect to march with the Bantry men. There was probably some confusion with Edward Roche who unquestionably was present at Tubberneering.

[1] Gordon, p. 140.
Taylor states that his destination was Hacketstown. See Appendix IV for the dispatch from General Loftus.

Gorey

MILES BYRNE STATES that during the retreat of the defeated
troops from Tubberneering, concern was felt as to the fate of
the prisoners known to be confined in the town gaol and the
loft of the Market House in Gorey. Accordingly, the pursuit
was hotly pressed in order that there might be no opportunity
for massacre if, as is not improbable, such was the intention.
The fugitives did, however, fire through the windows of the
rooms in which the prisoners were confined, but these, by the
instructions of Esmond Kyan, lay on the floors and the bullets
lodged harmlessly in the opposite wall.

Esmond Kyan was a decided acquisition, having had artillery
training, and it was he who, shortly after he was set at liberty,
fired a salvo which discouraged General Loftus from carrying
out any intention he may have had to attack the insurgent
camp on Gorey Hill.

The roads in all directions were patrolled by the insurgents
and outposts stationed to guard against surprise. This was the
only action of any military value whatsoever at what was,
perhaps the most critical period of the campaign. The delay
in advancing on Arklow, lasting from the 4th until the 9th,
was a demonstration of almost incredible ineptitude. Miles
Byrne's half-hearted apologies are unconvincing. He refers
to the possibility of attack by General Loftus from Carnew,

but he himself found Carnew undefended on the 7th, and could have found it deserted on the 5th. In addition, he admits that before dawn on the 5th, definite information had been received that Arklow had been evacuated. This delay, like that at Carrickbyrne (see page 110), was to lead to irretrievable disaster and the loss of many hundreds of lives.

The first day of the occupation of the camp on Gorey Hill, was spent in rounding up a number of persons of no military importance in the neighbourhood and lodging them in the town gaol; also, in burning down the adjoining residences of Ramsfort and Clonatin and, with more excuse, the house of the infamous Hunter Gowan, at Mount Nebo[1] (now Mount St. Benedict). Then apparently in deference to popular clamour and unaware that its evacuation had taken place on the 5th, the entire force marched out on the 7th to attack Carnew, camping on Kilcavan Hill, two miles north-east of the town. Finding the town undefended they burned a number of the houses and in the course of this futile operation, news was received that Arklow had been re-occupied by government troops. Accordingly, on the 8th the insurgents returned to Gorey Hill to prepare for an attack which should never have been necessary as that town could have been occupied without opposition three days before. It is possible that the fatal diversion to Carnew may have been undertaken in the hope of collecting some much needed powder and ammunition. An urgent application to Wexford had produced one barrel of powder only. In the event it was the complete exhaustion of their scanty ammunition supply which was one of the main causes of their withdrawal from Arklow.

A writer, signing himself George Tenor and stating he was from the neighbourhood of Gorey,[2] supplies the following description of the camp on Gorey Hill:

[1] Stephen Ram claimed £6,908 for the looting and burning of Ramsfort, Abel Ram, £4,143 for Clonatin, and Hunter Gowan £2,130 for Mount Nebo.
[2] Apparently a pen-name of George Taylor.

'The Rebel camp covered many acres of ground and their Numbers were very great. It was very distressing to my Mind to see their Colours flying, Drums beating, and Fifes playing, but no Military Force in the Neighbourhood sufficiently powerful to engage them.' He states that he was importuned frequently to accept Catholic baptism which he refused and was brought from the town to the camp (he thinks for execution), but was saved by the arrival of Bagnal Harvey's proclamation issued from the camp at Carrickbyrne on the 6th of June. He mentions that the insurgents pitchcapped some of the prisoners, but not himself.[1]

---

[1] *The Monitor*, Nos. 1 and 2, National Library, Dublin. For a description of the scene in Gorey a week after the battle of Arklow, see Appendix V.

The Freeman's Journal of the 6th of August, 1798, records that an entrenched camp had been established on Gorey Hill under the command of Colonel Skerrett, adding that 'this force is to be kept up in that quarter during the winter'.

The Battle of New Ross

BAGNAL HARVEY on his journey westwards, was accompanied by John Henry Colclough of Ballyteige, Father Philip Roche, late of Pollpeasty, John Kelly of Killann, Thomas Cloney of Moneyhore, Matthew Furlong of Raheen and his brother Michael Furlong of Templescoby, Walter Devereux of Bally-brittas, a young lad named John Devereux of Taghmon,[1] John Boxwell of Sarshill and Henry Hughes of Ballytrent.[2] It is difficult to estimate the actual number of effectives in this division, as considerable desertions took place both before and after the battle ground was reached and although many others joined on the line of march to Ross, a proportion of these had been forced into the ranks, or voluntarily accompanied the fighting men without any serious intention of risking their lives. The total has been placed as high as twenty thousand, but certainly a very much smaller number took part in the battle.

The first night was spent in the neighbourhood of Taghmon and the following day they reached Carrickbyrne. There is no tradition as to the exact site of the camp, but from collateral evidence it probably spread over the east slopes and on both

[1] He afterwards served with great distinction in the army of Bolivar, the liberator of South America from the Spaniards.
[2] Though Richard Grandy in his deposition suggested that Cornelius Grogan was also present, I have given reasons for believing that his information was misleading—see page 212.

sides of the old road which at that time crossed the centre of the hill in the direction of Old Ross.

Here for three days they waited and this extraordinary and unaccountable delay without any doubt whatever, was the principal cause of their failure on the 5th of June.[1]

The insurgent forces appear to have occupied this interval in collecting a number of men and women from the countryside further south, many of them from the vicinity of Tintern Abbey. These were lodged in the house and barn of Scullabogue at the foot of the hill.

On the 4th of June the march was resumed through Ballynabola and Cushinstown, and that evening Corbet Hill (now Talbot Hall), lying south-east of Ross and a mile from the outskirts of the town, was occupied as a battle station.

In the meantime, the experienced officer in command of the garrison, Major-General Henry Johnson, made good use of the opportunity provided by the military incompetence of his enemies. He had kept himself well informed of their movements by means of videttes operating as far afield as Lacken Hill. He received a valuable addition to his garrison by the arrival, at the last moment, of the Dublin Militia under Lord Mountjoy and he had time to strengthen the defences of the town. He considered that the main attacks would be directed against Irishtown and the Three Bullet Gate and accordingly 'upwards of one hundred labourers with spades, shovels and pickaxes were quickly pressed and under the direction of some gentlemen of the town, cast up two trenches, one in the Irishtown

---

[1] It has been suggested that simultaneous attack from the Kilkenny side was part of the original plan and that no serious resistance was anticipated. This may have been the cause of the delay at Carrickbyrne in order to allow time for concerted action, but it seems unlikely that liaison was sufficiently close to make such an explanation probable.

On the 2nd of June, Major-General Eustace at New Ross reported: 'This morning the Rebels were practising their artillery behind the hill of Carrick Burn.' (I.S.P.O.).

about thirty yards from the Bishop's Gate[1] and the other about six yards from the Three Bullet Gate on the outside quite across, and in such an angular direction as to command two passes'[2]— that is, the Wexford road towards Corbet Hill and the road running due south.

During the night of the 4th of June, there was ceaseless activity in the town and strong outposts were stationed in the fields between the outer defences and the insurgent camp.

The scene on Corbet Hill was in unhappy contrast. Having decided in a general way on the tactical scheme of attack on at least two main points at once, the commander and his staff seem to have shown no concern to keep in close touch with their very mixed force. Several witnesses declare that they passed the evening and part of the night at the hospitable board of Edward Murphy, the occupant of the house on Corbet Hill.

It is well to recall at this point that the only two men in the camp who appear to have made any serious attempt to create a force capable of united action—namely young John Kelly of Killann and Thomas Cloney of Moneyhore—had only been seven days in the field, having joined after Enniscorthy was taken. Each commanded a body of men from the barony of Bantry. Also, while there may have been up to ten thousand men in the neighbourhood of Corbet Hill on the 4th of June, a much larger number actually took part in the battle and a whole division under John Henry Colclough deserted before the attack began.

At 3.30 a.m., Harvey issued a summons to General Johnson to surrender the town and so avoid loss of life and destruction of

---

[1] Also known as Fair, East, Market, Ladies' and Maiden Gate. See Appendix VI.
[2] James Alexander: *A Succinct Narrative of the Rebellion in the County of Wexford* (1806).

On the title page of the volume I consulted is the following note in the handwriting of Lord Carleton: 'A coarse, not to say vulgar work, but the writer, though not a well-informed man is a very honest one'.

The book is dedicated by the publisher to General Johnson.

property. Any expectation which Harvey may have had of a favourable outcome to his ultimatum would have been better warranted had he been in a position to present it three days earlier.

Matthew Furlong of Raheen was entrusted with the summons under a flag of truce and in the half light he was shot dead at the first outpost he approached. I think it is likely that the outposts had pushed out very close to the insurgent position and that Furlong's death was immediately perceived. In any event, from that time all tactical plans of simultaneous attacks were forgotten in the fury of the moment. John Kelly of Killann, at the head of five hundred Bantry men drove in the outposts and the main body followed him to the region of the Three Bullet Gate.[1] Here an attempt was first made to overcome the defences by driving upon them a herd of cattle —a measure which had been found successful at the Duffrey Gate in Enniscorthy a week previously. On this occasion, however, it failed in its object, largely I think, on account of the angular trench outside the gate and the concentrated fire of the defenders powerfully aided by discharges of grape from two guns.

Fighting was very heavy at this point and here Lord Mountjoy was killed.[2] His place in command of the Dublin Militia was taken by Major Vesey. Following this, General Johnson ordered up the 5th Dragoons from their station on the quayside via Condon Street and Cross Lane. Having cleared a space outside the gate, the cavalry made a spirited sortie into the fields beyond, but here the pikemen got among them and inflicted heavy casualties, driving the survivors back into the town. The defence at this point then gave way and the victorious insurgents poured

---

[1] Also called Aldgate (Oldgate) and Bewley (buaile, a milking place).
[2] He was a loss to his country. As Luke Gardiner, he had been responsible for the passing of an Act of the Irish Parliament in 1778, relaxing portion of the Penal Laws to enable Catholics to lease and will land in the same way as Protestants.

into the streets. They rushed down Nevin Street[1] and on into Brogue Maker's Lane, pursuing the garrison beyond the line of Mary Street. They fought their way down Michael Street to the Barrack at the corner of Michael Lane and Bakehouse Lane. Here the gallant John Kelly was seriously wounded in the thigh and was carried back to the Three Bullet Gate.

Other parties succeeded in reaching the south end of the Quays via Cross Lane. Stubborn fighting with very heavy casualties took place near the junction of Brogue Maker's Lane and Mary Street. This approach was enfiladed and raked with canister and grape from a gun placed on the high ground in St. Mary's churchyard above Church Lane. Another gun firing from Chapel Lane caused great execution among the attackers who had reached Mary Street. Major Vandeleur and the Clare Militia, posted in Irishtown, had not so far been attacked and Sergeant Hamilton and fifteen men of the Donegal Militia held firm at the Main Guard. This latter strong point was formed by the Market House and the adjacent houses at the foot of Mary Street. Their swivel guns placed at the cross-roads withered every attack along Mary Street and South Street.

General Johnson had still a line of retreat via the old market and directly west across the bridge. By this time most of the town south of that line was in flames, the fire spreading rapidly owing to the thatched roofs and the long spell of dry weather. The arrival of further bodies of insurgents on the quays led to a precipitate retreat of the bulk of the garrison across the river, carrying their commanding officer with them in the general confusion, but leaving the defenders of the Main Guard and Major Vandeleur's party behind them. General Johnson succeeded after a time in rounding up most of the fugitives beyond Rosbercon and in due course returned. In the interval many of the attackers, exhausted by their prolonged exertions and convinced that victory was already theirs, threw themselves

[1] Also called Neville Street.

down to sleep, or entered the houses in search of food and drink.

Meanwhile, a determined attempt was made by a large party to sally from Barrack Lane (Bakehouse Lane) in order to carry the guns at the Main Guard by push of pike. As they assembled in this narrow thoroughfare they were shot down in large numbers by fire from the house of the Dowsley family in Mary Street facing the mouth of the lane and the attempt failed.

At this juncture the lack of cohesion, discipline and trained leadership was painfully evident among the insurgents. One obvious precaution would have been to raise the drawbridge and another to have had in readiness fresh bodies of men to relieve those who, hungry, thirsty and exhausted had survived the burden and heat of several hours of the heaviest fighting and who were now dispersed among the remaining houses.

Learning of the state of affairs in the town, General Johnson, having restored some semblance of discipline by extraordinary personal efforts, pushed his guns back across the bridge and clearing the lower streets with grape and canister, brought into action first his cavalry and then his infantry. Major Vesey and the Dublin Militia led the van of the latter, burning to revenge the death of Lord Mountjoy and in this second phase of the battle a number of civilian volunteers distinguished themselves, among them one named Devereux and another McCormick, who was conspicuous in a brass helmet.

This time it was the turn of the insurgents to be on the defensive and they fought under a grave disadvantage, having exhausted their ammunition. When a street had been cleared by gunfire those who sought shelter in the houses were able to put up no effective defence without musketeers against a fully equipped attacking force.

With their numbers sadly depleted, the pikemen fought on throughout the afternoon. Several times forced back to the Three Bullet Gate fresh attacks drove the troops from the upper streets, but at last a general retreat was ordered and an action in which courage of the highest order had been shown on both sides came to an end.

It has been alleged that Bagnal Harvey remained on Corbet Hill throughout the day, but this is not so. Cloney states very definitely that Harvey was at the Three Bullet Gate during the battle. Cloney himself seems to have made a last despairing effort to retrieve the day by a belated attack on Irishtown via the line of country now traversed by the Bohereen na Slanaigh, but he could muster only some forty men and the attempt was unsuccessful.

For obvious reasons many deeds of individual heroism on the insurgent side have had no chronicler, but the name of Mary Doyle of Castleboro, has not been forgotten. She appears to have borne a charmed life, moving from point to point where the fighting was heaviest. Also the prowess of a fifteen-year-old boy named James Lett, from near Wexford town, who rallied a party of men in a headlong charge is still remembered.[1]

Lieutenant-Colonel Robert Crawford, one of the most experienced officers in the garrison, wrote an account of the battle in a private letter to the commander-in-chief, General Lake. This letter was written on the day of the battle and after mentioning the march of the insurgents from Carrickbyrne, he proceeds:

> This morning General Johnston was about giving orders for advancing against them when they did it and made as severe an attack as is possible for any troops with such arms.—They were in great force, not many firearms and no guns at first. They drove in our right, follow'd the troops quite into the town and got possession of four guns.—By very great personal exertions of General Johnston, they were repulsed and the repeated attacks they afterwards made (being far less vigorous than the first) were beaten back—and the guns retaken. They certainly have given

[1] A son of Stephen Lett of Newcastle and a nephew of Newton Lett of Killaligan, near Milehouse. He was arrested and courtmartialled after the Rising. Having been compelled to join the British Navy, he died at sea four years afterwards. (See *The Past*, No. 5, 1949, Father Joseph Ranson's notes, page 148).

proofs of very extraordinary courage and enthusiasm; and it is, in my opinion very doubtful that the force under General Johnston's orders should be able to subdue the Wexford insurgents—should it spread now it would be very serious indeed. . . . The militia behaved with spirit but are quite ungovernable.[1]

It is impossible to arrive at a correct estimate of the number of casualties on either side. They were undoubtedly very heavy and in view of the great preponderance of artillery and small arms in the hands of the garrison, the insurgent dead and wounded must have been very numerous.[2] But unfortunately the losses of the latter were not all incurred in the heat of battle. Dr. R. R. Madden made some close enquiries on the spot and his remarks, based on the statements of two survivors, one aged eighty-four and the other eighty-six are as follows: 'They differed in their estimates of the number killed in action. They agreed in one particular—namely that after the battle was entirely over as many were shot and suffocated in the burned cabins and houses from four o'clock in the afternoon till night and were hanged the next day as were killed in the fight. . . . I visited the spot where their bodies were thrown into a hole on the side of a hill facing the town, immediately below the Carmelite Convent—six hundred and odd was the number mentioned by a man who saw the bodies thrown in and was forced to draw one of the cars used to carry the bodies to the pit'.[3]

[1] Crawford to Lake. I.S.P.O.
[2] James Alexander, who was present states that 'the greatest slaughter was in the Main Street (Mary Street), especially near the churchyard. The piece of cannon planted on an eminence just over the Church Lane did very much the greatest execution of any other. Next to the Main Street, the greatest slaughter was round the Town Wall where the battle raged. Next the Chapel Lane, 'twas horrible; next Brogue Maker's Lane, Michael Street and the Cross Lane'; He ascribed the feebleness of the insurgent musketry fire to 'inferior powder manufactured in Wexford'.
[3] R. R. Madden: *United Irishmen*, 4th series.
    The Reverend James Gordon, the 'loyalist' historian states (page 269): 'I have reason to think more men than fell in battle were slain in cold blood. No quarter was given to persons taken prisoner as rebels with or without arms. . . . How many fell in this manner, or were put to death unresisting,
(*Continued at foot of next page*)

This account of the battle of New Ross may be fittingly concluded by quoting the following extract from an article entitled 'Remarks on Street Fighting' by an anonymous military writer:

. . . the yeomanry and militia posted behind barricades, covered by artillery and powerfully aided by the loyal inhabitants who from their windows kept up an incessant discharge of muskets, pistols and blunderbusses [and] were enabled by their fire to repel the fierce onset of the insurgent pikemen, were forced from the town with the exception of a few regulars who held the Market House and were saved from destruction only by a headlong and over-whelming charge made by the 5th and 9th Dragoons supported by a considerable body of mounted yeomanry. Some idea of the desperate fury with which, during more than three hours the contest was maintained, may be drawn from the facts that some of the regulars fired *one hundred and twenty rounds per man*! and that the principal street was swept by twenty-three successive discharges of grape shot and that one of the insurgent leaders, confident in a charm which he wore, was actually blown away from the mouth of a twelve pounder which he attempted to seize. Had the dragoons and yeomanry engaged been armed with the light Indian twelve-and-a-half foot bamboo lance . . . the result of the day would never for a moment have appeared doubtful for they would thereby have been enabled to reach over the pikes of their opponents, few of which exceeded ten feet in length and to trample them down at first onset instead of having to sustain three repulses and at length only retrieving the victory when the insurgents had fallen into that state of disorder which with irregular combatants generally follows partial success.[1]

in houses, fields and elsewhere, would be as difficult to state with accuracy, as the number slain in battle.'

[1] *United Services Journal*, (September-December), 1835.

Note

For most of the topographical particulars in the foregoing account of the battle of New Ross, I am indebted to the excellent description written by Patrick Donovan in connection with the commemoration in June, 1948, and also to the kindness of his brother, Gerard Donovan of Rosbercon, who not only acted as my guide, but also placed his intimate local knowledge at my disposal.

In Appendix VII will be found a short, but valuable reference from the pen of an eye-witness which adds to our knowledge of the events of that disastrous day.[1]

---

[1] The 'loyalist' historian, Taylor, records the evidence of an eye-witness who stated that three thousand four hundred dead insurgents were buried and sixty-two car loads were thrown into the river. This takes no account of those burned in the houses or of the many car loads of wounded evacuated by the retreating insurgents.

The official casualties in General Johnson's force are given as follows: eight officers killed or missing; two officers wounded; one hundred and sixty-eight other ranks killed or missing; fifty-seven other ranks wounded.

Scullabogue

THREE EVENTS have clouded the fair face of the County Wexford —the many executions in the camp on Vinegar Hill, the massacres at Scullabogue on June 5th, and at Wexford Bridge on June 20th. Of these the second named was, if anything, the most lamentable and it certainly had the most disastrous and far-reaching results. One writer, in the following words, expressed an opinion which was fairly general in the north: 'The accounts of the bloody goings on in Wexford had their full share in bringing the Northerners to their senses.'[1]

When the news reached the north, the Antrim insurgents were already committed and they rose and fell on the 7th of June. County Down had not yet taken the field and the instigators of dissension between Catholic and Presbyterian had an easy time. Not only did fear and suspicion lead to the defection of many Protestants from the United Army, but large numbers crowded in as volunteers to swell the crown forces under the command of General Knox. Nothing could more completely have played into the hands of the Government.

When the fighting ceased in Ross in the late afternoon of the 5th of June, the point of assembly for the retreating insurgents was Carrickbyrne Hill. On reaching the camp they learned of the massacre at the house and barn, which had been

---

[1] *MS. Journal of a Field Officer*, quoted by Maxwell.

used as a prison.[1] When leaving Carrickbyrne on June 4th, on the march to Corbet Hill, Harvey had left a strong holding party at the camp and in charge of the prisoners at Scullabogue. Taylor states that the guard consisted of three hundred men under three captains—John Murphy of Loughnageer, Nicholas Sweetman of Newbawn and Walter Devereux.[2]

The latter was almost certainly not present when the massacre took place at nine o'clock in the morning. There is no reliable evidence of the actual determining cause of an act so foreign to our people. The accepted character of the population in County Wexford before and since the Rising has been that of industrious farmers and decent men. The sudden change in the official attitude designed to make them appear as devils incarnate during the insurrection surely calls for some explanation, apart from ingrained natural savagery which many authors and newspaper writers have laboured to suggest.

Those who take the necessary trouble to understand the whole story instead of a part only, may reasonably reach the conclusion that the true explanation is a measure of the unendurable provocation to which the people had been subjected.

There is reason to believe that at least three runaways, or parties of runaways from the battle of Ross, arrived at intervals with news of the slaughter there and with demands for retaliation on the helpless prisoners confined in the house and barn; and further that on the first two occasions the guards were able to control the mob, but that on the third occasion, the cry was that a priest had ordered the destruction of the prisoners.[3] I think

---

[1]   See the evidence of Richard Grandy of Ballyshan, at the trial of John Devereux, Junior, (*Howell's State Trials*, Vol. XXVII).

[2]   Cloney refers to the conspicuous humanity of Walter Devereux, to his bravery at the battle of New Ross and to his unjust execution on the charge of participation in the massacre. But see also page 170.

[3]   Gordon states: 'The runaways declared that the Royal army in Ross were shooting all the prisoners and butchering the Catholics who had fallen into their hands, feigned an order from Harvey for the execution of those at Scullabogue.'

it is quite possible that the third arrivals may have used this means of overcoming opposition.

In his deposition dated 13th of January, 1799, Michael Askins stated on oath that he 'was forced to join a party of rebels' and when about three miles from Ross they 'met a man riding very fast who seemed by his dress to be a priest'. He further stated that this man declared that Bagnal Harvey had ruined them and that he would go to Scullabogue and destroy every soul in it and that he threw down a firelock he had and galloped off to Scullabogue. 'Deponent saith he never saw the man before, but that the party he was with said he was the stoutest priest in Ireland, Father Murphy of Taghmon.'[1]

At the trial of Patrick Furlong at Wexford, on 12th September, 1799, it was stated in evidence that the messengers who conveyed the orders to Captain Murphy to put the prisoners to death said they were sent by Father Murphy. On the other hand, William Fleming, a member of the Taghmon yeoman cavalry, in a sworn statement dated 20th September, 1798, deposed that when a prisoner and in imminent danger of death he 'produced a pass which he had obtained from Brian Murphy, a priest of Taghmon, and that said pass saved the life of informant'.

I can find no support for the suggestion that Father Brian Murphy was at or near New Ross on the 5th of June and I think Fleming's personal statement should be regarded as more reliable than the hearsay evidence of the other witnesses.

Father Shallow of Newbawn and Adamstown, who lived in the townland of Ballyshannon, east of Carrickbyrne Hill and within a mile of Scullabogue, is stated by one writer to have been present at the massacre. Admittedly he visited the prisoners there and he certainly was instrumental in procuring the release of at least one boy, Benjamin Lett of Kilgibbon, and several women captives. He seems to have run some little risk in

---

[1] Bishop Caulfield suspended 'Father Bryan Murphy from all priestly functions whatsoever, except the recital of the divine office in canonical hours'.

doing so and he later complained of his lack of influence and that he 'went to the house at Scullabogue in fear and trembling'.[1]

Whatever the instigation may have been the melancholy fact remains that a large number of men, women and even children were shot, piked, suffocated or burned in the barn, while others, taken from the house, were piked or shot in the front garden. Scullabogue House, then the residence of Francis King, has changed little since that time. The walls are the same, but the house was re-roofed more than forty years ago. The barn stood directly behind the house in a corner of the present walled paddock where stones bearing the marks of burning are still turned up from time to time.[2]

The measurements of the barn (which was thatched) were thirty-four by fifteen feet, with a height of twelve feet. The balance of evidence and probability would indicate that about one hundred persons were murdered altogether. Taylor publishes the names of seventy-four, including sixty-five men and nine women, of whom eight were Catholics, six men and two women. In addition there is a list of twenty-one men who suffered in front of the house and he hints that there were others who were not identified.

The story of this tragedy would be incomplete without a reference to the opinion of one who took an active part in the Wexford fighting and who reached Scullabogue from Ross some time after the massacre had taken place:

As to the instigator of the disgraceful butchery . . . he was never really known. Rumour had it that his name was Devereux who.

[1] John Jones: *An Impartial Narrative* (1799), p. 47. It is perhaps significant that the reference to Father Shallow is omitted from the 1800 edition.

See also the deposition of Elizabeth Dobbyn of Oldcourt in Musgrave, Appendix XX. 5.

In the M.S., *Memoir of Charles Lett* (1773-1853), it is stated that 'two faithful neighbours of the Letts—Romanists—Thomas Murphy of Park and Brien of Ballymorris' took Benjamin and his sister out of the farm at Scullabogue, 'just after they were put into it and advised them to go to priest Shallow's house and claim his protection. This was not refused. . . .'

[2] The ruins of the barn were visible as late as 1814—see W. Shaw Mason: *Statistical Account*, Vol. I.

fled from Ross and reported that hundreds were burned in their houses in that town which set people delirious and incited them to the butchery. Walter Devereux was executed in Cork as the person suspected and most unjustly and a Mr. John Devereux was afterwards transported on the very same evidence,[1] and both alike innocent to an undoubted certainty. All that can be said in extenuation of the disgraceful transaction is that there was nothing premeditated in it. The sudden report from Ross was the sole cause.[2]

One Frizel, himself a survivor of Scullabogue, was examined later at the bar of the House of Commons. He stated that from opinions current among the insurgents, the cause of the massacre was the report that the military were murdering their prisoners in Ross as they had done in Dunlavin, Carnew and Carlow.

It is not my intention to multiply the details of individual cases from the depositions. I do not even know how far such statements are to be relied upon,[3] but the general facts are beyond dispute. It must suffice to mention one typical and most pitiful story on the authority of the Quakeress, Dinah W. Goff of Horetown House, who was fourteen years old in 1798 and who has left an account of her own experiences which she names *Divine Protection* after the Quaker manner.[4] She saw the smoke of the burning barn and mentions 'the strong and dreadful effluvium which was wafted from it to our lawn', three and a half miles away. She tells of the fate of two of her own acquaintances, John and Samuel Jones, who had attended Quaker Meetings though not actual members:

> Samuel was kindly supported by his wife, whilst he was un-mercifully tortured; one limb after another being broken and each time the question repeated 'Will you have the priest?' which

[1] Both Walter and John Devereux were charged at their trials with the murder, in the Ring at Kellymount, of prisoners taken at Goresbridge on the 23rd of June.

[2] Letter from Thomas Cloney to Dr. R. R. Madden, dated 3rd October, 1843. (Madden MSS., Library, T.C.D.).

[3] The 'loyalist' historian, Gordon, plainly referring to those depositions published so lavishly by Musgrave, describes them as 'a lumber of affidavits formed to his purpose among the dupes of his party'.

[4] *Divine Protection through Extraordinary Dangers* (3rd edition), Dublin, 1871, p. 16.

he steadily refused; looking calmly at his faithful wife and saying 'My dear, I am not hurt; I feel no pain'. His brother also bore his martyrdom with firmness and was put to death by slow degrees in a similar way.

The wife, with admirable fortitude stood between them when they were shot and held a hand of each. She then implored the murderers to take her life also; but they refused. . . .

. . . I saw her afterwards in deep affliction passing our gate as she sat in a cart with the remains of her husband and brother'.[1]

---

[1]   Musgrave mentions this case, but his account differs in some details.
    Mary Jones of Kilbreany claimed £169 compensation and was paid in full.

Slieve Coiltia and Lacken Hill

THE WEARY and disillusioned men who reached Carrickbyrne on the night of the 5th of June, rested there for two days. They had learned of the holocaust at Scullabogue and to increase their anxieties and responsibilities they had large numbers of wounded to be cared for. These were taken to Foulke's Mill, four miles south of the camp, six houses in that neighbourhood were converted into field hospitals and several doctors were placed in charge of them. A number of men with some knowledge of first aid were rounded up and compelled to assist, among them Richard Grandy of Ballyshan, who later gave much information to the Government (not all of it accurate), for which he received suitable remuneration.[1] A herd of milch cows were grazed in Caesar Sutton's demesne at Longraigue for their special use.[2]

At this juncture it became clear that such influence as Bagnal Harvey had possessed over his very mixed forces was waning rapidly. He was blamed for the failure at Ross and as commander he had, of course, to accept responsibility for much that was beyond his power to control. I think also that at this time Harvey suffered from the mounting fanaticism among his followers, who more and more cried out against the 'heretics'

---

[1] See page 212.
[2] Gordon.

in their midst. There is no doubt also, that he was horrified and depressed beyond description by the terrible events at Scullabogue.

On the 6th of June he issued his last general order, the outcome of the unhappy events of the previous twenty-four hours. Trial by courtmartial and condign punishment were resolved upon for all those who remained in their homes when ordered to join the forces, for all who deserted in the face of the enemy, for disobedience to orders and for robbery and murder.

This order was distributed throughout the county and surprising as it may seem it was not without its effect as far away as Gorey on an occasion which has already been mentioned.[1]

A proclamation issued in Wexford on the 9th of June called for the arrest of Hawtrey White, Hunter Gowan, James Boyd and Archibald Jacob—four magistrates who were adjudged guilty of cruelty and oppression and it expressed determination 'to protect the persons and properties of those of all religious persuasions who have not oppressed us'. The immunity of the Quakers throughout the Rising should be remembered in this connection.

On the 7th of June, Edward Roche of Garrylough had found it necessary to issue a proclamation from the camp at Vinegar Hill urging his followers to be particular in their conduct to their prisoners; to remember that numbers of them might not be guilty through principle but through necessity and that 'this is not a war for religion but for liberty'.

On the 7th of June the main body marched to Slieve Coiltia, a high hill three miles south of New Ross. It would seem that this move was decided upon as part of a vague plan to renew the attack on that town and also to command the river from Camlin Wood to Fisherstown in order to deny to the garrison the use of the water-way to and from Duncannon Fort and

[1] See page 108.

Waterford. In this latter object they were only partially successful. One gunboat was captured and casualties were inflicted
otherwise, but the river traffic continued without serious
interruption.

At Slieve Coiltia, Bagnal Harvey was compelled to resign
the chief command of the southern force and he was succeeded
by Father Philip Roche.[1] Harvey returned to Wexford, but
before he left, he wrote a letter to his old friend, Francis Glascott
of Pilltown House, at the foot of Slieve Coiltia, who had
appealed to him to protect his property. He declared that
although he wished to protect all property he could scarcely
protect himself.

On the 10th of June, leaving a holding party on Slieve
Coiltia, Father Roche moved his force to Lacken Hill, two miles
east of Ross, following the road through Carnagh and Cushinstown. This hill, though only 630 feet in height, commands a
remarkably extensive view of the surrounding country. Here
a camp was formed which continued to be occupied until the
19th of June. On the 12th, hearing that a large quantity of arms
and military equipment was stored in the house of Walter
Kavanagh at Borris, County Carlow, Father Roche sent a
detachment under Thomas Cloney to collect them. The
house was defended by the Borris yeomanry and a party of
the Donegal Militia. Without artillery it was, as usual, found
impossible to dislodge a garrison occupying a strong defensible
building and amply supplied with arms and ammunition. The
attackers suffered some casualties and eventually returned to
Lacken Hill before the arrival of strong reinforcements from
Kilkenny.

From that date until the evacuation of the camp on the 19th

[1] See page 192.

of June no further action took place there.[1] The events from the 19th of June onwards will be described in the Chapter on the engagement at Foulke's Mill, or Goff's Bridge.[2]

---

[1] Lecky writes: 'It should be remembered to the credit of Father Philip Roche that the camp at Lacken Hill, where he held the undivided command, appears to have been absolutely unstained by the murders which had been so numerous at Vinegar Hill'. *History*, Vol. IV, p. 428.
[2] See page 141.

The Battle of Arklow

AT TEN O'CLOCK in the morning of Saturday, the 9th of June, the insurgent forces left the camp on Gorey Hill to attack the town of Arklow. Their numbers, though very considerable, cannot be stated with accuracy. They have been variously estimated as between nineteen thousand and thirty-four thousand, but for reasons already given,[1] I think even the lesser figure is an overstatement and certainly whatever the gross number, the roll of effectives was smaller still. Only comparatively few had firearms of any description and fewer again, apart from the Shelmalier marksmen, had either the knowledge or the training to enable them to make full use of what they did possess. The remainder were nominally pikemen, but fighting had been in progress already for a fortnight and as many smiths had been arrested or otherwise disposed of, the problem of replacement and repair of arms was becoming increasingly difficult. Probably a majority were armed with various farm implements.

The route they followed from Gorey was along the Clonatin road, past Kilmurry cross-roads, through Inch and Coolgreany. Five hours after they had set out they were still more than a mile from their objective.[2] The fact that such a long period had been spent in covering ten Irish miles of ground requires some explanation. Luke Cullen's informant states that 'arriving

[1] See page 32 et seq.
[2] See Wheeler and Broadley, page 119.

at the seat of Mr. Perry [at Inch] the Wexford men would not pass it until they would halt and give some cheers for its proprietor. He endeavoured to bring them on, but to no purpose and they remained there some hours and got drunk in Coolgreany; during those hours reinforcements came into Arklow and more defences [were] thrown up.'[1]

The five days vouchsafed to government forces after Tubberneering had been utilised by a cautious re-occupation of Arklow and in the small hours of the morning of the 9th the defence was completed by the valuable addition of three hundred and sixty men of the Durham Fencibles commanded by Colonel Skerrett, a most capable officer—bringing the total to at least sixteen hundred.[2] These latter had been rushed from Dublin by means of improvised transport on receipt of news that an attack on Arklow was imminent. The garrison was commanded by Major-General Needham, Lord Kilmorey's son and heir.

At this time the present direct county road from Gorey to Arklow had not been constructed in its northern part. The main approaches from the south were through Inch and Coolgreany to the west, and to the east by an old seaside road which entered the town by the Fishery from the direction of Arklow Rock.

From early morning mounted patrols from the garrison probed southwards along both these roads, and also up the Pollahoney road on the right bank of the river.

About 3.0 p.m. they brought the news of the insurgent advance and shortly before 4.0 p.m. the battle commenced. Needham posted his men, correctly anticipating that the main weight of attack would come from the west side. Three of his five guns were placed in position to command the Cool-

---

[1] Madden MSS., T.C.D. Library. Michael Dwyer is credited with the statement: 'We lost Arklow by drunkenness and insubordination at Coolgreany'.
[2] See Lecky, but Castlereagh mentioned to Pelham on the 8th that Needham had then one thousand, six hundred men and we know that he received further reinforcements on the 9th.

greany road. The right flank of the defending force rested on the barrack, which then stood between the ravine and the present Parade, while the camp was located on the other side of the street and just east of the present railway. The camp was covered by the Durham Fencibles and upon them the main attack was made. At the same time a large force advanced on the Fishery from the Rock road, reinforced by detachments moving east along the road now known as the Yellow Lane and across country in the same direction.

The attack on the Fishery, in the course of which a number of houses were set on fire, was checked by a strongly held barricade at the eastern end of the Main Street, where also a gun was mounted which raked the approaches. There were, in addition repeated cavalry charges from this strong point, in one of which Thomas Grogan Knox was killed.[1] There was a subsidiary strong point in an adjoining graveyard.

One of the defenders described the position at the opening of the battle as follows: 'I first saw in a moment thousands appear on the tops of ditches, forming one great, irregular circular line from the Gorey road through the fields quite round to the Sand Banks near the sea as thick as they could stand'.[2]

The action commenced with an artillery duel—an expensive exchange from the insurgent standpoint as their principal gun was manned by a prisoner named Shepherd, captured at Three Rocks on the 30th of May. This man, torn between the order of his captors and loyalty to the coat he wore compromised for a time by misdirecting his fire until detected by Esmond Kyan who, with Dick Monk took over the duty with better results.[3]

Miles Byrne viewing this battle in retrospect after a lifetime of military experience was of opinion that the insurgents

[1] He was a younger brother of Cornelius Grogan of Johnstown, but signed his name as given here.
[2] See Appendix VIII.
[3] It is pleasant to recall that Kyan later succeeded in saving Sergeant Shepherd's life.

would have been better without any artillery on this occasion, as it kept the pikemen too long out of action. He also appears to deprecate the orthodox attacks from east and west where they were obviously expected and provided against and he would have favoured diversionary tactics which he states were urged by Matthew Doyle.[1]

With ample numbers to draw upon, it is strange that simultaneous attacks were not made all along the defensive perimeter instead of persisting in mass attack against canister and grape which 'tumbled them by twenties'.[2] Had this plan been adopted, together with diversions in strength it is most probable that some weak points would have been found in the thinly held salient and once the pikemen broke through and reached the houses in the town, retreat of the garrison across the bridge could hardly have been avoided. As it was, the balance of evidence goes to show that General Needham in the course of the battle consulted Colonel Skerrett on the advisability of retreat, but was told that their only chance was to stand and fight.

Garrett Byrne of Ballymanus[3] is mentioned repeatedly in various accounts of this engagement as having taken a prominent and gallant part, together with Esmond Kyan and Father Michael Murphy. The latter, who is said to have rounded up a number of stragglers[4] headed an attack from the direction of the Charter School. He was killed within a few yards of the main road block;[5] Esmond Kyan was wounded and insurgent

[1] Matthew Doyle of Pollahoney, near Woodenbridge, was a most determined fighting man. He later became Holt's second-in-command and eventually a front line grenadier in the British Army in the Egyptian War. He stated that he fought against the French with readiness as he regarded their failure to effect a timely landing in Ireland as the cause of his country's misfortunes.

[2] See Appendix VIII.

[3] He commanded a contingent of one thousand Wicklowmen.

[4] Taylor.

[5] There is mention by several writers of mutilation of Father Michael Murphy's decapitated body, but it was at least identifiable by his friends who later removed it for burial in Castle Ellis graveyard, where his grave may still be seen. For further information on this subject, from a new source, see Appendix III.

casualties were very heavy. About 8.00 p.m. when the ammunition of the gunsmen was exhausted, they broke off the engagement and retreated to the camp on Gorey Hill.[1]

Miles Byrne considers that if they had held their ground until dark and then by the lighting of fires intimated that they were still in a position to attack, the garrison would have evacuated the town during the night.

It might have been possible, one would think, to rush small parties of pikemen through the lines into the town during the hours of darkness, an exploit which might easily have succeeded in spreading panic in a force which was not by any means all of the quality of the Durham Fencibles; but such commando tactics call for careful training and cohesion, both of which were sadly lacking in the insurgent forces. In addition, there was no unity of command and when the design of overwhelming the defenders by weight of numbers failed, there seems to have been no alternative plan. Nothing is more daunting and discouraging even to disciplined troops than the realisation that they are engaged in a struggle without competent leadership or tactical control.

It is notoriously easy to be wise after the fact, but it is, I think, permissible to condemn the insurgent leaders for making their main attack where it was expected and where most of the garrison's artillery swept the open approaches. A reconnaissance in force sent out from Gorey in advance of the main body could with ease have driven in the patrols and ascertained the dispositions of the defence. The main body could, therefore, have been directed to the Fishery with a simultaneous feint attack from the Coolgreany road. By this means it is probable the bridge would have been seized and the town entered in force by the pikemen. In such an event it is difficult to see what the alternatives would have been to the garrison except to surrender,

[1] There is a good topographical account of this engagement by Dr. G. A. Hayes-McCoy in *The Irish Sword*, Vol. I, No. 1.

or to gather their forces and fight their way out of the town up the river by the Pollahoney road.

The failure at Arklow was the beginning of the end. Thereafter the isolation and encirclement of County Wexford proceeded without serious opposition.[1]

. . . .

There is a difference of opinion as to whether or not Father John Murphy was present at this battle. Miles Byrne states that he was and he gives a circumstantial account of his conduct there, but this is unsupported by any other writer and it is probable that he was not present, but remained at Castletown. It has been suggested that he did not approve of Wexford men fighting outside their own county and that he considered that each county should do its own fighting. I think this a most unlikely explanation. In less than a fortnight he was himself fighting in County Carlow and if he held such foolish views it would have been inconsistent on his part to have accepted the help of Wicklow, Carlow and Kildare men. It has not been hitherto suggested, but it seems possible that the real cause of his absence on this occasion was illness.

For details of this battle see eye-witnesses' accounts in Appendices V, VIII and IX.

Skinner's map (1777) shows four roads out of Arklow—1, North across the bridge; 2, West up the right bank of the river; 3. South-east towards Tara Hill; 4, South-west to Coolgreany.

From Arklow to Vinegar Hill

THE FIRST PROBLEM which presented itself to the insurgents retreating from Arklow, was the disposal of the large number of wounded. Many of them were conveyed to Gorey on cars commandeered for the purpose, but Miles Byrne states: 'The numbers could never be rightly ascertained; we brought some hundreds of wounded men away from the field of battle and from the night coming on, it appeared that many more were not brought off. When those unfortunate men were discovered by the enemy next day, they were instantly slaughtered.'[1] He records with regret that the dead were left unburied.

No attempt appears to have been made to dress the wounded before transporting them over the ten Irish miles of what must then have been indifferent roads. Many, no doubt, died of haemorrhage and shock, apart from the numbers who must have developed fatal complications at a later date. Those not seriously wounded were taken to their homes by relatives and the remainder were looked after in Gorey with such meagre facilities as the place and the time provided.

From the night of the 9th until the 12th of June the insurgent force was based on Gorey Hill. A field court was set up, organised by Captain Patrick Redmond of Coolgreany and the prisoners who were confined in the Market House were brought to trial. Those found guilty were marched under escort to

[1] *Memoirs*, (1906), Vol. I, p. 108.

Wexford town and lodged in the gaol there, but later, four of the most obnoxious of these were returned to Vinegar Hill and there executed.

Among those dispatched to Wexford was the Revd. Roger Owen, the rector of Camolin. Miles Byrne states that he had been an active magistrate and addicted to the use of the pitch cap. This painful process he himself now experienced and this treatment, the fear of death and the fatigue and indignity of the long march to Wexford unhinged his reason.[1]

Leaving a garrison on Gorey Hill the main body moved four miles due north to Limerick Hill[2] on the 12th of June. On the 15th they marched through Wicklow Gap to Mountpleasant where they camped on the 16th, having had some desultory skirmishing on the way. Tinahely was also occupied and there seems to have been some intention of pushing on to Hacketstown.[3] At this juncture, however, Lord Roden appeared with a force chiefly of cavalry, but finding the insurgents in such numbers and full of offensive spirit, he retreated hastily towards Hacketstown to inform General Dundas of the situation. The latter thereupon advanced on Tinahely and as he approached the insurgents moved three miles to the south and occupied a strong position on Kilcavan Hill on the 18th,[4] at eight o'clock in the morning.

General Loftus had by this time reached Shillelagh from Tullow and General Dundas ordered him by express from Tinahely to march on the Carnew road and to begin the attack on the insurgent position on Kilcavan Hill from that side,

---

[1] It has been suggested that his mental breakdown was simulated in order to save his life, but the reference to him in the narrative of his sister, Mrs. Jane Adams of Summerseat, who described his condition after his arrival in Wexford leaves no room for doubt that it was genuine.

[2] The corps from this neighbourhood had especially distinguished itself at Arklow under the command of Michael Redmond (who was killed there) and of Murt Murnagh.

[3] One recognises the hand of Garrett Byrne in this design. He eventually did make his attack in very different circumstances on the 25th of June.

[4] Miles Byrne states that Kilcavan Hill was occupied on the 19th.

while he himself moved on the hill from the north or west. It is easier to understand what followed if we assume that Dundas marched from Tinehely soon after the dispatch of the express to Loftus and that he was thus some distance on his way before the latter left Shillelagh.

The intention to attack from two sides simultaneously was frustrated by the failure of Dundas to reach his assigned position, for having travelled a considerable part of the journey, he found himself in a 'deep hollow road' and fearing attack in such difficult country and with the recollection of the fate of Walpole at Tubberneering, he decided to turn back and follow a safer, if less direct route. Accordingly, he sent orders to Loftus to support this retrograde movement and the two met at Coolattin, two miles and a half from Kilcavan Hill. Soon afterwards they were joined by General Lake and his staff.[1]

All authorities who mention this incident agree that the junction of Dundas and Loftus took place *before* the advance was made to attack the hill. Miles Byrne states that as this combined force approached the insurgents were formed in line, 'the most formidable one I had yet seen since the commencement of the war'. He added that 'those prudent generals kept at a certain distance, no doubt to induce us to quit our strong position on Kilcavan Hill. Thus we had to move forward to bring the enemy to action on the direction of Carnew.' This seems to indicate that the insurgents came down off the hill in sufficient strength to establish a series of outposts on the Carnew road. 'Here great skirmishing between our gun-men and the enemy's rifle-men commenced and our little artillery that followed in the rear was brought to the front and opened a smart cannonade on the enemy. This, with our formidable line of pikemen moving forward like a wall, made the King's troops retrograde.'

This desultory fighting and cannonading lasted some hours

[1] See Note at the end of this Chapter.

and Miles Byrne admits that the insurgents 'had some fine fellows killed and a great number wounded', among the latter being his brother Hugh. It seems probable that most of the fighting took place in the region of the long triangle between the old road from Kilcavan Gap (where five roads meet) to Carnew on the east side and the Coolattin-Carnew road on the west.

Jones records that an advancing column had only just swung into line when the insurgents opened fire and had not the troops changed formation a moment before 'the first shot would have raked the column from the front to the rere and did actually plough up the ground which had not been a minute receded from by the troops'.

There is evidence showing that the action commenced at 2.30 p.m.[1] The harrassing tactics above mentioned continued throughout the evening. Lake refused to become involved in a general engagement at this point in order to avoid dislocation of the concerted strategic plan of encirclement and when he eventually reached Carnew and night fell, the insurgent outposts were withdrawn to the camp on the hill. Here a meeting held to decide upon the next move revealed divided counsels. Anthony Perry and Garrett Byrne urged a night march to Rathdrum, in order to cut one of the main supply routes from Dublin to Wexford and to preserve their mobility and freedom to manoeuvre. Edward Fitzgerald and Edward Roche, supported by a majority, favoured a concentration of all forces at Enniscorthy. The result was what the experienced Miles Byrne afterwards referred to as 'our silly march to Vinegar Hill'.

Sir James Duff arrived in Carnew from Bunclody (Newtownbarry), during the night and fresh preparations were made to attack the camp on Kilcavan Hill. In the meantime, however, the insurgents had marched off south-east and then south to Camolin and Ferns where they spent the remainder of the

[1] General Needham (writing from Arklow) to Lieutenant General Craig (commanding at Dublin). He confirms that the engagement took place on the 18th. (I.S.P.O.).

night. The following morning, they moved slowly to Vinegar Hill which they reached late the same evening.

. . . .

Those left behind on Gorey Hill when the main force moved to Limerick Hill on the 12th of June, detached from their number a large party who occupied Ask Hill, two miles northeast of Gorey, on the 16th. This was, no doubt, in order to establish a strong outpost, or advance guard to keep patrols from Arklow at a safe distance from the camp. Gordon mentions[1] that frequent desertions occurred from this post. On the 17th of June there is an entry in the Camolin yeomanry Detail Book[2] recording that a strong mixed party with officers was ordered to patrol from Arklow through Coolgreany and towards Ask Hill to ascertain the nature of a fire which had been reported by a patrol from the post at Arklow Rock the previous night. Gordon states that those on the hill were without a leader and did not exceed one hundred men, half of whom disappeared on the approach of the cavalry, 'while the rest of them, stripping to their shirts that they might be more expedite for the business, ran full speed to charge the cavalry with their pikes; but the latter avoided the attack and retreated to Arklow with expedition'. This account is confirmed from the Detail Book.

On the advance of General Needham from Arklow two days later, those holding this post and those remaining on Gorey Hill withdrew to Carrigrew Hill and thence to Vinegar Hill.

[1] *History* (2nd Edition), pp. 164-5.
[2] Wheeler and Broadley, pp. 145-6.

Note

The fact that Loftus was able to meet Dundas in Coolattin at short notice, might be explained by the former having only reached the neighbourhood of Cronyhorn crossroads on his way to Carnew. He would then have merely to turn left past Tomacork Church. The route followed by Dundas and the exact place referred to as the 'deep hollow road', is more difficult to identify and the references are distressingly scanty and vague. I have carefully examined this whole area under the expert guidance of the late Thomas Fleming of Shillelagh who spent a lifetime there and possessed an unrivalled knowledge of the old road system now partially obliterated. I agree with his opinion that Dundas had traversed part of the country now included in Coolattin Park and was approaching, if he had not already entered, the difficult region between the present park and Kilcavan Gap known as Paulbeg, when he decided to turn back, forking left to Coolattin along the Shillelagh road.

The route which Dundas had followed from Tinehely in order to reach this turning point is merely a matter of conjecture. Thomas Fleming was of opinion that the most probable direction would have been from Tinehely to Ballyraheen crossroads, then to the left across the river at Greenhall bridge, then to the right along an old road skirting Tomnafinogue Wood and now practically disused, through Ballykelly and across the present Coolboy-Coolattin road to Paulbeg.

I think, however, that another possible route may be mentioned. It seems to me at least conceivable that Dundas would cross Kilcommon Bridge to satisfy himself that Mountpleasant was in fact evacuated as had been reported. From that point he could then march south west for two miles to join the road from Greenhall bridge at Tomnafinogue and thence as already described.

The Battle of
Goff's Bridge, or Foulke's Mill

THE TITLE OF Goff's Bridge for this engagement is the more correct, as most of the fighting took place in the region lying between Horetown House and Raheenduff House to the north and between Goff's Bridge and Stoneenrath Cross Roads to the south.

Brigadier-General John Moore,[1] in command of nine hundred Light Infantry, the 60th Yagers and fifty Hompesch Cavalry (the so-called Hessians) arrived in New Ross on the morning of the 18th of June to take part in the encircling movement on Vinegar Hill and Wexford town. He states in his diary that he had some difficulty in discovering what part he was supposed to play as everything was in a state of confusion. At last he marched out early in the morning of the 19th of June through Irishtown, taking the direct road to Old Ross which skirts Lacken Hill to the south. At the same time Major-General Johnson approached the same hill by the road on the other side of Newtown House and towards the present forge of Lacken. Threatened with encirclement the insurgents evacuated the camp and retreated to the east. Cloney who was present states

---

[1] His promotion to Major-General did not appear in orders until the 7th of July—see letter to his father in *The Life and Letters of Sir John Moore*, edited by Beatrice Brownrigg, (1923).

that there were only four hundred men in camp at the time
and not three rounds of ammunition each for those who had
firearms. Moore states that the Germans killed sixty or seventy
in the retreat; Hay claims that there were no losses and Cloney
mentions none. This probably means that the actual fighting
force suffered no casualties, but that numbers of unarmed
country people were murdered by the Hessians.

Moore joined Johnson at Old Ross and together they marched
to Carrickbyrne which they found abandoned. From that point
Johnson returned to New Ross while Moore moved south to
the neighbourhood of Foulke's Mill to await reinforcements
from Duncannon before proceeding to Wexford and to prevent
the escape of insurgents eastwards through the three mile gap
between Foulke's Mill and the estuary at Clonmines. He took
post that night in Caesar Sutton's house at Longraigue, half-a-
mile west of Foulke's Mill.

With sadness he noted in his diary: 'The country through
which we had passed was rich and beautiful, but perfectly
deserted. The soldiers, contrary to all orders, quitted their
divisions and set fire to many houses. It was shocking to see
a fine cultivated country deserted by its inhabitants and in
flames. I have prevented this from happening since then. . . .'

In the meantime Father Philip Roche had marched his men
as far as Templenacroha crossroads. Here it was decided to
make for Wexford rather than Enniscorthy in order to obtain
a supply of ammunition.[1] They reached Wexford that night
after a march of twenty miles.

When it was learned there that Moore was camped only
twelve miles off, the advisability of an immediate night attack
was strongly urged, but ultimately it was decided to summon a
corps of Wexfordmen (who had recently been moved to
Enniscorthy) to rejoin them and to await their arrival. The
men who had marched from Lacken proceeded to the camp

[1] Cloney.

at Three Rocks for much needed food and a night's rest.

The reinforcements arrived during the night and at dawn on the 20th of June, the insurgents under Father Philip Roche, Thomas Cloney and John Henry Colclough, set out to engage Moore's force. It has been suggested by Musgrave that this advance was part of a larger design which included the capture of New Ross, but I think, in all the attendant circumstances this is altogether unlikely and Cloney makes no reference to it.

Early on the 20th Brigadier-General John Moore dispatched Colonel Wilkinson in the direction of Clonmines and Tintern to patrol the gap south of Foulke's Mill and to make contact with the reinforcements expected from Ballyhack under Lord Dalhousie. Moore himself spent part of the morning personally examining the ground between Longraigue and Goff's Bridge. When Wilkinson returned he reported having met and killed 'straggling parties of rebels',[1] but saw nothing of the expected reinforcements.

As Moore was working to a time-table and was due in Taghmon that evening he marched at 3.0 p.m. When he had reached the top of the hill east of Foulke's Mill, he saw the clouds of dust raised by the long column of insurgents approaching across the valley beyond Goff's Bridge. He at once advanced two rifle companies of the 60th regiment in skirmishing order, ran forward a howitzer and a six pounder gun to Stoneenrath crossroads and posted flanking parties of light infantry north and south of this position. Meanwhile the insurgent approach was somewhat confused. The chief authority on the insurgent side is Thomas Cloney who had a command there, but his account is, in parts, difficult to follow. He mentions separation of the gunsmen from the pikemen and the advance of the former in column formation. He also states that at this critical juncture one of the leaders[2] led his division off to the

[1] Probably unarmed home-biding folk.
[2] Not named, but clearly John Henry Colclough.

right without orders from the officer in command (Father Philip Roche) who sent Cloney to summon him back to the main body. He replied to Cloney that he intended to get between the enemy and Ross and so cut their line of retreat! In my opinion Colclough turned off to the right at the three-roads on the highest point of the hill before descending to Goff's Bridge and quite possibly his action gave rise to Musgrave's statement that the main body had proceeded towards Cullenstown Bridge and moved down on Moore's left flank as the battle developed. Cloney relates that by the time he reached Goff's Bridge he found both the road to Foulke's Mill and the road running north through the woods of Horetown House crowded with men and he was unable to learn in which direction Father Roche had gone! For some reason which he does not make clear, he led his own men along the crowded road to the north and actually reached a crossroad at Tottenham Green more than a mile away! He then discovered that Father Roche had advanced along the half-mile of road towards Stoneenrath Cross and had made a frontal attack on the troops stationed there. By this time Moore's left flanking companies had extended some distance and Cloney found himself separated from the main body by these infiltrating parties. His difficulties were not diminished by the dense cloud of smoke which hung over the field of battle. He eventually succeeded in rejoining Father Roche with his little force reduced by desertion and having suffered some casualties.

Moore in his dispatch to Major-General Johnson and in his diary gives the best available account. He states that 'the rebels attempted to attack the guns, but they were repulsed by such a tremendous fire of musketry and grape shot as made them retreat in confusion over the bridge'.[1] But at the same time he confesses that when the attack began 'the companies of light infantry being unaccustomed to fire, hesitated a little. I was

[1] That is Goff's Bridge.

obliged to get off my horse and put myself at their head, to jump over a high ditch and advance on the enemy. We drove them down hill. . . .' He posted Colonel Wilkinson with orders to prevent the insurgents from re-crossing the bridge. He then ordered 'Major Aylmer with three companies of Light Infantry to march against a large body which were going round upon my left'. This can hardly refer to Cloney's small force which had been partially surrounded and which was with difficulty attempting to regain contact with his main body from the direction of Tottenham Green. I suggest that it may possibly have been at least part of the force which Colclough had led off earlier and which, having reached Cullenstown Bridge, hurried back due south to the region of Raheenduff Park and so presented a direct threat to Moore's left. In any event Major Aylmer reported that the insurgents were in a wood near him 'and seemed in such numbers that he was afraid to advance on them'. Major Daniel was dispatched to Aylmer's assistance with two more companies and a field gun.

Moore states: 'I was afraid to go from the front opposite which the enemy were in great numbers and where I thought they were waiting for a favourable moment to fall upon me. The fire grew hotter upon the left and messages for reinforcements were continually coming in. I ordered the brigade-major Anderson to go and let me know the true state of the left. He returned and told me that it was absolutely necessary for me to go to the left immediately. I set off at a gallop[1] desiring him to stay and watch the movements at the front. I met the Light Infantry, the Yagers and some dragoons all in the woods[2] mixed and retreating. The enemy was following close and firing. I succeeded in stopping some immediately and got them to jump out of the road and make a front on each side of it. I then encouraged the rest first to halt, then to advance and when I

[1] Apparently along the road from Stoneenrath crossroads towards Raheenduff.
[2] Of Raheenduff Park.

saw them ready for it, I took off my hat, put my horse into a trot, gave a huzza and got them to make a push. The tide immediately turned and we drove the rebels before us and killed a great many. They attempted two or three times afterwards to make a stand but failed. The fire of the rebels was well supported. I was surprised at the number of muskets which I have since learned amount to six hundred. The numbers of the whole, five or six thousand including pikes. We lost ten killed and forty-five wounded, besides Major Daniel,[1] Captain de Villers and Lieutenant Green. I pursued the rebels till they dispersed. Whilst we were pursuing a messenger came up to me with the news of the arrival of two regiments under Lord Dalhousie.[2] It was now near eight o'clock; too late to proceed. I took post for the night on the ground where the action had begun'.[3]

The insurgent retreat probably followed the by-road north of Tottenham Green and through Taghmon.

So ended a battle the issue of which was determined by the exertions and courage of that fine soldier, Brigadier-General John Moore. That the government forces would have been defeated on that occasion had they had a less brave and capable commander hardly admits of doubt.[4]

An incident referred to by Miss Dinah Goff[5] and relating to insurgent casualties is worth recording. She writes:

[1] Major Daniel died of wounds.
[2] Cloney is at variance with this account in two particulars—he states that news of the reinforcement came before and not after the retreat had commenced and that Moore lost nearly two hundred killed and more than that number wounded! No prisoners were taken on either side.
[3] *Diary*, pp. 296-8.
[4] An attorney, named John Tench, in a deposition dated 24th November, 1798, stated that Nicholas Gray (also an attorney and former secretary to Bagnal Harvey) had informed deponent that he was a commander in the insurgent army at Goff's Bridge and that if the pikemen had obeyed his orders the force under General Moore would have been surrounded and cut to pieces. (I.S.P.O.).
[5] *Divine Protection*, pp. 23-4.

Two [insurgents] soon came to the house to have their wounds dressed, which my sister Arabella did as well as she could; one had a ball in the cap of his knee, and both bled profusely; they expressed much thankfulness and hoped they might soon be able again to fight for their freedom. A fine young man coming, who had received a wound in his side and shoulder, my dear mother used means to relieve him and dressed him comfortably in clean linen, while he frequently exclaimed 'Do, ma'am, try to stop the blood. I don't mind the pain so that I may but fight for my liberty.' Observing him in danger from the great injury she spoke to him in a very serious strain and also recommended his going to the Wexford Infirmary. We heard afterwards that he died on the way, a few hours after he left us. This battle was at Goff's Bridge. . . . Several hundreds of the insurgents were killed, but not many of the military.

On the 21st of June Moore resumed his march to Taghmon and on the road met emissaries from Wexford town with letters from Lord Kingsborough and the Governor, Matthew Keogh. As he proceeded from Taghmon towards Wexford, along the road which skirts the north-western flank of Forth mountain, he saw with his glass crowds of people on the summit who were armed. These were probably in the vicinity of the camp at Three Rocks. He sent a strong advance guard and followed himself in support. The people, however, were by this time entirely disorganised and leaderless and they dispersed on his approach.

Wexford Bridge

IN A PREVIOUS CHAPTER events in the town of Wexford were described up to the point when the fighting men marched off northwards and westwards, leaving a garrison under the command of Matthew Keogh. Except for the hasty visit of a division under Edward Roche and Garrett Byrne from the night of the 19th to the night of the 20th of June, these men did not return except as individuals and in small parties, until after the battle of Vinegar Hill. The town was therefore, for the first three weeks of June, in a state of unstable equilibrium with numbers of prisoners confined in the gaol and elsewhere, or under open arrest, while at the same time there were crowds of people who had contrived to avoid any kind of active service, who merited no higher title than that of town rabble and who constituted a standing menace to the safety of the prisoners. It is no small tribute to Keogh and his lieutenants[1] that, except for the deaths of the four persons already mentioned, no lives were lost until the chaotic and terrible events of the last hours of the occupation.

There were at least two hundred and sixty prisoners in actual confinement.[2] The conversions and pseudo-conversions continued and Mrs. Brownrigg states in her diary that Matthew Keogh was compelled to conform to save his life during his

[1] Especially William Kearney and later Bagnal Harvey, who joined Keogh when superseded in his command by Father Philip Roche after the battle of New Ross.
[2] See Gordon. Jones states that there were five hundred.

tenure of office !¹ This practice had become widespread. Thus Gordon, the least fanatical of the so-called 'loyalist' writers, mentions the case of Father Corish of Mulrankin,² 'who being requested by a Protestant lady to baptize herself and family replied that except for protection from the fanaticism of the ignorant multitude the ceremony was useless; that he would be on the watch for her safety and give her timely notice if he should find the performance of that rite necessary'.³ The same writer refers to the kindly conduct of Father Rogers of Killegny (where Gordon later became incumbent of the Protestant parish). He states that Father Rogers 'without any hint of a wish' for the conversion of his Protestant neighbours encouraged the belief of it 'among his bigoted flock'. He adds that some of those conforming hesitated for some time to revert afterwards, 'probably through fear of a second insurrection', but eventually all did so except one young man. A good many of the prisoners must be accounted fortunate in surviving—among them Lord Kingsborough, the son and heir of the Earl of Kingston, captured at sea and landed at the town on the 2nd of June. This officer commanded the notorious North Cork Militia, who were popularly regarded as responsible for the introduction into County Wexford of that particular form of torture known as the pitch cap and who were among the most active in the use of the whip and other methods of extorting 'confessions'. Taylor is indignant at the treatment which Lord Kingsborough received on being landed at Wexford. He states: 'So little did the rebels respect his rank that they confined him in a common dram shop'.⁴

---

¹ She may have been misled by the fact that to show their freedom from sectarian bias, both Keogh and Harvey appeared from time to time at Catholic services. Keogh was attended before execution by the Rev. John Elgee, the rector of Wexford.

² North of Bridgetown in the barony of Bargy.

³ Page 264.

⁴ This was known as *The Cape of Good Hope* and was in the Main Street, near the Bull Ring.

His life was often threatened by the mob, but by the combined efforts of the Governor, Keogh and his lieutenants and also, it is stated, of Bishop Caulfield, his life was preserved. Other and possibly unofficial bodies of men seem to have been enrolled for the purpose of preserving order; for example, the so-called 'John Street corps' of three hundred men, commanded for a time by Richard Monaghan (Dick Monk).

As early as the 7th of June a proclamation was issued, signed by Edward Roche, clearly with the object of stemming the rising tide of fanaticism among his followers. He reminded the people that their principal object had been 'to promote an union of brotherhood and affection amongst our countrymen of all religious persuasions', adding that 'to my Protestant soldiers I feel much indebted for their gallant behaviour in the field where they exhibited signal proofs of bravery in the cause'.

On the 9th of June, a second proclamation called for the arrest of four magistrates—James Boyd, Hawtrey White, Hunter Gowan and Archibald Hamilton Jacob, who had 'committed the most horrid acts of cruelty, violence and oppression against our peaceable and well affected countrymen' and stating further that they were 'determined to protect the persons and properties of those of all religious persuasions who had not oppressed us and are willing, with heart and hand to join our glorious cause, as well as to show our marked disapprobation and horror of the crimes of the above delinquents'.

It was not until the 14th of June that it was decided to introduce the United Irishmen's oath[1] and this seems to me a further indication that the mass of the Wexford people were inspired more by the spirit of the Defenders than that of the United Irishmen.

On the 19th, panic reigned in the town. Gunboats were seen hovering outside the harbour. Crowds of refugees had

---

[1] Hay. The same author states that on the 19th of June two small camps, at Carne and at Rastoonstown were broken up and the men sent to Three Rocks.

been pouring in from the north and west before the advancing front of the encircling troops. In the course of that night came the news of Father Philip Roche's retreat from Lacken Hill, followed by his appearance at Three Rocks, while Edward Roche arrived from Vinegar Hill to collect reinforcements, thus confirming the report of an impending and critical battle there.

On the 20th, a rumour reached the town that the camp at Three Rocks was being attacked. This may have arisen owing to the hasty departure that morning of Father Philip Roche's force to meet Brigadier-General Moore at Goff's Bridge.

It has been stated[1] that with the object of saving the town from direct assault, the Catholic bishop and clergy prevailed on the greater part of the active insurgents remaining there to march out to the camps on Windmill Hill and Three Rocks. This well intentioned action had, however, the most unfortunate result of placing the town and the prisoners in the power of a bloody-minded remnant headed by one Thomas Dixon[2] and his no less blood-thirsty wife. Hay, the historian, states that Dixon brought in seventy men during the night 'from the northern side of the Slaney' and plied them with whiskey to induce them to remain under his orders in the town. He commenced the work of massacre at two o'clock in the afternoon and in less than five hours ninety-seven defenceless prisoners, brought down in batches to the bridge, were either piked, or shot and their bodies thrown into the sea.[3]

Edward Hay was in the town during this terrible time and his account of it is, perhaps on the whole, the most reliable as he

---

[1] Plowden.

[2] He was referred to by Mrs. Brownrigg as 'a very large man', is stated to have been the proprietor of an inn in Wexford and to have spent some time at sea. His cousin Father Dixon had been sentenced to transportation on the evidence of one of the Murphy's who paid the informer's penalty earlier in the month. See also Appendix XIII.

General Lake in his dispatch dated the 22nd states: 'They murdered above seventy prisoners and threw their bodies over the bridge'. Hay states that the number did not exceed thirty-six.

describes incidents of which he was an actual eye-witness. He refers to the decline of the authority of the committee which had been entrusted with the public safety and he makes it manifest that, surrounded as they then were by the uncontrollable rabble the committee's functions were disrupted by the influence of Dixon and a kindred spirit by the name of Morgan Byrne.[1] He tells an unpleasant story about Charles Jackson and a man named O'Connor who, he states, volunteered to point out to Dixon and company, which of the prisoners were 'Orangemen' and this 'information apparently relieved those gentry of the labour of trial or enquiry'.[2]

Esmond Kyan was at this time in a house on the Ferrybank shore, suffering from a severe wound in the shoulder received at Arklow. He struggled across the bridge and succeeded in saving some of the prisoners. Later Father Curran, the parish priest and other clergy intervened with success and finally Edward Roche arrived and put an end to the orgy of murder. He and Garrett Byrne and their men must have been out of reach at the camp at Three Rocks during the afternoon, as it is impossible to believe that the butchery would otherwise have continued unchecked for five hours.

It appears to me that the determination of these men, insofar as they were actuated by any motive other than blind revenge, was to ensure, since they realised that all was lost, that those among the prisoners whom they thought most deserving of death should not be permitted to escape. I do not know whether Dr. Caulfield and the other clergy then in the town could have prevented the massacre, but there is at least a possibility in

---

[1] A son of Luke Byrne, who was a farmer and maltster of Castlesow and Enniscorthy. Hay had a poor opinion of this family. Luke Byrne escaped to America as, in 1804, Lord Mount Norris enquired from the Lord Lieutenant whether 'the American States' if applied to would give up Luke Byrne, a noted murderer who was the instigator and perpetrator of most of the massacres at Vinegar Hill'. (I.S.P.O.).

[2] Jackson was an Englishman who had been five years in Ireland and had settled in Wexford in 1797 as a 'carver and gilder'.

view of the drunkenness and blind ferocity of Dixon's followers, that they would have lost their own lives had they made the attempt.

Gordon makes a shrewd comment on the allegation that the Catholic clergy refused to interfere, or at all events, did not interfere until five hours of butchery had occurred and the news of the menacing movements of Lake's forces had reached the town 'though their influence might be supposed as powerful at two o'clock when the massacre commenced, as at seven'. He observes that an attempt on the part of a Protestant clergyman to stop the slaughter of rebels where loyalists were victorious would be not only useless but dangerous and although the influence of the Catholic clergy over their followers was greater than that of Protestant clergy over theirs, yet how far they would be likely to influence an infuriated rabble, or how far fear might be admitted as a plea for their inaction he felt unable to determine.

I have never heard anyone attempt to defend the massacres at Scullabogue and Wexford Bridge—what Miles Byrne refers to as 'those abominable cold-blooded reprisals', but it would be more becoming as well as more honest if certain authors laid equal stress and pronounced equal condemnation on the much more numerous murders of defenceless people throughout the county by the forces of 'law and order'.

On the night of the 20th the division defeated at Goff's Bridge (Foulke's Mill) returned to the camp at Three Rocks bringing the news that Brigadier-General Moore was at Taghmon and might be expected to attack the town.

Between five and six o'clock in the morning of the 21st, Edward Roche and Garrett Byrne marched their division north and at Darby's Gap met the main insurgent forces retreating from Vinegar Hill. Though late for the battle itself this force performed signal service by forming a rear-guard and fighting off the pursuing cavalry.

Meanwhile, back in Wexford town in the early hours of the 21st, before it could have been learned there that the battle of Vinegar Hill had been fought and lost, it was decided by the town 'authorities' to put into immediate operation a scheme which had been maturing for some time. This included the vesting of control in the hands of the former mayor, Dr. Ebenezer Jacob and of Lord Kingsborough. With the object of preventing destruction of the town which would inevitably follow a direct assault, envoys were dispatched to the various army commanders bearing letters from Lord Kingsborough. Thomas Cloney accompanied by Captain John O'Hea of the North Cork Militia were appointed to intercept the troops advancing from the north; Edward Hay and Captain MacManus of the Antrim Militia were to proceed to General Needham then thought to be at Oulart, while Robert Carty of Birchgrove and Captain Bourke[1] of the North Cork Militia, were to meet Brigadier-General Moore advancing from Taghmon. Hay and MacManus succeeded in entering Enniscorthy after an adventurous journey and there they spent the night in company with Cloney and O'Hea who arrived soon after them. Learning that Needham had advanced as far as Ballinkeele, Hay, this time accompanied by O'Hea, reported to him there. It must have been a painful experience for Edward Hay to revisit his dead father's house in such circumstances. On his return to Wexford he found that the town had already surrendered to Brigadier-General Moore.

[1] Cloney states that Carty was accompanied by Lieutenant Harman of the North Cork Militia and that the latter was met on the road and shot dead by a man named Whelan.

The Battle of Vinegar Hill

IT HAS ALREADY been emphasised that once the insurgents were forced to take the field the only real hope of success lay in a timely French landing in sufficient force to supply sorely needed arms and ammunition and the still more necessary experienced leadership. Up to the date of Vinegar Hill, this help was confidently believed to be imminent and for that reason alone it was folly for the insurgents to risk a final battle and a scattering of their forces. Every dictate of military prudence cried out against their allowing themselves to be surrounded by an immensely superior enemy. Had the division on Kilcavan Hill moved north-west instead of south on the 19th and had Father John Murphy's command, then at Vinegar Hill, broken through the closing ring in the same direction on the 18th or 19th, then a very useful force could have manoeuvred readily enough in that difficult country.

As it happened, however, the French did not land until the 22nd of August and it would hardly have been possible for the insurgents in such numbers to have continued together in the field unsupported for such a length of time; but that does not alter the fact that the decision to stand and fight on Vinegar Hill was a fatal blunder.

Alexander Hatterick of the Dumbartonshire Highlanders, who had been a prisoner since Tubberneering and who was on the hill when it was attacked, stated that the insurgents 'had the impudence to entertain some hopes of victory',[1] but it is difficult to believe that anyone possessing the elements of military understanding can honestly have cherished any such illusion.

Vinegar Hill, viewed from the town of Enniscorthy, has the appearance of a strong defensive position. This is, however, deceptive as, approached from the east, all appearance of elevation disappears and the whole hill lies vulnerable to attack from that side.

Crowded on and around the summit and the adjoining ground to the east were about fifteen thousand men. In addition, large numbers of women and children had accompanied the fighting men for protection and were congregated nearby, probably in the vicinity of the Wexford road east of the river near 'Beale's Barn'. The anxieties of the insurgents on the hill must have been multiplied by the knowledge that if the day went against them their wives, sisters and children would assuredly share in the general butchery.

The defenders were armed for the most part with pikes and similar weapons, some hundreds provided with firearms, but with very scanty supplies of ammunition and according to Miles Byrne (who was present) they awaited 'the arrival of the English army, now moving after us in all directions, with vast parks of artillery, well supplied with everything necessary for battle, whilst we had with us but two six pounders and a small mortar or howitzer, with scarcely a round of ammunition for these cannons. The town of Enniscorthy had placed on the hill a few small one-pounders, which were of very little use, not having any cartridges prepared to fit them.'[2]

Edward Roche, Byrne states, had been 'the principal instigator of the false manoeuvre of marching our army from the strong

_____

[1]   See Appendix V.
[2]   *Memoirs*, Vol. I, p. 123.
    Lake later reported the capture of three six pounders, one three pounder, seven one pounders and two small howitzers.

military position we occupied in the County of Wicklow', but he, with a detachment stated to have numbered about four thousand, marched away on the night of the 19th to Wexford, accompanied by Garrett Byrne, ostensibly to round up reinforcements for the final trial of strength, but possibly also to deal with those known to be anxious to employ their prisoner, Lord Kingsborough, as an intermediary with General Lake. The absence of Edward Roche and his force was sorely felt when the battle commenced, not only on account of the loss of his services as a leader, but also as his detachment included most of the famous Shelmalier marksmen. The battle was over before he succeeded in rejoining the main body at Darby's Gap.

It is appropriate at this point to summarize Lake's plan of encirclement. The design was to drive the insurgents towards Wexford town and the advance on Enniscorthy from the north, north-west, west and south-west was incidental in this general plan.

It will be recalled that General Loftus had retreated to Tullow after the battle of Tubberneering on the 4th of June and he was there on the 17th. General Dundas was at Hacketstown on the same date and he and Loftus reached Carnew with General Lake on the 18th, Sir James Duff joining them there during that night.

Dundas was ordered south to reach the Slaney at Ballycarney and thence by the east side of the river to be at the general assembly point at Scarawalsh Bridge by noon on the 20th. Loftus arrived at the same point at the same hour having marched through Camolin and Ferns. Duff, who had apparently returned to Bunclody from Carnew on the 19th joined the others at Scarawalsh Bridge following the road on the west bank of the river.

The movements of Brigadier-General Moore have already been described, including the delaying action at Goff's Bridge

(Foulke's Mill) on the 20th. General Johnson and General Eustace were in Old Ross on the 19th and moved on the 20th by Clonroche and Ballymackesy Bridge to the western approaches of Enniscorthy.

General Needham, who had been in Arklow from the date of the battle there on the 9th, was in Gorey on the 19th and in Oulart on the 20th.

During the afternoon of the 20th, Lake with the force which had assembled at Scarawalsh Bridge, advanced down the road on the east of the river to Solsborough, the residence of Solomon Richards, where he halted for the night.

It is tempting to speculate on what would have been the outcome of a night attack on Solsborough. A couple of thousand determined pikemen moving in silence and darkness across country might easily have succeeded in getting to close quarters with the troops, their artillery would have been useless and in that wooded region organised defence against sudden and unexpected attack would have been difficult. With complete success the prize might have been very great and in any event the grand strategy would have been seriously dislocated. The insurgents on the hill would in consequence have been enabled to fight with infinitely greater prospects of success than when they found themselves attacked at dawn on the 21st simultaneously from three sides.

Thomas Cloney records as follows: 'Had a proposal been acceded to which was made on Vinegar Hill the evening before the battle by some of the leaders to pour down on Lake's army at Solsborough, where in consequence of extraordinary fatigue, by forced marches, they lay prostrate on the ground and unable to offer any formidable resistance, they would certainly have defeated the General, for several officers who were there with General Lake assured me, if they had been attacked that night from Vinegar Hill, they must have been inevitably destroyed'.[1]

[1] *Personal Narrative*, page 71.

When the attack opened on the hill, the road towards the south-east—that is, the road to Wexford town east of the river through Darby's Gap, was unaccountably left open. It should have been occupied by General Needham who received his final orders in Oulart to march at dusk on the 20th and reach his assigned position astride that road before dawn on the 21st. His objective was not more than six miles off as the crow flies, he had six or seven hours at his disposal and his failure to reach this objective has never been satisfactorily explained.[1] It appears to have been accepted in some quarters that he would have succeeded had he not been diverted by an order from General Lake at Solsborough. Then shortly before dawn, he was again directed to proceed as originally intended, but by a circuitous route which made it impossible for him to get his division into position in time.

Several alternative explanations have been suggested. Gordon states that 'the commonly received opinion' was that General Lake, in his great mercy, contrived matters so as to avoid the slaughter of the defeated insurgents! Apart from its inherent absurdity in view of the known character of Lake, this fairy tale can be finally disposed of by quoting Lake's own biographer who writes:

Needham did his best by throwing his cavalry forward; but although the latter did some execution, the gap caused by the non-arrival of Needham's infantry prevented the total destruction of the rebels that had been intended and would have taken place.[2]

Miles Byrne thought Needham was deliberately held back by Lake to keep open the road to Gorey in the event of his defeat and retirement to the north. I think this is unlikely

[1] The incident gained for him the title of 'the late General Needham' and the open road was referred to as 'Needham's Gap'.

[2] Colonel Hugh Pearse: *Memoirs of the Life and Military Services of Viscount Lake*, (1744-1808), 1908, p. 107. It may be mentioned that on the 24th of May, Lake had written to Loftus as follows: 'I cannot believe these rascals dare move, though there seems to be little doubt of their being in motion. If you have an opportunity of attacking the villains, take no prisoners.' See a collection of letters from General Lake, microfilm, National Library, Dublin.

also and it would seem more probable either that Lake, for some unknown reason, diverted Needham and then changed his mind, or else that during the night march Needham's guides either by accident or design, led the division too far along the wrong road to enable them to remedy their mistake in time.[1]

In justice to Needham, it should be mentioned that he had in his charge the entire commissariat of Lake's force, comprising four hundred wagons and his diversion to Solsborough (if it took place) may have been necessary for reasons of supply. In addition the wagons had been commandeered and presumably the drivers also. In any event Needham was censured for his failure to close the gap.

No serious attempt had been made by the insurgents during their three weeks' occupation of the hill to deal with the question of defence. Miles Byrne was 'surprised to find that scarcely anything had been done to make it formidable against the enemy; the vast fences and ditches which surround it on three sides and which should have been levelled to the ground for at least a cannon shot, or half-a-mile of distance, were all left untouched. The English forces availing themselves of these defences advanced from field to field, bringing with them their cannon which they placed to great advantage behind and under cover of the hedges and fences, whilst our men were exposed to a terrible fire from their artillery and small arms without being able to drive them back from their strongholds in those fields.'

The disposition of the opposing forces immediately before the battle was as follows. The insurgents held the town of

---

[1] See also Appendices V and X. Earl Stanhope in his *Life of William Pitt*, states that there were thirteen thousand government troops actually engaged at Vinegar Hill. He also refers to Needham's non-arrival as *accidental* and suggests that the fact of the Gap being there may have lessened the insurgents' will to fight (Vol. III, p. 146). In this battle Lake had under his command no fewer than eight general officers.

Enniscorthy, Vinegar Hill itself, and the ground extending a mile from the summit in an easterly direction towards the Clonhasten crossroads and south of the present Oulart road. The limit of their position in this region was just east of the existing quarry.

General Henry Johnson and General Eustace were in charge of the attack on the town of Enniscorthy from the west.[1]

General Lake, with the main body, moved out from Solsborough in the early hours of the 21st of June and before dawn they had reached a point on the road to Enniscorthy, a mile from the outskirts of the town where a by-road branches to the left. At this point the force divided. General Sir James Duff, with his division, marched a quarter of a mile further ahead and then halted, posting his infantry on both sides of the road and planting his four guns on the road itself. General Loftus turned left up the by-road and having reached a point nearly half-a-mile distant from the main road he brought his four guns to a low green hillock just east of the by-road. Half the force of Light Cavalry was posted behind the hillock. When the cannonade commenced at dawn, Loftus soon left this position and pushed his guns forward towards the insurgent lines aided by the shelter of fences and walls and by the feebleness of the artillery retaliation from the hill.

Lake, accompanied by Dundas and Wilford with four guns, the Light Infantry and the rest of the Light Cavalry proceeded to their assigned positions on the west side of the present Clonhasten crossroads.[2]

---

[1] In the *Cornwallis Correspondence* (Cornwallis to Ross, 15th July, 1799), there is the following extraordinary passage:

'Johnson, Gardiner and Eustace are all put off the staff ... Johnson, although a wrong-headed blockhead, is adored for his defence at New Ross, and considered as the Saviour of the South, and poor Eustace after forty-three years' service is reduced to his company in the 33rd. . . .'

[2] The route they followed to reach this point is uncertain as the road system has changed somewhat and the present road from Enniscorthy to Oulart did not then exist.

Dundas and the Light Cavalry were posted seven hundred yards to the east of the nearest insurgent position and north of the road, with two guns on the road itself, while Wilford with the other two guns lay south of the road. Lake and the Light Infantry took up their battle stations a short distance in front. From the nature of the ground in this region, Lake had a clear view of the entire battlefield north and east of the hill. The actual fighting seems to have commenced west of Enniscorthy. William Barker and Father Kearns who were in command of the town's defences had stationed outposts at Bloomfield House on the main road to New Ross and in the vicinity of Cherry Orchard on the Killann road. These were attacked and eventually driven into the town through the Duffrey Gate. A gun mounted later by General Johnson at Cherry Orchard Rock was knocked out in the course of the battle.[1]

In the bitter fighting which followed, with alternating attack and counter-attack and heavy casualties, the streets were eventually cleared with grape and the contest developed into a house to house struggle at close quarters. Many houses had been burned when the insurgents stormed the town on the 28th of May and many more now suffered the same fate. Gradually the insurgents were forced down the hill to the river side and across the bridge into the suburbs of Templeshannon and Drumgold. Father Kearns was wounded, but escaped during the general retreat along the Wexford road east of the river. Barker was wounded and made prisoner in circumstances detailed later.[2]

Almost simultaneously with the attack on the town, the battle for the hill commenced with a prolonged cannonade at dawn. The insurgent guns were soon silenced chiefly on account of lack of ammunition. The artillery fire, now one-sided, continued unabated until 7.0 a.m., during which time the

[1] See the *Narrative* of Mrs. Newton Lett.
[2] See page 207.

guns were moved forward and the insurgent defenders decimated with grape and canister.

Oddly enough, there is no reference in any account of the battle to the old high banked lane which crosses the hill nearly east and west, passing not far from the summit and to the north of it. This must have been strongly held and here the casualties were no doubt, extremely heavy.

At 7.0 a.m., the infantry commenced their advance and the engagement became general. The most formidable infantry attack came from the east under the leadership of Colonel Campbell and gradually the insurgent outposts extending in that direction were driven back on to the hill itself. As the concentration here became greater, the easier were the targets for the artillery firing from two directions and casualties mounted rapidly. Charge after charge of pikemen withered in the face of the combined fire of artillery and small arms. Miles Byrne records that at one period it was suggested that an all-out attack should be made to turn the enemy's left wing, that is, along the Oulart road, and so break through northwards towards County Wicklow. This attack, however, did not materialise owing, Byrne states, to reluctance to desert their companions fighting in defence of the town of Enniscorthy.

Finally, after an hour and a half of this most unequal contest it was decided to retreat along the Wexford road past Beale's Barn towards Darby's Gap. At this latter point Edward Roche's force returning from Wexford town intervened as a rearguard and succeeded in preventing any further considerable interference.

In the course of the first two miles and a half, however, many of the wounded left the road and lay in the adjoining ditches; while the old and infirm and many women and children lingered by the wayside, or sought concealment in the fields and so lost touch with the main body. All such were systematically slaughtered by the pursuing troops.[1]

Thomas Cloney, a temperate chronicler, records that when he came within about a mile of Enniscorthy (as an envoy from the town of Wexford) he actually saw many of the soldiers still busy on the work of extermination. 'The dead and dying were scattered promiscuously in the fields, in dykes, on the roads, or wherever chance had directed their last steps. ... In one place we beheld some men with arms and some with legs off, and others cruelly mutilated in various ways; horses with their necks broken, and their cars with women and children under them, either dead or dying in the road and ditches, where in their precipitate flight they had been upset.'

Edward Hay who passed along the same road two hours earlier and Miles Byrne, who was with the retreating force, both tell the same story. The former adds that after his arrival in Enniscorthy he noted that 'the house which had been used as an hospital by the insurgents, and which was set on fire with all the patients in it, continued burning until next morning, when I saw a part of a corpse still hissing in the embers'.

Father Thomas Clinch of Enniscorthy who was wounded on the retreat, died on the roadside between Darby's Gap and Mye Cross, where a monument has been erected in his memory. He was buried at Kilmallock, a mile south of Ballinkeele House.

It is difficult to estimate the insurgent losses in this action. Lake's biographer states that the army losses were eight officers and eighty-seven other ranks killed and wounded. Sergeant McLaren (an eye-witness) gives them as six officers and eighty-one other ranks,[2] so it is likely that these figures are approximately correct.

Lake's biographer thinks the insurgent losses may have

[1] Lord Roden's 'Foxhunters' distinguished themselves here as they had previously done at the massacre of unarmed men on the Curragh of Kildare.
[2] See Appendix V.

been three hundred, most of them cut down in the retreat. This is, unfortunately, an under-estimate. Lake himself wrote from Wexford town on the 22nd: 'From enquiry the numbers killed yesterday were very great indeed'.

Apart from the heavy casualties in the town of Enniscorthy, guns had been pouring grape from two sides for several hours into a crowd of some fifteen thousand men on an open hillside with practically no protective field works and when the casualties inflicted in close combat with small arms are added the total must have been large.

Sir Jonah Barrington mentions in his *Recollections* that he visited various places in County Wexford a short time after the end of hostilities. Enniscorthy which had been twice stormed he found 'dilapidated and nearly burned . . . the numerous pits crammed with dead bodies on Vinegar Hill seemed on some spots actually elastic as we stood upon them'.

During the first two miles and a half of the retreat between the hill and Darby's Gap the losses in men, women and children in the general massacre were great beyond doubt and in addition an unknown number of sick and wounded were burned to death in the hospital in Enniscorthy.

Retreat

THE DEFEATED INSURGENTS kept together from Darby's Gap, through Oilgate to Ferrycarrig Bridge. Here there was a division of forces; the larger number, including most of the leaders, entered Wexford town, while the smaller, led by Father John Murphy, turned off to the old camping ground at Three Rocks. Edward Roche kept his own men together at Windmill Hill while the remainder for a time dispersed through the town. These latter were at length collected and without waiting for the result of the various missions and having been rejoined by Edward Roche, they crossed the bridge and marched north through Blackwater and Kilmuckridge to Peppard's Castle where they halted for the night.

Further reference to this division will be found at page 174.

Cornelius Grogan, a sickly old man, had returned from the town of Wexford to his house at Johnstown. Matthew Keogh remained in the town apparently confident that the envoys' mission would be successful. Bagnal Harvey retired to Bargy Castle and John Henry Colclough to Ballyteigue, inspired by the same confidence. The two latter, on learning through a messenger that their optimism was misplaced, sought concealment on the greater Saltee Island, where they were betrayed, arrested and brought back to Wexford.[1]

Miles Byrne with a contingent who placed themselves under

[1] See also biographical notes, pages 191 and 205.

his leadership, left the town to join Father John Murphy at Three Rocks, but before he had gone far he learned that Father John had decided to move further south. Byrne joined him, stopping at Johnstown for a short rest and much needed refreshment for his men, before pushing on a further two miles to Sleedagh where they halted for the night. It had been found necessary to leave Father Kearns in a house on the way, suffering as he was from loss of blood, the result of a wound received in the defence of Enniscorthy that morning. Father Philip Roche, who had accompanied them thus far, now rode back to Wexford having persuaded himself of the possibility of obtaining terms. On his arrival he was recognised, dragged from his horse and unceremoniously hanged. Father John Murphy refused to consider surrender.

Miles Byrne records that at dawn on the 22nd, they resumed their journey 'greatly encumbered as usual with our wounded and vast numbers of females who were following their brothers, or other relatives, not having any place of refuge or other means of escaping from the monsters then ravaging their homes'.

As the route they followed covered no less than forty-five miles of ground and as at the end of this formidable march they fought a skirmish, it may be taken as fairly certain that most of such followers were shed on the way. It is probable also that there were numerous desertions and that it was a sadly diminished force which rested at last four miles on the Carlow side of the Scullogue Gap.

There is no detailed information available as to the actual line of march except that they traversed the battlefield of Goff's Bridge or Foulke's Mill where they saw the countryside littered with the bodies of those killed two days before and that later they passed through the village of Killann.[1]

According to one account they commenced their march by a detour southwards to Moyglass and from there to the Moor

[1] Miles Byrne.

of Mulrankin. To reach Goff's Bridge from Mulrankin would have brought them through Bridgetown and Baldwinstown and on by Tullycanna and Ballymitty crossroads.

This achievement and that of the other division which marched from Vinegar Hill to Wexford and back to Peppard's Castle (more than thirty miles) immediately following an uneasy night and a hard-fought battle, are worthy of remembrance as two of the most remarkable feats of endurance in the annals of war.[1]

At Killann they had their first brush with cavalry patrols, but they met with no serious opposition until they reached the Gap. There are at present two roads between Wexford and Carlow at this place. 'The road followed by the insurgents is the old road which runs close to the foot of Knockroe . . . on the right hand side as one comes from County Wexford. This is the ancient road through the Gap. The other road, which is now used by travellers, was made in 1847. The Aghabrisky River runs between the two roads. . . . The traveller will observe that almost all the houses in the Gap are built along the ancient road. . . . The local tradition is that the insurgents, having come through the Gap, proceeded through the bogs at the back of Rahanna Chapel in order to prevent the English forces at Killedmund from escaping through Crumlin Gap which is to the north of Killedmund. Some of the Killedmund Yeomanry did nevertheless escape through this Gap.'

Killedmond village contained a military barracks and this and the village itself were defended by infantry and cavalry, but a charge of pikemen cleared them from both, after which, by order of Father John Murphy, the barracks was burned, no doubt in order to prevent its re-occupation.

[1] In the description which follows I have freely drawn upon the account, compiled partly from local tradition, by the Revd. Brother Luke, (formerly of Muine Bheag) which he embodied in a lecture delivered in Gorey in 1938. I am grateful for his permission to quote from this valuable work.

Miles Byrne states: 'By this time our small army was quite exhausted from so long and so fatiguing a march and stood much in need of both refreshments and of sleep'.

They bivouacked that night in the townland of Tomduff, half-a-mile north of Killedmond and the field in which they lay is still known as the Camp Field.

The following morning (the 23rd) it became necessary to dislodge the garrison at Goresbridge (Newbridge) in order to force a passage across the Barrow. 'The insurgents approached the town of Goresbridge by the old road now disused, over Knockmanus Hill and down by the [present] railway station of Ballyellin. Their route from Kilcloney Bridge lay a little to the south of the road now leading from Kilcloney Bridge to Ballyfeanan Cross. The present road from Kilcloney Bridge to Ballyfeanan Cross and from Ballyfeanan Cross to Goresbridge was not there in 1798.'

Miles Byrne describes what followed: 'Coming near the town we were met by a company of the 4th Dragoon Guards and after a short skirmish we forced them to retreat and fall back on their infantry, the Wexford Militia, which began a brisk fire and a sharp engagement ensued during which we had several wounded. But now, whether from a fear of disaffection in his troops, or a terror of another kind, the commanding officer of the militia[1] hastened to mount behind a dragoon soldier, galloped away and left his men to do the best they could. Abandoned by their officer, their fire soon ceased, when they were surrounded and made prisoners.'

According to local tradition some foraging parties of the insurgents crossed the river a little higher up at Duninga and at Slyguff Lock (now called Byron's Lock). 'A road led from this ford through Fenniscourt and Ballytarsna to Cnocan na gCros, now . . . called Black Acre and thence by the line of the present road to Paulstown, Boherboy and Kellymount. . . .

[1] Lieutenant Dixon.

The main body who had crossed at Goresbridge, followed the road which runs northwards along the western bank of the river Barrow past Red Mill and through Barracore and Duninga to Cnocan na gCros, Paulstown, Boherboy and Kellymount. Thus the insurgents who crossed at Byron's Lock may have met the main body at Cnocan na gCros. There is evidence from tradition and history that some insurgent detachments passed through Shankill' which they reached before noon.

The night of the 23rd was spent on the high ground known as the Ridge, between Old Leighlin and Castlecomer and the traditional site of the camp is on the Commons of Baunreagh lying four miles north-west of Kellymount in an eight-acre field owned (in 1938) by William Bergin.

Of the prisoners taken at Goresbridge seven were murdered at Kellymount. At the trial by courtmartial of John Devereux, junior, of Shelbeggan[1] held at Cork on the 27th of November 1799, where he was charged with high treason, some interesting particulars were supplied. For example Sergeant Benjamin Tuttle of the Wexford Militia stated that there were twenty-five prisoners. Two of the 4th Dragoons (Fowkes and Hawkins) were piked and of the five Wexfordmen killed, three were piked and two shot. It was plainly stated in evidence that the murdered men were all Protestants. Sergeant Tuttle stated further that he himself was brought into a circle formed of the insurgents and marked for death, but that his life was saved by the intervention of Richard Monaghan (Dick Monk— see pages 208 and 209).

Further evidence was given that there were six persons named Devereux present, including the prisoner and Walter Devereux who was executed in November, 1798.

There was a good deal of hard swearing at this courtmartial, some at least of which was proved to be false. The court

[1] Before the rising he had been groom to General Fawcett.

obviously discounted much of it as is shown by their sentence of transportation for life instead of death.[1]

Neither Father John Murphy nor Miles Byrne was present when these murders took place and they were probably committed by details left behind in charge of the prisoners after the main body had moved on to the Ridge.

At 2.30 a.m. on Sunday, the 24th, they advanced on Castlecomer, passing through the Butts and Croghtenclogh to Doonane. From Doonane the attack on the town was made along both sides of the river—Miles Byrne leading the assault through Crottyard and Coolbawn, while Father John Murphy crossed the river at Massford and came down the west bank. The town was carried with little difficulty except for one strong point, Lady Ann Butler's house which commanded the bridge from the west side. Sir Charles Asgill made his appearance from Kilkenny and there was a good deal of skirmishing in the neighbourhood, but eventually the town was abandoned by both parties, Sir Charles Asgill retreating to Kilkenny and Father Murphy marching away rather unaccountably northwards through Doonane and on to the townland of Slatt Lower, three miles further north where the night of the 24th was spent.

The following day there was a tentative advance towards Athy, but except for a number of colliers there was no support such as had been expected from the people of that county.

It was therefore reluctantly decided to turn back, re-cross the Barrow, re-enter County Wexford through the Scullogue Gap and join the other division which had marched northwards on the 21st from Wexford town.

That night they formed camp on Kilcomney Hill.[2] When morning came it was discovered that the collier recruits had deserted, bringing with them many of the precious firearms of which the now much reduced force stood so greatly in

[1]   *The Trial of John Devereux, junior, of Shelbeggan.* Joly Pamphlets—National Library, Dublin.
[2]   A mile east of Goresbridge.

need. Sir Charles Asgill at this critical juncture suddenly reappeared with a largely increased force and compelled the insurgents to retreat through the Scullogue Gap, the two Fencible detachments stationed there by General Lake being unable to stop their progress.

The wrath of the troops fell, however, on the unfortunate unarmed inhabitants of that countryside. Sir Charles Asgill claimed that 'upwards of one hundred were killed and that his own casualties numbered seven', but Gordon, the 'loyalist' historian, stated that the loss of the insurgents 'may have amounted to two or three hundred as they were pursued six miles by some of the cavalry. . . . I am informed that great part of the slain were inhabitants of the country . . . who had not joined the rebels nor left their houses; and that the great part of the plunder was taken from people of the same description. The behaviour of the army in other places renders this account very probable'.[1]

Such wholesale butcheries as this did not escape the notice of Lord Cornwallis, who made the following comment:

> The accounts you see of the numbers of the enemy destroyed in every action are, I conclude, greatly exaggerated. From my own knowledge of military affairs I am sure that a very small proportion of them only could be killed in battle and I am much afraid that any man in a brown coat who is found within several miles of the field of action is butchered without discrimination.[2]

Having forced their way back into County Wexford, the insurgent leaders decided to make for the Gold Mines region in County Wicklow, in order to link up with their companions who had marched north before them. There were further considerable desertions on the way, as numbers of men preferred what they regarded as the security of Killoughrum Forest to continuing the forced marches of the past few days.

. . . .

[1] Pp. 204-5 and note.
[2] Cornwallis: *Correspondence*, Vol. II, p. 355.

Brother Luke supplies the following detailed and most interesting account of the movements of Father John Murphy from the field of Kilcomney until his arrest and execution:

Father John and one companion, Gallagher, became separated and proceeded northwards by the foothills of Mount Leinster, making for County Wicklow. There is a well established tradition in south County Carlow that Father John, on the evening or night of 25th June, called to the house now occupied by Daniel Tierney in Killoughternane. The house was, in '98, occupied by Mr. O'Connell. Here his torn clothes were mended by Miss O'Connell, then aged twelve. The next place Father John called was at Ballyreel House, occupied by Mr. Kepple, a Protestant farmer, about a mile and a half from Ballon. It is thought he travelled from Killoughternane to Ballon via Knockinadrane, Drumfea, Straduff, Taylor's Cross Roads and Killane Cross Roads. Father John and Gallagher approached Kepple's house from the back and hid at first in a stable, but later were brought into the house. The stable is still known as 'Father John's stable' or 'The Priest's Hole'.

From Ballyreel they travelled to Castlemore, by an ancient road or track, part of which is now called 'the long tochar'. In '98 it was 'very narrow . . . a mere track'.

It is generally held that Father John and Gallagher called to O'Toole's—a small farmer living near Castlemore Cross Roads.[1]

Here they were discovered and brought to General Duff's headquarters at Tullow and there recognised, tried and hanged on the Market Square outside the house of a Mr. O'Callaghan, now owned by Dempsey. Father John's body was then burned in a barrel of tar and his head spiked at the Sessions House, now Henderson's of Mill Street.

After some time the head was taken down and buried in the Mullawn, Tullow.

---

[1] The site of this house is still pointed out. It is a few perches from the crossroads, on the road running north-west and opposite the woods of Castlemore House.

Gorey Again—Bloody Friday

As ALREADY MENTIONED, there was a division of the insurgent forces in the vicinity of Wexford town on the evening of the 21st of June. Those who headed northwards comprised the larger party and were led by Anthony Perry, Edward Fitzgerald, Esmond Kyan, Garrett Byrne and Edward Roche. As they rested for the night at Peppard's Castle, young John McAuley son of Daniel McAuley the proprietor of the inn at Oulart, rode over to visit his parents. There he was arrested and summarily hanged.

The following morning disquieting news reached them of recent events in the Gorey neighbourhood. It is somewhat difficult to disentangle the facts from the propagandist reports of writers on both sides. It appears, however, that when Gorey was evacuated first by the insurgents who marched south to Vinegar Hill and later by General Needham on his way to Oulart, there was a gradual return of refugees who had earlier fled for safety into south Wicklow. Some yeomanry also made a cautious approach to the town and finding it deserted they resumed their former conduct of ranging through the country, shooting every man they could find on the roads, in the fields, or in the houses.[1]

Anthony Perry and Edward Fitzgerald immediately set out to deal with the situation. The yeomen 'and their associates'

[1] The 'loyalist' historian, Gordon, states that fifty men lost their lives in this foray.

made some slight resistance, but soon fled and were pursued as far as Coolgreany. In the pursuit a considerable number of the fugitives were killed; Hay puts the number at forty-seven and James Rowsome, who was overtaken on Kilmurry Hill, ill-treated and left for dead, later stated in a deposition that the number 'he heard and believes' was 'thirty or forty'. James Pippard, sovereign of Gorey, in a deposition stated that the losses of the loyalists numbered thirty-six by shooting and piking. Hay states that Pippard was discovered in the town after the pursuit was over, was brought before Edward Fitzgerald and set at liberty. Pippard himself stated that he 'was one of the number that retreated from Gorey and narrowly escaped with his life'.[1]

While in the town Fitzgerald learned that all his worldly possessions, including his house at Newpark, his farm buildings and malt-house had been destroyed by fire on the orders of General Needham.

The detachment which had made the detour to Gorey now followed their companions in their march northwards. At White Heaps, on the southern slope of Croghan mountain, they met the shattered remnant of Father John Murphy's force led by Miles Byrne who refers to 'the heartfelt delight we experienced on meeting at the White Heaps the other division of our army, which we so much longed to join. . . . We returned with it to Ballyfad where we bivouacked for the night'.

The further fortunes and misfortunes of this force belong chiefly to the history of County Wicklow and the reader will find an account of them in the present author's *Life of Michael Dwyer*.

---

[1] Pippard's deposition was sworn before Hunter Gowan on the 31st December, 1798.
See Musgrave, Appendix XX, 21.

Aftermath

DURING THE LAST DAYS of June, 1798, the scattering of the insurgent forces had made it clear that, except for the stubborn resistance maintained for so long in County Wicklow under the leadership of Joseph Holt and Michael Dwyer, the end of active hostilities was in sight, albeit after an expenditure of rather more blood and treasure than had been anticipated. For some time preparations had evidently been in train for putting the finishing touches to the long term plan which was to end with the Union. It was considered that the time was approaching when the 'softening up' process should have produced the desired effect although the time-table had been somewhat disturbed.

As early as the 15th of June the Lord Lieutenant wrote: 'General Lake is certainly frequently inadequate to the situation he now fills'.[1] That General who had issued orders to take no prisoners, was obviously not the man to handle the delicate situation which would arise when the time came to switch from a policy of bloody massacre to one of loving kindness and tender mercy.

As it happened, neither was Lord Camden, who had advocated the appointment of a soldier to the vice-royalty and so it came about that on the 20th of June, Lord Cornwallis arrived

---

[1] Camden to Pelham. I.S.P.O.

176

in Dublin to take over the combined functions of Viceroy and Commander-in-Chief.[1]

The first step that was taken after Lake was got rid of, was to regularise the Wexford courtsmartial. At first they had been of the drum-head variety and in some cases not even conducted in accordance with King's Regulations. They were assembled merely for the purpose of giving an appearance of legality to fore-ordained death penalties. The new departure demanded other methods and the freshly constituted military court presided over first by Colonel Lord Ancram and later by Lieutenant-Colonel Sir James Foulis, brought in verdicts in accordance with the evidence and many of the prisoners were acquitted.

Not long after the end of hostilities a well known agricultural authority observed that in County Wexford 'all the farmers who have leases exhibit great proofs of industry'. He also makes the following statement: 'Far would it be from us to offer any palliation of the conduct of the rebels in this country in the year 1798; but we cannot help observing that, as sudden and general as was the rising by the inhabitants of this county, in the month of May of that year, no less sudden and general was the return of these people in July following, to their industry and their homes (for houses thousands had none). . .'[2]

Such a state of affairs was, however, to be rudely disturbed. The new appointment and the new procedure were fiercely assailed by the Orangemen who realised that, henceforth, there would not be the same measure of support for the Irish executive and therefore, indirectly for themselves. Changes were made in the military commands in the county—General Hunter to Wexford, Brigadier-General Grose to Enniscorthy

---

[1] Efforts to induce Cornwallis to accept the vice-royalty at an earlier date had been abortive. He held strongly that Catholic concessions were necessary, but this the Government would not then concede. His avowed object was to separate Catholics from Dissenters.

[2] Robert Fraser: *Statistical Survey of the County Wexford* (1807), p. 56.

and General Gascoigne to New Ross and the career of the terrorists, so successful only a few weeks before, received a check. The Government in a flutter of virtue even permitted the arrest of Hunter Gowan of Mount Nebo and Hawtrey White of Peppard's Castle—the first on many charges of murder and robbery and the second of oppression and the spreading of rumours calculated to cause disturbance and loss of confidence in the then intentions of Government. It was too much to expect, however, that two magistrates to whom the executive was under such exceptional obligation should be allowed to suffer merely for continuing their loyal activities beyond the allotted time and on one pretext or another the release of each was effected.[1]

It had not taken Lord Cornwallis long to find out that the yeomanry and militia, so long accustomed to being given a free hand and no questions asked, were unwilling to forego their former privileges. He felt compelled to express himself as follows: '. . . in too many cases the militia and yeomanry were not to be restrained. Free quarters were freely indulged in: floggings to extort confessions were often inflicted; nay even death itself was sometimes not withheld. . . . These men have saved the country, but they now take the lead in rapine and murder.'[2]

In spite of official anxiety that the country should be allowed to settle down, there were very many who thought otherwise and acted accordingly. There were the so-called 'Babes in the Wood' based on Killoughrum Forest, then an extensively wooded tract of land five miles west of Enniscorthy. These men were mostly deserters from militia regiments who could expect no mercy on surrender and who, instead of joining Dwyer and Holt in Wicklow as many of their companions

---

[1] Hunter Gowan later claimed £2,130 and was awarded £2,044, for losses as a 'distressed loyalist'.
[2] Quoted by Stanhope: *Life of William Pitt*, Vol. III, p. 149.

had done, elected to prey upon their neighbours instead. The chief offenders, however, were the yeomanry and militia as Lord Cornwallis admitted. They roved the countryside chiefly, but not always, at night and kept the inhabitants in a state of chronic terror *for several years.*[1] Chapel burning continued until well on in 1801; in fact of thirty-three set on fire in County Wexford, only five suffered during the fighting.[2]

The curious reticence of the Wexford people as a whole and the comparative absence of tradition among them relating to '98, are characteristics which are familiar to all who have a knowledge of the county and this has been attributed to the multiplied horrors of the insurrection itself.[3]

While this is, no doubt, true in a general way, I feel that in addition, during the long drawn out terror of the after period, men must have feared to speak freely of their experiences even to their children and this would tend to result as time went on, in a blurring of memories and a fading of tradition.

One prominent Wexfordman has drawn my attention to 'a horrible blank' in the folk memory of the period immediately after '98, and this he attributes to the deportations which continued 'by the cart load' at frequent intervals for upwards of two years after fighting ceased.

---

[1] See the important Appendix XI.

[2] It may be mentioned that when a chapel, usually thatched, was 'burned' the structure was not necessarily destroyed. Thus Derrylossery Chapel in County Wicklow, was burned, but it was estimated that the damage would be made good for the sum of £42.14.6d.

[3] See an article on the parish of Bree, by the Revd. P. Shiel, P.P., in *The Past*, No. 2.

A Summing Up

IN THE FOREGOING PAGES I have endeavoured to set down dispassionately the causes of the outbreak in County Wexford in 1798. The conclusions are the outcome of many years study of every available source of information in manuscript and in print and of an intimate knowledge of the county. Also an attempt has been made to describe the events of the brief campaign which followed so that it may be possible for the reader to reconstruct on the spot the actual incidents which took place in each locality.

The evidence as a whole, in my opinion, supports the view that in some measure County Wexford was, in comparison with the other so-called 'fighting counties', in an exceptional position. It is not, I think, sustainable that the strength of the membership of the Society of United Irishmen there was in reality large, but concealed by the non-attendance of the county secretary at the meeting of the Leinster Directory on the 23rd of March, 1798, when nominal rolls of certain other counties were captured. I have found no sufficient support for the belief that the numbers sworn in County Wexford at the outbreak of hostilities were comparable with those in the surrounding counties and the evidence now available in the deposition of Anthony Perry seems to me conclusive that so far as any considerable body of the people was concerned the efforts of the Society met with no enthusiastic response except perhaps in the north of the county and especially in the area of which Gorey is the centre.

That a resistance movement was in being in other baronies also is undeniable, but I think this had its origin in the anti-tithe or Defender organisation which was particularly strong in County Wexford where there had been much activity accompanied by bloodshed only five years previously. This, I feel sure, was one reason why pikes and other rude weapons were in the hands of the people and which they surrendered in considerable quantity at the instance of the clergy during the months preceding the outbreak.

This may also, to some extent, explain the mounting sectarian bitterness which showed itself later and which was so repugnant to the whole conception of the Society of United Irishmen. I suggest also that the sudden and almost complete quiescence of the insurgents after four weeks of the heaviest fighting may have had a similar explanation and this is supported by the contrast with the neighbouring county of Wicklow, where the resistance movement under the leadership of Michael Dwyer continued for five and a half years, unquestionably encouraged and sustained by the reconstituted United Irish Directory until the hope of French intervention had been finally relinquished.[1]

As I have stated elsewhere, it is likely, had the French landed towards the end of May, especially if such landing had taken place on the coast of any one of the Leinster counties, Wexford, unprepared though it undoubtedly was, would have caught

[1] It has already been pointed out that an oath of one kind or another was extensively imposed during the later stages of the fighting in Wexford and that a state of apprehension continued for years afterwards. That at least it was desired in some quarters to create the impression that a genuine cause for apprehension existed, is indicated by a letter written from Duncannon Fort as late as the 11th of July, 1803, by one E. C. Moncrieffe to the Viceroy, Lord Hardwicke, stating that he had been informed by a magistrate named Glascott 'that the County of Wexford except two baronies are sworn to secrecy to aid the French and to rise when called on'. (I.S.P.O.).

fire and joined its neighbours in a general uprising. The deficiencies of arms and trained leadership would thus have been remedied, the fatal isolation of the county would have been prevented and hostilities would have taken an altogether different course.

The Government, determined to force an issue before the expected landing could take place, were successful in their object by the application of methods to which reference has already been made. It must be borne in mind, not only that French intervention was an essential part of the scheme of the revolutionary movement in Ireland, but that the Government were fully aware of this and of the fact also that the port of Wexford was regarded as a likely landing place. In addition the Government were kept informed through their agents of the active preparations which were ostensibly being made in France for the invasion of England during the early months of 1798 and they viewed the situation with the deepest anxiety.

Napoleon, however, lured by his ambition to emulate the conquests of Alexander the Great in the east, lacking command of the sea and never fully convinced of the adequacy of the revolutionary preparations in Ireland, set sail for Egypt at the head of an army of forty thousand men on the 19th of May, when those parts of Ireland where some kind of preparation had been made were already fully committed and only *four days* before the men of Kildare, Carlow and Wicklow actually took the field.

In County Wexford, once hostilities commenced and apart from the lack of equipment and training, the want of some one outstanding and acknowledged leader with military capacity and experience was immediately felt. It is true that William Barker, John Hay and Esmond Kyan had all seen service and when decisions had to be taken their advice was usually sound, but they were out-voted by inexperienced men whose opinions were often based on considerations other than those of strategic necessity. This was especially exemplified on at least three critical occasions—the failure to occupy New Ross at once after the fall of Enniscorthy on the 28th of May, the failure to occupy Arklow immediately after the capture of Gorey on the 4th of June and the fatal concentration of their forces on Vinegar Hill to be pounded to pieces on the 21st of June.

Of the remainder and apart from the clerical leaders to whom I have already referred on page 23, there seems to be no evidence that Bagnal Harvey, Edward Fitzgerald of Newpark and John Henry Colclough, were any more than political sympathisers with the constitutional aims of the United Irishmen in the direction of reform and emancipation. If all three had not been arrested on the information of Anthony Perry and brought as prisoners to the town of Wexford, they would not have been placed at the most critical moment in such a position as to be left with no alternative to being swept into the insurgent ranks.

PART III

Biographical Notes

I HAVE NOT BURDENED the text by attempting to ascribe success or failure to individual leaders. Information on this subject is unreliable and writers are frequently in error in mentioning even the presence of this or that prominent person in certain places—for example, Father Philip Roche at Tubberneering, or Cornelius Grogan at New Ross, or Father John Murphy at Arklow.

In the notices which follow there is no claim to completeness, but it may be of interest to place on record some personal particulars relating to those who in County Wexford have been referred to in varying degrees, as leaders.

The following list of such, curiously incomplete, has been published.[1] It is stated to have been found by General Lake in Matthew Keogh's house in Wexford:

Colonel Edward Roche of Garrylough.
Esmond Kyan, Major of Brigade.
Colonel Edward Fitzgerald of Newpark.
Colonel John [sic] Perry of Inch.[2]
Captain Nicholas Dixon, of Castlebridge.
Captain Martin Myrna of Limerick.[3]
Captain Nicholas Murphy of Moneyseed.
Captain William Carton of Ballyclough.
Captain Rossiter of Saunders-court.

} County Wexford

[1] Musgrave. Appendix XXI, 5.
[2] Anthony Perry.
[3] Usually referred to as Murt Murnagh of Little Limerick.

Father Nicholas Stafford of River-Chapel.
Captain Denis Doyle of Gorey.
Captain James Doyle of Gorey.
Lieutenant John Tissin of Coolatore.
Captain Martin Quin of Clough.
Captain Edward Synnot of Kilrush.
Captain Philip Murphy of Peppard's Castle Gate.
Captain Patrick Redmond of Coolgreany.

County Wexford

About several of those mentioned in this list I have been unable to obtain any detailed information, but on the other hand reference will be found to thirteen additional individuals.

It is difficult to determine with certainty whether all these persons were willing or unwilling insurgents. My own opinion is that it is impossible to describe any one of them as a *willing* insurgent, though no doubt when they were finally compelled to take the field there were varying degrees of reluctance.

. . . .

FATHER JOHN MURPHY

Curate of Boulavogue and Monageer in the parish of Kilcormick. Born in Tincurry in the parish of Ferns. Educated at a hedge school and abroad. Age at least forty in 1798. Father Kavanagh describes him as under ordinary height, but broad chested and strong limbed. 'His white forehead rose over bright blue eyes.' Another writer describes him as 'about forty-five years old, light complexioned, bald pated, and about five feet nine inches high'.[1] In common with other clergy in north County Wexford, he took the oath of allegiance on behalf of himself and his congregation, made protestations of loyalty between November, 1797, and April, 1798 and induced his people in large numbers to surrender such arms as they possessed and receive 'protections' from Lord Mount Norris. He clearly held the view that engagements of this

[1] Musgrave: Vol. II, p. 90.

kind are two-sided and that surrender of arms on one side should be accompanied by effective protection on the other. He recognised at last that the authorities on whose behalf Lord Mount Norris acted were more concerned with disarming the people than with affording them protection when disarmed. Towards the end of May, the 'activity' of the local magistrates, particularly Hawtrey White and Hunter Gowan and the growing persecution of the people by the yeomanry, forced many to desert their houses during the night and take to the fields for safety. This and the news of the massacres at Dunlavin (on the 24th of May) and Carnew (on the 25th) brought matters to a head and both Father John Murphy and his friend Father Michael Murphy were swept into the field on a wave of warm sympathy with their unfortunate parishioners.

There is some difference among the various writers as to whether the affair at the Harrow preceded or followed the burning of Boulavogue chapel. The Detail Book of the Camolin Yeomanry[1] states clearly that after the discovery of the bodies of Bookey and Donovan at the Harrow, (on the 27th of May) various corps of yeomanry 'took a circuit thro' the country, killed a great number of Insurgents who seemed as if collecting in a body and burnt upwards of one hundred and seventy houses belonging to Rebels whose inhabitants had fled and also the Popish chapel of Boulavogue'.[2] Loftus Richards in appealing to Father John for terms in the camp at Three Rocks, on the 30th of May, was met with the reply that he 'did not know what terms they could expect from the treatment which he had received; for that, by burning his house and property and obliging him to take shelter in the ditches, he was under the necessity of raising the whole country'.[3]

I think, therefore, what actually happened was that Father John's house was burned on the 26th and his chapel on the 27th.

[1] See Wheeler and Broadley.
[2] See also page 269.
[3] Musgrave: Appendix XXI, 3.

It must be mentioned, however, that John Rossiter of Grange and Peter Crawley of Clondaw, in depositions sworn on the 27th of July, both state that Bookey and Donovan were killed 'many hours before said Murphy's house was set on fire'. The point is important—so important in fact that it is conceivable that Rossiter and Crawley (both ex-insurgents) were induced to swear what they did as the price of their lives and liberty.

Father John Murphy, in circumstances described elsewhere, was captured after the break at Kilcomney Hill and suffered at Tullow on or about the 26th of June.[1]

Father Patrick F. Kavanagh prints as an appendix to the centenary edition of his history, a letter from Patrick Murphy of Knockaree, Strahart, stating that he is a grand-nephew of Father John, who had three brothers, Philip, Patrick (killed at Vinegar Hill) and Mogue, the writer's grandfather.

FATHER MICHAEL MURPHY

Curate at Ballycanew. Born either in Ballinoulart, or in Castleannesley,[2] it is uncertain which. Father Kavanagh, however, who states that he was related to him, believes he was born at Kilnew, a mile and a half south-west of Kilmuckridge. Educated at a hedge school and abroad. Age probably about fifty-five in 1798. Ordained on the 15th of May, 1785, on the same day as Father Philip Roche. An unwilling insurgent like Father John. On the 27th of May, his chapel was ransacked and he made his way first to Gorey and then to Kilthomas Hill. He escaped from the massacre there and joined Father John's force on Ballyorril Hill. He was killed at Arklow leading with great gallantry a frontal attack on a gun position defending the western approach to the town. He was buried at Castle Ellis.

---

[1] A short sketch of the life of Father John Murphy was published in *The Redemptorist Record*, Nov.-Dec., 1938. by T. D. Sinnott.

[2] Two coastal townlands near Kilmuckridge.

Some new information relating to the manner of his death will be found in Appendix V.[1]

BEAUCHAMP BAGNAL HARVEY OF BARGY CASTLE

He was small in stature, of proven personal courage as a duellist. Aged thirty-six in 1798. Had been called to the Irish Bar. Married Miss Steevens of Arklow in 1797. A man of liberal principles and wide sympathies who, like many others expressed himself freely on occasion, but was no willing revolutionary. A United Irishman of some years standing, with the object of promoting reform of the legislature and emancipation. Arrested at his own house at 11.0 p.m. on the 26th of May, on the information of Anthony Perry and lodged in Wexford gaol. Hay states that Harvey had collected the arms of all his tenantry and brought them to Wexford on the 26th, but I think Hay is in error in stating that Harvey was arrested in the town.[2] He remained in Wexford until its occupation by the insurgents, whereupon he was pitch-forked into the position of Commander-in-Chief, probably sorely against his will. He wore his own clothes with the addition of silver epaulets. He was in command at New Ross where his plans miscarried. He was overwhelmed by the magnitude of the disaster there and by the massacre at Scullabogue the same morning. On the 6th of June he issued a proclamation with the object of enforcing obedience to orders and prescribing punishment for murder, plundering and un-authorised house-burning. This proclamation was widely distributed and undoubtedly checked excesses on some subsequent occasions, for example at Gorey Hill on the 8th of June.[3]

[1] See also a comprehensive account of Father Michael Murphy by T. D. Sinnott published in *The People* newspaper, 11th December, 1948.
[2] See Mrs. Jane Adam's *Narrative*, published as an Appendix in Crofton Croker: *Researches in the South of Ireland* (1824).
[3] See deposition of George Taylor of Ballywalter; Musgrave. Appendix XX, 2.

On the 7th of June he was displaced in the chief command by Father Philip Roche and returned to Wexford where he was appointed president of the town committee and where he exercised his very limited jurisdiction to save life and protect property. He lodged on the west side of Selskar, near the junction with George's Street.

When the envoys were dispatched with letters from Lord Kingsborough, Harvey retired to Bargy Castle, apparently confident that the terms would be accepted. On the receipt of disquieting rumours he, accompanied by John Henry Colclough, made his way to a cave on the Greater Saltee Island whence they planned to escape by sea. Their whereabouts was betrayed and they were arrested, brought to Wexford and hanged.

Harvey's headless body was recovered from the sea and buried in St. Patrick's Churchyard in Wexford. Sir Jonah Barrington states that when he visited the town, three heads, those of Harvey, Keogh and Colclough were, at his request to General Hunter, taken down and buried.

FATHER PHILIP ROCHE

Late of Pollpeasty, two miles west of Clonroche. Ordained on the 15th of May, 1785. A big-bodied, boisterous man who, when the occasion demanded it, could assume an expression of great ferocity. This faculty was probably what led to such widely differing descriptions of his personal appearance. To Miles Byrne he appeared as 'a clergyman of the most elegant manners and fine person, tall and handsome', while Brigadier-General Moore, who was no bigot and who saw him shortly before his execution, described him as 'a great fat vulgar looking beast'.[1]

The Bishop of Ferns (Dr. Caulfield) mentioned him in the following terms in a letter to Archbishop Troy: 'He had been

[1] *Diary*, Vol. I, p. 300.

curate to the Rev. John Synnott of Gorey: had been a proper man and would be useful, but indulging in excess of drinking and beginning to agitate he became obnoxious and was removed. He was afterwards sent curate after reprehension, admonition and instruction by his superior, to Rev. Thomas Doyle in Bantry, the other extremity of his Diocese, last winter. I heard nothing of him until he joined the rebels and soon became a leader.'

There were times in the course of the short campaign when he was more or less incapacitated from the same drinking habit. Cloney plainly so states when describing a critical moment on Lacken Hill and there was another similar incident on his return to Wexford. It was a time, however, when men drank freely and no stigma was attached to excess of that kind.

Father Roche gained a reputation, even among his enemies, for merciful conduct and my own view is that opinions to the contrary have been formed largely on account of his manner which I feel sure was assumed in order to conceal his merciful intentions from certain of his followers. The Rev. James Gordon, the 'loyalist' historian, stated that Father Roche 'was in appearance, fierce and sanguinary, yet several persons now living, owe their lives to his boisterous interference.'[1]

The same author mentioned that Roche was acknowledged to have been humane by some who previously denied it and adds: 'It will be acknowledged by all when the system of terror shall have ceased to exist'.[2]

[1] Gordon, page 167.
[2] Ibid. p. XXVIII. (Note).

According to Dr. Ebenezer Jacob, when Keogh, Carty, Harvey and others discussed the surrender of the town of Wexford on the 21st of June, Father Philip Roche's voice alone was raised against it.

Gordon's estimate was as follows: 'I knew Father Roche for some years before the rebellion, and he was certainly not a favourite with me, as I disliked his rough familiar manner and his two frequent indulgence of ebriety; but his behaviour in the rebellion has convinced me that he possessed a humane and generous heart, with an uncommon share of personal courage. My information comes from numbers of Protestants who were protected in his camp.' (Page 399).

His final return from Sleedagh to Wexford to await in confidence the outcome of the negotiations, however quixotic it may have been, was certainly not the act of a man conscious of any blood-guiltiness.

He was hanged on Wexford Bridge.

ANTHONY PERRY OF INCH

The only son of Anthony Perry of Dublin, Cardmaker, who died in 1770.

In a sense the most tragic figure of the insurrection. He lived at Perrymount, half a mile south of Inch. It has been stated that he came from County Down, (but see Appendix I). Married Eliza Ford of Ballyfad. A United Irishman and an active organiser in his district. Miles Byrne and others came under his influence.

The torture he underwent drove him into the insurgent ranks where he held high command and exerted great influence. He was one of the most consistently determined of the leaders until his capture at Clonbollogue with Father Kearns on the 12th of July and his death by hanging at Edenderry.

He has been referred to as 'the Screeching General' from his adoption of a very ancient device for spreading alarm and despondency in the ranks of his enemies during a headlong attack.

Further particulars about Perry are given in a special Chapter (see page 43), and in Appendix I.

EDWARD FITZGERALD OF NEWPARK

Born in 1770. Newpark is in the townland of Curclough, nearly three miles due west of Blackwater. In 1798 the house in which Fitzgerald lived was situated behind the present dwelling (which was built nearly ninety years ago) where some of the brickwork of the original house is still traceable in the outbuildings. He also owned a malt-house. He was a noted horseman and kept a pack of hounds.

His mother was a Hay of Ballinkeele. Edward Hay, who was an intimate friend both of Fitzgerald and of a neighbouring magistrate named Edward Turner of Newfort, states that on Saturday, the 26th of May Turner agreeed to issue 'protections' to all who surrendered any kind of weapon and he arranged to meet the people for this purpose at Newpark as the most suitable place in the district. Large numbers attended from a distance of several miles in every direction and each man who handed in a weapon received a 'protection' signed by Turner. Hay decided to remain at Newpark that night, but before morning a detachment of yeoman cavalry, under Percival the high Sheriff [1] arrested Fitzgerald and lodged him in Wexford gaol.

Edward Fitzgerald enjoyed not only an excellent reputation, but he seems to have inspired real affection amongst the people in his own part of the country. He had no intention of taking an active part in any conflict, but when he consented to act as intermediary between the Wexford garrison and the insurgents on Vinegar Hill on the 29th of May, his popularity caused his detention in the camp and thereafter he had no alternative to acting as he did in the capacity of a leader. Among many to whom he was not known personally, he was often referred to as 'Lord Edward'. His popularity, however, did not prevent murmurings against him; thus his good faith was called into question in the camp at Three Rocks when he accompanied one of the envoys back to the town; and again when he left Wexford for a flying visit to his home:

> They dispatched a messenger after him to say that if he did not immediately return he would be put to death and his property destroyed and in consequence of these threats he arrived the following day in Wexford.[2]

[1] Acting as we now know on information supplied by Anthony Perry.
[2] Cloney, page 206.

Once engaged, he did not spare himself and no insurgent leader was held in higher regard. He made mistakes, when for example, he supported Father John Murphy in the proposal to head for Wexford rather than New Ross after the first battle of Enniscorthy and again when he sponsored the fatal concentration on Vinegar Hill.

When the last remaining parties of Wexford insurgents were scattered in County Meath, he and William Aylmer of Kildare had the good fortune to be able to surrender to General Dundas on the 12th of July on condition that they went into exile. With Garrett Byrne of Ballymanus (who obtained the same terms from Major-General John Moore)[1], he settled in Hamburg where, it is stated, he died in 1807.

Fitzgerald and a number of others were detained in Dublin Castle for nearly six months, but twelve days after his surrender, that is, on the 24th of July 1798, the Under-Secretary, Edward Cooke, wrote to William Wickham as follows:

> I conversed a good deal with Fitzgerald, one of the Wexford leaders, he said that at first his men fought well, but latterly would not stand at all; that he and the other leaders had but little command; that the mob were furious and wanting to massacre every Protestant; and that the only means they had of dissuading them from burning houses was that they were destroying their own property.[2]

EDWARD ROCHE OF GARRYLOUGH

A farmer and maltster, living two miles and a half north of Castlebridge. Married to a sister of the infamous Thomas Dixon. He was permanent sergeant in the Shelmalier Yeoman Cavalry, commanded by Colonel Le Hunte of Artramont.

---

[1] His promotion had come through on the 7th of July.
[2] Cornwallis: *Correspondence* (2nd Edition), Vol. II, p. 372.

Note: Edward Roche of Garrylough in a sworn statement before Dr. Ebenezer Jacob, on 18th of April, 1799, mentioned that 'the rebels vowed vengeance against Mr. Edward Hay for aiding and assisting the late Edward Turner (of Newfort) who was a magistrate for said county, in the surrender of their arms and pikes at Newpark, on Saturday, the 26th May 1798, thereby supposing him their enemy'.

Aged about forty in 1798. Stoutly built. He joined Father John Murphy dressed in his regimentals on the 27th of May, at Oulart Hill along with several of his corps. He was nominally in command during the engagement there. In the camp at Three Rocks three days later Cloney found him reluctant to assume the responsibility of command, but on the 1st of June, he is referred to as General Roche and is described as wearing 'a snuff-coloured coat, black waistcoat, corduroy breeches and a round hat; but for distinction he had two most enormous gold epaulets and a silk sash and belt in which he carried a large pair of horse pistols and he wore a sword by his side'.[1]

(The reader must be careful in using the various authorities as there is some confusion among them between Edward Roche and Father Philip Roche).

He took a leading part in the engagements in the north of the county and acted for a time as Commandant of the camp at Vinegar Hill where he issued and circulated a proclamation emphasising that 'this is not a war for religion but for liberty'. He visited Wexford with Garrett Byrne on the 19th of June to collect reinforcements for the impending battle and is one of those credited with having put an end to the massacre on Wexford Bridge the following day. His return northwards with his division to form a rearguard for the force retreating from Vinegar Hill has already been described.

He marched north again with Anthony Perry, Edward Fitzgerald, Esmond Kyan, and Garrett Byrne on the evening of the 21st of June and shared their many adventures until hostilities ceased. He then succeeded in remaining in concealment until the thirst for blood had somewhat abated when he surrendered to General Hunter, on terms of transportation, towards the end of August.

Taylor states that he was 'sent to Newgate with other convicts; but before the vessel was ready to convey them

[1] Jackson: *Narrative*, p. 35.

abroad, he, with some others died suddenly; it was thought they had taken poison'.

The similar 'sudden death' of Oliver Bond in the same prison on the 6th of September, 1798, will be recalled and the reader is at liberty to draw his own conclusions.

THOMAS CLONEY OF MONEYHORE

The son of Denis Cloney, a well-to-do farmer, living about three miles west of Enniscorthy. The house and the long tree-shaded avenue are still very much as they must have been in 1798. Thomas Cloney was twenty-six years of age at that time. Most of the particulars of his early life are derived from his own memoirs published thirty-four years afterwards. According to his own account he was 'like many other peaceably disposed persons unexpectedly carried away by the torrent that overran the county of Wexford'. He was not a United Irishman. Miles Byrne describes him as 'this splendid young man . . . six feet four in height'.

On the 29th of May he was compelled to march via the Leap to Enniscorthy, which he did 'without authority or command'. He played a leading and distinguished part in the action against General Fawcett's advance guard below Three Rocks and later at New Ross. He relates a touching incident which took place just before the latter battle, when Philip Lacey and John Doogan, two of his father's tenants, 'put their arms about me with such feeling that they could scarcely speak', saying, 'you are now going into battle and we declare if you fall we shall not survive to carry home the sad tidings to your father and sisters'. Both Lacey and Doogan were killed in the assault on the Three Bullet gate.

Cloney continued under Father Philip Roche's command at Lacken Hill, marched with him to Wexford on the 19th of June and back to Goff's Bridge (Foulke's Mill) on the 20th.

As already related, he accompanied Captain O'Hea from Wexford to Enniscorthy on the morning of the 21st, where, at the instance of Captain O'Hea, he obtained a safe conduct pass from General Lake.

On his return to Wexford he proceeded to his father's house at Moneyhore where he remained for some time in concealment and was joined by Father Kearns. While there he accidentally shot himself in the thigh and nearly died of haemorrhage. He was removed secretly to the house of Joshua Lett and thence to Enniscorthy where he obtained a 'protection' from General Hunter, having taken an oath of allegiance. He remained there until March, 1799. Before leaving the town he was savagely attacked with a bayonet by a yeoman as he was leaving the house of Thomas Lett of Templeshannon. He returned home, but two months later he was arrested and lodged in Wexford Gaol, courtmartialled on a charge of being accessory to murder, found guilty by a majority of one and sentenced to death. Lord Cornwallis commuted the sentence to two years of exile. On the 12th of February he was liberated and crossed to England. On the expiration of the prescribed period of exile he returned to Ireland in February, 1803 and took a lodge at Graiguenamanagh.

With respect to his subsequent movements there and in Dublin he is lacking in candour. The most he will admit is that 'indifferent to that state of espionage in which I felt myself placed, I continued to attend to my affairs in Dublin, lodging in the same place, receiving the same associates and visiting them openly in return until the latter end of July'. He does not mention, however, that one of these associates was Miles Byrne and another was Robert Emmet, nor does he mention having remarked to Byrne after a prolonged conference with Emmet, that the latter's 'powers of reasoning and persuasion are such that an objection can scarcely be made to any of his plans'.

Needless to say, the Government were made aware of all
this and Cloney was again arrested. He states that when asked
by the Attorney General as to his meeting with Emmet or
Russell, he answered that he had not any acquaintance with
either! He was imprisoned, first in the tower of the Castle
and later in Kilmainham, until the beginning of November,
1804, when he was finally liberated. In after years he was
associated with Edward Hay in the affairs of the Catholic Board.

He died at Graiguenamanagh on the 20th February, 1850,
at the age of seventy-six. The house he lived in is still occupied
(by Thomas Joyce, in 1952), and named Whitehall. I am
informed by John O'Leary of Graiguenamanagh, that the
old residents always refer to it as 'Cloney's House'.

See also Appendix XIV.

Esmond Kyan

The fourth son of Howard Kyan of Mount Howard about
a mile south-east of Carrigrew Hill, and a first cousin of Sir
Thomas Esmond, their mothers being sisters. Aged about
fifty in 1798, 'rather a handsome man, of a very genteel appearance, but somewhat awkward on account of the loss of his
left arm which was cut off near the elbow some years ago
and a cork one substituted. . . . He was liberal, generous,
courageous and merciful.'[1] Luke Cullen states that he lost
his arm having been fired on by a debtor from whom he was
trying to recover a debt. He had served as an officer of artillery
in the British army. He lived in the parish of Monamolin.

He distinguished himself in several battles and at Arklow
where he had command of the guns, the stump of his left arm
was carried away by a cannon shot. From this wound he
never fully recovered and as already related, he was in a house
at Ferrybank suffering great pain when, hearing that massacre

[1] Taylor: pp. 203-4.

was in progress he crossed the bridge and was instrumental in saving several lives.

Marching north with the contingent which headed for County Wicklow on the 21st of June, he found his broken health unequal to the rigours of guerilla warfare and ill-advisedly he returned to the neighbourhood of Wexford. Here he was arrested, tried and hanged all in less than twenty-four hours. Had he reached the sanctuary of Glenmalure, or had his execution not been carried out with such indecent haste, his life would have been saved under the terms made by Edward Fitzgerald with General Dundas, which covered Kyan's case as well as his own.

It is not clear why both Esmond Kyan and Father Philip Roche should be credited with having declared that their lives would be forfeit if the insurgents prevailed, unless they had been threatened on account of their efforts to prevent murder.

JOHN KELLY OF KILLANN

His father was a prosperous merchant in the village of Killann, eight miles west of Enniscorthy, at the foot of the Blackstairs Mountains. History has been both kind and unkind to this remarkable young man. Alone among the prominent insurgents he is eulogised by friend and foe alike. Gordon refers to him as 'worthy of a far better cause and better associates —his courage and humanity being equal and conspicuous'. Among his friends he was always acclaimed as the bravest of the brave and he has been fortunate as the hero of a stirring ballad by P. J. McCall, set to a fine marching air.

On the other hand tradition is provokingly silent about the details of the exploits which earned for him so great and no doubt, so well-deserved a reputation. He marched with the men of his district through the Leap to the camp at Vinegar Hill on the 29th of May after the battle of Enniscorthy. He,

Cloney, Robert Carty of Birchgrove and Michael Furlong of Templescobey led the contingent from the Three Rocks which overwhelmed General Fawcett's advance guard on the 30th of May. He was seriously wounded in the thigh at the battle of New Ross, after fighting his way at the head of the Bantry pikemen to the vicinity of the barrack. He was carried back to the Three Bullet Gate and thence to Wexford. There he lay until General Lake entered the town when he was taken from his bed, hastily tried by courtmartial and hanged.

I do not know if instances of his humanity were put forward at his trial, but if they were, they would, as Gordon points out, merely have been regarded as proof of guilt and as showing a commanding influence among the insurgents.

Edward Hay who was in the town at the time, states that Kelly's severed head was kicked about the Custom House Quay before being placed above the door of the Courthouse.

It will be seen, therefore, that his active service lasted no more than a full week and during that time he was in action only twice. We are left to speculate on the individual deeds of heroism which raised him above the stature of his companions and which inspired such unstinted admiration in so short a time.

FATHER MOSES (MOGUE) KEARNS

Curate in Enniscorthy and previously in Clonard, County Meath. Like Father Philip Roche, he was a man of powerful physique. He had been in France during the Terror there and had actually been hanged from a street lamp-post when his height and weight saved him from strangulation by bending the iron until his toes reached the ground! Such an experience as this can hardly have inspired him with any great affection for 'French ideas', and the facts that the United Irishmen were assuredly inspired by such ideas and that Father Kearns threw himself whole-heartedly into the contest in Wexford, would suggest that for him at least (and as I believe, for most others in that county), the resistance movement had another origin.

Like Father Philip Roche, he seems to have had a taste for soldiering and to have been fitted more for the camp than the cloister. Although he showed little evidence of military capacity at Bunclody (the only occasion on which he had an independent command) it would be unfair to place the blame for ignominious failure on the leader alone when his followers were completely untrained and unaccustomed to understand and obey orders.

He shared with William Barker the honours of the defence of Enniscorthy on the 21st of June, where he was wounded. In the early days of July he had sufficiently recovered to join Thomas Cloney near the latter's house at Moneyhore, from which place he moved to the woods of Killoughrum. With a considerable body of men whom he found there, he joined the force under Anthony Perry, Edward Roche and Garrett Byrne, forming part of the ill-fated expedition into the plains of Meath. Father Kearns is blamed by Holt for insisting on leaving the safe shelter of the mountains and venturing into the flat open country to be cut to pieces by cavalry.

After an unsuccessful engagement at Summerhill on the 12th of July, he and Anthony Perry were captured at Clonbollogue in Offaly and hurried to summary execution at Edenderry.

MILES BYRNE OF MONASEED

Born in the townland of Ballylusk, about a mile north of Monaseed crossroads, on the 20th of March 1780. His parents removed to the Fox Cover a short distance west of Monaseed, where the foundations of the house are still traceable. He was enrolled as a United Irishman in 1797, apparently influenced by Anthony Perry of Inch. That was the only part of County Wexford where the Society of United Irishmen made much progress before the Rising.

In his *Memoirs*, written with becoming modesty, he gives no hint of the exploits which won for him a position of acknowledged leadership in spite of his youth, especially among those from his own district. He took part, during that brief campaign, in several hard fought battles, including Bunclody, Tubberneering, Arklow and Vinegar Hill and he accompanied Father John Murphy on the advance to and retreat from Castlecomer. Unlike some of the other leaders, he continued in the field until the end, eventually escaping to Dublin where he remained undetected, employed by a builder in the neighbourhood of Booterstown.

When Robert Emmet returned to Dublin in 1803, Byrne immediately joined him and became one of his most faithful lieutenants. When all was over he was entrusted by Emmet with the perilous duty of making his way to France in order to explain to Thomas Addis Emmet the causes of failure.

He was commissioned as an infantry officer in the Irish Legion in the service of France in December 1803; Captain in 1808; became a naturalised Frenchman in 1817; thrice decorated for gallantry on the field of battle; chef de bataillon (lieutenant-colonel) in the 56th regiment of the line. In 1830 married Fanny Horner, a sister of Francis Horner. Died in Paris, in January 1862.

His wife in a preface to his *Memoirs*, published in 1863, refers to his book as 'the truthful narration of a modest, brave, high-minded soldier. One who possessed the soundest understanding and the most tender heart and who was ever disinterested and humane'.

He, himself towards the end of his life made the following manly declaration:

I now most solemnly declare in the presence of the Almighty, that I never regretted the part I took, and that if it were to be done over again I should do the same; the only difference would be that from the experience I have acquired as a military man (who has had the honour to serve in the French Army), I might be enabled to do it better.

JOHN HENRY COLCLOUGH OF BALLYTEIGUE

Ballyteigue lies in the extreme south of the barony of Bargy. Colclough was aged thirty in 1798 and he possessed a medical qualification. He was a man of liberal principles and a most unwilling insurgent. He was arrested by James Boyd on the 27th of May, on the information of Anthony Perry and brought to Wexford gaol. He accompanied Edward Fitzgerald as envoy from the Wexford garrison to the insurgent camp at Vinegar Hill on the 29th of May. He was permitted to return to announce the failure of his mission while Edward Fitzgerald was detained.

He was present in the vicinity of New Ross on the 5th of June and of Goff's Bridge (Foulke's Mill) on the 20th of June, but on neither occasion did he take part in the fighting and his reputation has suffered in consequence. I think, however, his conduct on these occasions was not due to lack of courage (he died bravely enough when it came to the bit) but rather was a measure of his anxiety not to commit himself too deeply. Cloney states that at the battle of New Ross he retired early 'as he was not disposed to favour the progress of the insurrection'.

When the negotiations were proceeding on the 21st of June he returned home and later, with his wife and Bagnal Harvey, was arrested on the Greater Saltee Island, courtmartialled and hanged on the 28th of June. He appeared up to the last moment to expect a reprieve and it is possible that had he had the good fortune to evade arrest until after General Lake had left the town, both he and Matthew Keogh and perhaps others might have succeeded like Edward Roche and Edward Fitzgerald, in saving their lives by surrendering to some general officer who was not obsessed, as Lake was, with the military necessity of exemplary execution, irrespective of well proven pleas of forced participation and irreproachable personal conduct.

WILLIAM BARKER

A brewer and merchant in Enniscorthy. He had served with distinction on the continent in Walsh's regiment.[1] He joined the insurgents after the fall of Enniscorthy. He advised immediate advance on New Ross instead of Wexford, but was out-voted. He acted as member of a kind of Committee of Public Safety in Enniscorthy.[2] Shared with Father Kearns the command of that town's defence on the 21st of June.

On the 12th of November, 1798, he memorialised the Lord Lieutenant, protesting his loyalty,[3] stating that before the attack on Enniscorthy he had agreed to become a member of the dismounted Yeoman Cavalry, that on the morning of the day the town was attacked (28th May) he voluntarily gave gratis, large quantities of flour and wine to the wives of soldiers of the North Cork Militia and others; that when the town was in flames he protected loyal inhabitants of both sexes and religions in his own house until about ten o'clock in the evening of that day he was seized by the rebels and compelled by menaces of death and destruction of his property to join them. He refers to the testimony of those he protected 'who being Protestants of character and rank in life (and your memorialist a Roman Catholic) their testimony must be considered as free from suspicion and prejudice'.

He 'ever avoided having any concern whatever, directly or indirectly, in the cruelties, murders and atrocities committed by them, but did, to the utmost of his power and at the imminent hazard of his life, interfere when present to save and did save the lives of many persons . . . sacrificed to private pique and religious resentment'.

[1] Miles Byrne.
[2] See Mrs. Newton Lett's narrative. She states that he told her he regretted having taken a command.
[3] See Frazer MSS. Public Record Office, Dublin.

On the morning of the 21st of June, he was forced to join those defending the hill, but through the confusion then reigning, found means to escape from them and secreted himself in an adjoining wood, where he was found by four soldiers 'who robbed, fired at and desperately wounded him and broke both bones in the lower part of his right arm. . . . Nineteen days after his arm was amputated on account of gangrene by the surgeon attached to the Waterford Militia'. He further stated that he never interfered in political or party matters, or was a United Irishman. That after an interval of nearly four months, a woman named Stacey was prevailed on by threats of being deprived of the means of subsistence to lodge information against him for being accessory to the murder of her husband.[1]

To this memorial there is appended a statement signed by thirty inhabitants of Enniscorthy and neighbourhood including Letts, James Brett, Sparrows, Philip Hay, Pounders, etc., testifying him to be 'a remarkable loyal subject'.

At his courtmartial in January, 1799, he was acquitted on all charges and set at liberty.

In the light of the above, the account given by Miles Byrne makes strange reading when, following Cloney's reference, he declares that Barker lost his arm on the bridge of Enniscorthy and was carried away, to be succeeded in the Command by Father Kearns, who was himself wounded soon after. He further states that *before his courtmartial* could take place, Barker's brother Arthur, a Waterford merchant, succeeded in having him provisionally released from Wexford prison on health grounds and later, with his wife and family conveyed to Hamburg. Byrne depicts him as a man consumed with anxiety to join any expedition destined for Ireland and concludes: 'I met him in 1803 in the Irish Legion at Marlaix, when I learned from

[1] Benjamin Stacey of Templeshannon, murdered on the 1st June.

him all the details of his sufferings and fortunate escape from
Wexford Jail'[1].

It will be noted that these two accounts disagree sharply,
especially in relation to the circumstances in which the wound
was received and on the fact of courtmartial. On the latter
point Byrne was certainly in error and the reader must judge
for himself on the former.

RICHARD MONAGHAN (DICK MONK)

This man deserves more attention than he has hitherto received
and the following notes have been collected from various
scattered sources. On reaching manhood he was engaged in
the corn trade in some subordinate capacity and was considered
'a fellow of wit and humour'. He had acted as a recruiting
sergeant and is referred to later as a captain in the insurgent
forces. According to one writer, Monaghan came into the
gaol in Wexford on the 31st of May and put the prisoners
through 'part of the United Irishman's Catechism' and other
questions designed to ascertain if the person addressed were a
Roman Catholic.[2] On the other hand (and more probably,
from other evidence) Taylor, the 'loyalist' historian states that
during the period of hostilities he was considered 'a very
generous, well-minded man'. He took a prominent part in
the battle of Arklow, serving the only gun which caused any
damage to the enemy. Taylor describes him as dressed in a
'light horseman jacket of green with silver lace cross-banded
in front, pantaloons to match with silver seams; and a green
helmet cap with a white ostrich feather across the top'.

In the early days of the occupation of Wexford, according
to Mrs. Brownrigg, he commanded a body of men in the town

---

[1] *Memoirs*, Vol. I, p. 132.
[2] Charles Jackson: *A Narrative of the Sufferings and Escapes, etc.*, (1802). His
pamphlet is full of inaccuracies.

known as 'the John Street Corps'[1] and she refers to him as 'a Derry boy', adding that 'he had the most truly ferocious countenance I ever beheld. Henry John asked whether it was God Almighty put *that face* on him'.[2]

Taylor states that Monaghan was responsible for stopping the massacre at Wexford Bridge. He relates that in the middle of that bloody business, Monaghan rode into the town from Vinegar Hill shouting: 'Damn your souls, you vagabonds, why don't you go out and meet the enemy that are coming in, and not be murdering in cold blood?' He then went on to the convent and 'shortly after, priest Corrin was seen running towards the bridge', and with difficulty succeeded, with others, in putting an end to the butchery.

Monaghan accompanied Father John Murphy and Miles Byrne in the retreat, first to Sleedagh and thence through the Scullogue Gap and we hear of him again intervening to save life on Kellymount Hill after the battle of Goresbridge. At the trial of John Devereux, junior, of Shelbeggan, Sergeant Benjamin Tuttle of the Wexford regiment stated in evidence that seven prisoners were piked or shot at Kellymount and that he himself was brought into the ring marked for death when 'a man of the name of Monaghan whom I knew in Wexford came into the circle and told me he would take me out. . . Monk was shoved out of the circle and remained away for about three minutes and then brought me to the edge of the circle the second time'. More opposition was encountered, but eventually 'Monk told me my life was saved'.[3]

On his return to County Wexford, after the expedition to Castlecomer, he was wounded. In the neighbourhood of

[1] Gordon refers to him as 'Mayor of John Street'.
[2] See Wheeler and Broadley, p. 178.
[3] See R. Radford Rowe: *Reports of Interesting Cases* (1824). For further evidence of Monaghan's humanity see deposition of Blackney Ormsby—Musgrave: Appendix XX, 3.

Bunclody (Newtownbarry) he was met by a party of the
local yeomen and shot dead.

JOHN HAY OF NEWCASTLE

The second son of Harvey Hay of Ballinkeele. He had been
an officer in the Irish Brigade in the Service of France (Dillon's
Regiment). On the 28th of May he was visited by a party of
men with a written order from Anthony Perry requiring him to
join the camp at Vinegar Hill. A most reluctant insurgent.
His first act was to point out how defenceless they were with
neither ammunition nor other warlike stores. He is next heard
of in the camp at Three Rocks where Cloney found him and
Edward Fitzgerald 'disinclined to assume authority or avow
their rank, if they had been invested with any'. Later the same
day, according to the statement of Loftus Richards[1] he apparently
shared the prevailing belief that Richards was guilty of double
dealing and deserved death. He possessed enough military
capacity to suggest the dispatch of a force from the camp to
intercept the fleeing garrison before they could reach the Scar
at Barrystown, but he was not supported and nothing was done.

There is remarkably little mention of him in the various
contemporary narratives, but Miles Byrne refers to his modesty
and to the fact that 'he fought bravely until he met his untimely
end'. On the other hand Cloney states (with probably more
truth) that 'he cannot be considered otherwise than as an
unwilling spectator of actions in which he had no participation,
and the witness of other deeds which he had not the power to
prevent . . . he gave himself up to a gloomy mood of mind'.

On the 21st of June he left Wexford and foolishly returned
to his own house with his faithful servant, John Carty. They
concealed themselves in a wood nearby and here their presence
was betrayed to a detachment of General Dundas's force and

---

[1] Musgrave, Appendix XXI, 3.

they were arrested and brought to Wexford. Anthony Perry's order was found on his person and he was hastily tried and hanged. His servant narrowly escaped sharing the fate of his master. The body was thrown into the sea from which it was recovered by a relative and brought for burial to Kilmallock Churchyard—a mile south of Ballinkeele. For further information about the Hay family, see Appendix XII.

CORNELIUS GROGAN OF JOHNSTOWN CASTLE

A wealthy landowner; unmarried; aged seventy in 1798.[1] A martyr to gout. He had been High Sheriff of the county and had represented Enniscorthy in the Irish Parliament from 1783 to 1790. A Protestant of liberal principles and an advocate of reform and emancipation. As was the case with many others like him at that time he was given to a certain imprudent expansiveness and the expression of extreme views over the dinner table and so, no doubt was regarded with suspicion in 'loyalist' quarters.

When the garrison retreated from Wexford, he endeavoured to escape to Duncannon and rode with them as far as the cross-roads of Rathmurry, but then returned to his own house. Here he was visited later by a large body of insurgents who compelled him to accompany them to Wexford town. He was allowed to function for a time in some undefined way in connection with supply.

A younger brother (who signed himself Thomas Grogan Knox) was killed at Arklow serving with the Castletown Yeoman Cavalry and another brother, John Grogan, was wounded with the Healthfield yeomanry.

Cornelius Grogan was charged at his trial with having been present at the battle of New Ross, chiefly on the strength of the deposition of Richard Grandy of Ballyshan, dated the

[1] His age is so given by Sir Jonah Barrington who knew him intimately.

23rd of June, 1798, who stated that when he and Loftus Frizzel (survivors from the massacre of Scullabogue) had been brought within a mile and a half of Ross they met Bagnal Harvey, Cornelius Grogan and others 'retreating from the battle of Ross'. He further stated that he heard and believed it to be a fact that the 'said Cornelius Grogan had the command of the Barony of Forth rebel troops at the battle of Ross'.

Richard Grandy's evidence must be regarded with suspicion as he was a paid swearer[1] and on this occasion his statements are false and probably made for the purpose of obtaining the conviction of Grogan. In this connection the following facts are of interest. During the passage of the Bill of Attainder, through the Irish House of Commons in relation to Grogan's extensive property certain witnesses were heard and among them one William Barry who was apparently one of a number *conducting Grogan under open arrest towards Ross on the 5th of June.* He stated: 'Having got within two or three miles of Ross, Mr. Grogan complained that he was then very ill from pains of the gout and violence of exercise and not able to ride further; which appeared to me to be the fact from his appearance, whereupon, not having met Mr. Harvey, we agreed to let him return to Fook's Mill where his carriage was ordered to go from Scullabogue. The four men that guarded him with me took the charge of him back'. Barry added that he himself proceeded towards Ross, *met Harvey returning from the battle*

---

[1] In the account of Secret Services Money (I.S.P.O.), £100 was paid to Grandy on 27/5/1802, £50 on 7/2/1803 (per Loftus Tottenham) and £50 on 13/2/1804 (per Loftus Tottenham). In his statement quoted above he deposed 'that every Protestant that was admitted into the rebel corps was first baptized by a priest; and that every Protestant that refused to be baptized was put to death; and that many to save their lives did suffer themselves to be baptized'. This is only partly true. Pressure of this kind did come at times from the ignorant and fanatical elements among the insurgents against which the priests themselves were powerless and were compelled to comply. Grandy was in possession of passes from Bagnal Harvey, Father Edward Murphy of Bannow and Father James Collins of Duncormick. He had some knowledge of first-aid and was employed for a time as a medical orderly in the insurgent field hospital at Foulke's Mill.

'and when he saw me he immediately asked me what I had done with Mr. Grogan. . . . I was then directed by Mr. Harvey to return to Mr. Grogan and detain him a prisoner at Johnstown till further orders'.

There the unhappy old man was arrested on the 23rd of June and brought into Wexford. Johnstown was occupied by troops including the King's County Militia. The house was pillaged and Grogan's property purloined. A 'loyalist' historian makes the following devastating comment: 'Doubtless Lord Kingsborough thought his conduct blameless when he went, the day after his liberation from Wexford, to Mr. Cornelius Grogan's house and took out of the stable two coach horses to sell. But if we should find the attention of any general officer so absorbed in a system of plunder as to leave him no leisure for fighting, perhaps we might think him not entirely blameless'.[1]

At his courtmartial the defence was the obvious and true one, namely that he had always been a loyal man and that his participation was forced upon him. The court was illegally constituted, the number being deficient and the members not sworn. In addition, the services of Judge Advocate were not available. The inevitable sentence of death was passed and the execution which took place on the 28th of June was, in the circumstances, murder.

He died bravely and his decapitated body was thrown into the sea. This was later grappled, brought ashore and conveyed to Rathaspick Churchyard adjoining Johnstown. His head is stated to have been recovered after a time by an old family servant named Devereux and buried with the body.

MATTHEW KEOGH

His residence was in George's Street, Wexford, on the south side, two-thirds of the way down. He had been Captain-

[1] Gordon: p. 240 (Note).

Lieutenant in the army, and in 1798 was living in Wexford on half-pay. After its occupation by the insurgents he was appointed 'military governor' and with his second-in-command, William Kearney, controlled with some measure of success, the unruly elements for three weeks, until the mob took charge on the final day of massacre. Mrs. Brownrigg in her narrative[1], states that apparently some time before the middle of the month, he narrowly escaped being murdered on the charge of being an Orangeman. She says that he became a Catholic to save his life, but this is mere surmise on her part from the fact that both he and Bagnal Harvey attended Mass from time to time to show their freedom from bigotry. Certainly he was attended in his last moments by the Rev. John Elgee, the rector of Wexford.

When the rabble broke loose on the 20th June, Keogh relinquished his now merely nominal command and when Lake arrived he was arrested, tried and sentenced to death. At the place of execution his speech was so affecting and convincing that Brigadier-General John Moore who heard it, immediately appealed to Lake to defer the carrying out of the sentence. The latter, however, refused, Keogh was hanged and his head placed above the court house door.

[1] See Wheeler and Broadley.

Bibliography

It is significant that the earliest accounts of the Rising in County Wexford are from the pens of 'loyalist' writers. These commenced to reach the public comparatively soon after the end of hostilities and the best known are *Memoirs of the Different Rebellions in Ireland* by Sir Richard Musgrave, *An History of the Rise, Progress and Supression of the Rebellion in the County of Wexford* by George Taylor and *History of the Rebellion in Ireland in the year* 1798 by the Rev. James Gordon. Later came *History of the Irish Insurrection of* 1798 by Edward Hay, a cautious author on the 'popular' side and later still (1832) *A Personal Narrative of* 1798 by Thomas Cloney, who makes some use of his predecessor Hay. Then in 1863 came *Memoirs of Miles Byrne* in three volumes, edited by his widow and published in Paris. Lecky's references to the insurrection are included in Volumes IV and V of his *History of Ireland in the Eighteenth Century*.

I propose to give here brief notices of the chief sources and add a list of others.

Sir Richard Musgrave

Sir Jonah Barrington[1] described him as a man 'who (except on the abstract topics of politics, religion, martial law, his wife, the Pope, the Pretender, the Jesuits, Napper Tandy, and the

[1] *Personal Sketches*, Vol. I, p. 205.

215

whipping post) was generally in his senses'. His work is a monument of remarkable, if misdirected industry and he missed little of any importance which emanated from Government sources. He undertook this laborious task with the avowed object of proving that the insurrection was a Popish plot and that while union between Catholic and Protestant 'in the bonds of brotherly love and Christian charity' was to be hoped for, 'incidents which daily occur afford incontestable proofs that the tenets of their religion and the conduct of their priests will always make it impracticable'. He dedicated the first edition, by permission, to Lord Cornwallis, Lord Lieutenant and Commander-in-Chief, but when the book appeared an order signed by the Military Secretary dated the 24th March, 1801 was issued withdrawing the 'permission' and stating that 'had his Excellency been apprized of the contents and nature of the work he would never have lent the sanction of his name to a book which tends strongly to revive the dreadful animosities which have so long distracted this country'.

It should be added that this was merely an expression of the change in Government policy. The insurrection having been fomented in order to terrify the landed gentry into accepting the Union and what is now known as the 'softening up' process having been completed by methods which have been referred to in the foregoing pages, it was the aim of Government to reverse their former policy and Lord Cornwallis was sent over to direct this new departure and to reconcile with the destruction of their liberties those whose interests were represented in Parliament.

George Taylor

He lived at Ballywalter, between Gorey and Ballycanew. He was a zealous 'loyalist' with very obvious evangelistic leanings. His work is chiefly valuable where he describes events of which he was an actual eye-witness, particularly in the Gorey neighbourhood and in Wexford town where he had a very narrow escape from death on Wexford Bridge. He refers to the arrest of Anthony Perry on the 24th of May, but does not mention either his torturing, or his information. He states that Harvey, Fitzgerald and Colclough were arrested 'by an order from Government' on the 26th, but he does not associate these arrests with Perry's information.

The compilation 'from authentic documents' published in *The Monitor*, Nos. I, II, and III, dated 18th July, 1798, and signed 'George Tenor' is, it would appear, by the same author.

THE REVEREND JAMES GORDON

For many years he was Episcopalian curate of Clogh, midway between Gorey and Camolin and he lived at Marlfield near Gorey. After the Rising he became rector of Killegny near Clonroche. Though unmistakably a 'loyalist' with two sons in the yeomanry, he makes an honest and on the whole, a successful attempt to be fair to both sides. As a consequence he was attacked, as he states in the preface to the second edition, on the grounds that although his book was admittedly a true account of events it was 'such as a loyalist and particularly a Protestant clergyman ought not to have published!'

I think, however, that he was less than fair in his reference to Anthony Perry, stating that 'this man of amiable manners and well-informed understanding' had been 'weak enough to be seduced into the conspiracy' and that he was always 'meditating his escape from the insurgents'. He also plainly hints that Perry was tortured *after* and not before giving information. In both these latter opinions I think he was mistaken.

EDWARD HAY

The first of the 'popular' historians of the period. He was the eldest son of Harvey Hay of Ballinkeele (who died in 1796).

Harvey Hay left his property to his youngest son Philip, an officer in the British Army (See Appendix XII). Edward Hay seems to have had the intention of leaving the country before the Rising took place. He succeeded in surviving the period of hostilities without taking up arms, although his abstention nearly cost him his life on more than one occasion.

His presence and the influence of his name in the town of Wexford were the means of saving the lives of many of the prisoners and he had no difficulty in obtaining the testimony of a number of them including Lord Kingsborough which no doubt carried great weight at his trial during the Wexford Assizes in July, 1799, when he was arraigned before a jury on a charge of high treason and acquitted. In his charge Baron Smith expressed himself with remarkable emphasis, declaring that the prisoner had undergone the most violent persecution, that his loyalty was unimpeachable and that if the jury attempted to find him guilty 'as some juries had acted contrary to law and justice at those assizes in Wexford', the prisoner might take advantage of the Amnesty Bill, by moving arrest of judgment and that he should be instantly discharged, so that they might as well give him at once the acquittal he deserved!

In later life he devoted himself to Catholic affairs and acted as Secretary to the Catholic Board.

His book, though coloured by his predilections, is a valuable document dealing as it does for the most part with his own personal experiences. His omissions are less commendable; he is ominously silent about the fate of his brother John and Miles Byrne makes an unpleasant reference to him in this connection.[1]

It is noticeable that Hay borrows extensively from Gordon, occasionally using whole expressions of the latter without acknowledgment.

[1] *Memoirs*, (1906), Vol. I, p. 40.

Thomas Cloney

His narrative is the modestly told story of a brave and single minded man. Its chief value lies in his descriptions of the engagements in which he personally took part, namely Three Rocks on the 30th of May, New Ross on the 5th of June and Goff's Bridge (Foulke's Mill) on the 20th of June.

Miles Byrne

His *Memoirs* were first published in three volumes in Paris in 1863, the year after his death. That they had been in preparation for many years is shown by a letter he wrote from Rue Montaigne, Paris, on the 18th of February, 1854: 'I have made notes of the principal events and transactions that came within my knowledge during the insurrection of 1798, as well as that of 1803. If I thought this publication could in any way tend to benefit my native country I would cheerfully get them printed; but I am well aware that the present time is not a propitious moment. I trust a time may come when the publication of such documents will be encouraged. They will show the efforts and sacrifices that were made to procure the independence of Ireland'.[1]

He had not completed the work before his death, but the unfinished volume deals only with foreign affairs of little present-day interest to us.

When writing the portion of his book which relates to Ireland, he had before him the works of Musgrave, Hay and Cloney and he makes use of all of them. He must be read with caution, as, ever generous-minded, he is apt to gloss over certain events and occasionally refers to others more favourably than the known facts warrant. But on the whole it would be difficult to over-estimate the value of his work, not only for the wealth of personal and local detail, but also as the

[1] Miles Byrne to W. J. Fitzpatrick, quoted in *The Sham Squire*.

commentary of a man with a lifetime of distinguished military experience behind him.

A new edition in two volumes was published in Dublin in 1906, edited by Stephen Gwynn and notable for the inclusion, as an appendix, of a letter from Paris to the *Irishman* newspaper, Dublin, dated the 15th January, 1860 and containing a description of Miles Byrne in language at once noble and unforgettable.

WILLIAM HAMILTON MAXWELL

This author hardly merits special mention for his *History of the Irish Rebellion* first published in 1845, but his book has passed through many editions and has had a very wide circulation. It is an uncritical compilation of the work of others, chiefly Musgrave and the extracts he gives from the 'MS. of a Field Officer', are almost valueless. Its importance lies in the regrettable fact that countless readers have formed their conception of the Wexford people from the illustrations which mar its pages. They are the work of the Cockney caricaturist, George Cruikshank (1792-1878), whose libels on humanity itself have disgusted so many readers of Charles Dickens.

WILLIAM EDWARD HARTPOLE LECKY

No one who has worked through the mass of manuscripts and other documents relating to this period, can fail to be impressed by the scrupulous fairness of this great historian in his choice of material. But when he comes to deal with stirring events like those of '98 it is well that the reader should bear in mind that Lecky's whole life was spent in the shelter of the study. He never stood on the rough edge of war, nor had he ever felt 'the blood rush behind the eyes and the void of courageous alarm at the pit of the stomach'! He never knew the horror of a desolate home, the men scourged or murdered, the women violated—and his whole mind recoiled from the

contemplation of such barbarities; yet those were the instruments
employed by the agents of Government which forced a
practically unarmed peasantry into the field. Lecky was, at
the same time, firmly of opinion that at no matter what cost,
the rights of property and the privileges of what he termed
'the landed gentry' must be preserved as the only alternative to
chaos. This conviction was the foundation of his political
opinions throughout his life.

For these reasons he turned a cold, unsympathetic eye on
the whole idea of insurrection, but nevertheless, it is easy to
trace in his pages the design of Government to withhold any
measure of Parliamentary reform until the country was in a
ferment and then when a partial concession had been obtained
and the further step of Catholic and Presbyterian emancipation
seemed inevitable, to complete the design by forcing the
constitutional movement into armed revolt in order to terrify
'the landed gentry' and others into sacrificing their country's
hard won liberties and accepting the Union.

Books and Pamphlets

In addition to those mentioned above I have included only
such as have been found of special value. Any serious student
of the period, will, of course, consult the various biographies
and volumes of correspondence of persons associated with
military activities, or civil administration, such as Cornwallis,
Castlereagh, Pitt, Grattan, Holland, Lake and so on.

1. Reports from the Secret Committees of the House of
   Commons (1798) and of the House of Lords (1798). The
   appendices of these reports include numbers of proclamations,
   orders, informations and returns and the latter report
   contains verbatim evidence of the examinations of Thomas
   Addis Emmet, Arthur O'Connor, Dr. McNeven, Samuel
   Neilson and Oliver Bond.

2. John Jones: *An Impartial Narrative . . . from Authentic Letters.*
3. Philip Harwood: *History of the Irish Rebellion of* 1798. (1848).
4. James Alexander: *A Succinct Narration of the Rebellion in the County Wexford, especially in the vicinity of Ross* (1800).
5. William Snowe: *Statement of Transactions at Enniscorthy on 28th May.* (Written from Bray in 1801).
6. A Wexford Freeholder: *Observations on Mr. Hay's History.*
7. William Shaw Mason: *A Statistical Account and Parochial Survey of Ireland* (1814-19).
8. J.M.R. (Richardson): *Six Generations of Friends in Ireland* (1893).
9. Dinah Wilson Goff: *Divine Protection . . . during the Irish Rebellion,* 1798.
10. Joseph Haughton: *Narration of Events During the Irish Rebellion in* 1798.
11. Thomas Hancock: *The Principles of Peace* (2nd. Edition), 1826.

This book is chiefly derived from *Six Generations* and Joseph Haughton. The author was of opinion that different objects commended themselves to two great classes of insurgents. 'By some, civil liberty—a spacious pretence in all ages, to the warm and enterprising—by others, uniformity of religious Faith—an imposing object to the dark and bigotted . . . it appeared obvious that a deep-rooted animosity was concentrating its forces on either side, nothing short of a dreadful conflict would extinguish their mutual hatred in mutual slaughter.'

12. Charles Jackson: *A Narration of the Sufferings and Escape of Charles Jackson.* (4th Edition, 1802).
13. Anonymous: *Minutes of Proceedings of a Court of Inquiry against Colonel Henry Peisley L'Estrange* (1802).
14. Rev. Patrick F. Kavanagh: *A Popular History of the Insurrection in* 1798.
15. Wheeler and Broadley: *The War in Wexford* (1910). This work is chiefly useful for the inclusion of extracts from the

Detail Book of the Camolin Yeoman Cavalry and also the personal narrative in its entirety of Mrs. Brownrigg of Greenmound.

16. R. Radford Rowe: *Reports on Interesting Cases* (1824).
17. Sir John Moore: *Diary*, Two Volumes, (1904).
18. Sir John Moore: *Life and Letters*, (1923).
19. Patrick Donovan: *A Commentary written for the Commemoration of the Battle of Ross* (1948).
20. Archibald M'Laren: *A Minute Description of the Battles of Gorey, Arklow and Vinegar Hill* (1798).
(From British Museum Copy, British Microfilm Service, P.14464. Microfilm in National Library, Dublin.)
21. Jordan Roche, L.R.C.S.: *A Statement and Observations, etc.*, (1798).
22. R. R. Madden, F.R.C.S.: *The United Irishmen—Their Lives and Times.*
23. Verax: A letter addressed to the printer of the *Dublin Journal* (probably in August, 1798).
24. Veritas: *A Vindication* of the Roman Catholic Clergy of the Town of Wexford in reply to Verax. (1798).
25. Veridicus: *A Reply to the Vindication of Veritas* (1799). The author was Sir Richard Musgrave.

MANUSCRIPTS

Rebellion Papers and State of the Country Papers in the State Paper Office, Dublin Castle.

Tithe Applotment Books, Public Record Office.

Fraser MSS., Public Record Office.

Luke Cullen MS. relating to County Wexford, included in the valuable collection of Madden MSS. in the library of Trinity College, Dublin.

DIARIES AND OTHER FAMILY DOCUMENTS

Ainsworth Transcriptions. National Library, Dublin, including extracts from Bayly papers, quotation from the Diary of Elizabeth Richards of Rathaspick (Orpen papers), etc.

The *Narrative* of Mrs. Brownrigg of Greenmound, published in Wheeler and Broadley: *War in Wexford* (1910).

The *Narrative* of Mrs. Jane Adams of Summerseat (Somerset), County Wexford. Published as an appendix in Crofton Croker: *Researches in the South of Ireland.*

The *Narrative* of Mrs. Newton Lett of Killaligan. The original is in the National Library, Dublin, 70 pp. of MS., marked 'purchased from Mr. O'Toole, Dec., 1942'—published in *The Past*, No. 5, 1949.

Reminiscences of a Fugitive Loyalist, 1798. *The English Historical Review*, Vol. I, (1886), pp. 536-544.

The author was a clergyman and magistrate and a newcomer to Enniscorthy.

M.S. account of the life of Charles Lett (1773-1853) in County Wexford. In the possession of Mrs. John Ainsworth (formerly Lett).

Appendix I.

ON THE 10th of June, 1795, a deed was executed between Andrew Forde of Ballyfad and Anthony Perry of Inch 'confirming onto the same Anthony Perry that part of the lands of Inch then in the possession of Anthony Perry and whereon Anthony Perry erected a dwelling house and offices consisting of forty-three acres, two roods and also that part of the lands of Inch called Ballyoak, then in the possession of the said Andrew Forde containing seventeen acres'.

This apparently relates to Perry's marriage settlement. Andrew Forde was his father-in-law.[1]

This settlement had an interesting sequel, for little more than seven months later—namely on the 19th of January 1796, Perry mortgaged these same lands to John Doran of Arklow! The reason for raising money on the security of his property may be surmised from the fact that the deed of mortgage is witnessed by two Dublin attorneys—Edward C. Keane and Matthew Dowling.[2] The latter was Perry's first cousin and swore him into the Society of United Irishmen in 1797. He suffered prolonged imprisonment in Fort George as a result of Perry's information.

On the 13th of June, 1810, there is the memorial of an indented deed between Richard Hetherington of Dublin and Peter Murray of Woodmount. Apparently between 1798 and 1810, Perrymount either came into the possession of, or reverted to Hetherington because this deed records a leasing of these lands to him for £137.12.9d. per annum during three lives—namely those of Mary Forde, daughter of Andrew Forde of Ballyfad (aged thirty-two years), M. Talbot son of William Talbot of Wexford (aged twenty-two years) and Roger Talbot of

[1] Registry of Deeds, Dublin—Book 492, No. 319122.
[2] Ibid—Book 502, No. 319633.

Castle Talbot (aged twenty-two years).[1] As already stated Anthony Perry was the only son of a Dublin Cardmaker of the same name, who died in 1770. His father's brother was 'Francis Perry of Dublin, Gent' and Anthony was a beneficiary under his uncle's will (Probate 7th June, 1794) to the extent of one-third share of property in Dublin at Usher's Quay, Arran Quay, Aungier Street, Hoey's Court and York Street. This Francis Perry had apparently no children, but he had three nephews, Matthew Dowling, Anthony Perry and Ambrose Moore of Dublin, a silversmith and a niece, Margaret Hoey, the wife of a stationer.

The Will of Anthony Perry of Perrymount is dated 9th February, 1798 and it was proved on 16th August, 1798. Mention is made of his late father Anthony Perry, his late Uncle, Francis Perry and his sons Andrew, Francis and Anthony.[2]

---

[1] Ibid—Book 262, No. 428520.
[2] These latter particulars are derived from *Betham's Genealogical Abstracts*. Public Record Office, Dublin.

Appendix II.

THE FOLLOWING is from an important MS. containing a commentary by a man who was in Wexford during the early days of the rising and who accompanied the insurgents until he succeeded in escaping on the march from Gorey to Arklow.

Wexford } The Information of Robert Edwards—who had been with the Rebels.

27TH MAY. Left Dublin alone a month since to go to Wexford, about some business with Mr. Le Hunte—on the morning of the 27th May saw numbers of men preparing Pikes and taking them out of the Ditches where they were concealed, and proceeded to the house of a Mr. Fitzgerald who lives four or five miles on the North side of Wexford and who had collected numbers of Pikes, with the assistance of a Magistrate, which he then had in his house—The Rebels attacked the house and got the Pikes.

Informt. proceeded to the house of Col¹ Le Hunte to acquaint him of what he had seen and the Col¹ sent round to his Yeomen in the neighbourhood to meet him at Castlebridge—Inft. went there likewise where he saw a Captain of the North Cork Militia who had brought one hundred and thirty-five men (as Inft. was told) out from Wexford and who proceeded by the low road to Oulard, while the Cavalry took the upper road.

Inft. returned to Colonel Le Hunte's and has heard that the same eveng (Sunday) the Infantry attacked the Rebels at the hill of Oulard with great bravery, but were all cut off except five, who returned—Inft. saw five officers brought into Wexford dead.—The Cavalry did not engage, but Lieutt Cavanagh of Le Hunte's Corps made

227

a cut at a person of the name of Roach who commanded the Rebels, and one whom Cavanagh had been particular in making a good soldier while he was with the Corps.

28TH MAY. On Monday morn^g Inft. went into the town of Wexford and remained there untill Thursday—on the Monday what he chiefly observed in Wexford was numbers of people coming into the town from the country around and particularly from Enniscorthy, which had been attacked by the Rebels about eleven o'clock, and which they succeeded in taking—was told that only a few of the Army were killed there and that but for the people in the town setting fire to their own houses, as he says, the Army could have maintained their ground there.

29TH MAY. During Tuesday there did not any disturbance take place in Wexford—the army kept all quiet and many of the townspeople armed themselves to act with the army and assisted in building walls across the streets which were the principal avenues into the town.

30TH MAY. The following morning at 3 or 4 o'clock an alarm was given that the Bridge was on fire—it was set on fire by the Rebels on the North side and about 100 feet of it consumed—as the wind blew from the North the whole would have been burned but that the soldiers cut down a part of the work to prevent the communication of the flames.—They were not fired upon while doing this, nor does Inf^t believe that the Rebels were there in much force on the North side, but were chiefly in the town and on that side.

This was considered as a signal for the Rebels to attack the town, to prevent which the Army and Yeomen marched from the town to the mountain of Forth, which lies south of Wexford about three miles and where it was understood the Rebels were in great force—having heard that a party of the Army were coming towards Wexford from Duncannon Fort the troops who had proceeded from Wexford endeavoured to form a junction with them, but before this could be effected the rebels had attacked them[1] to the amount of about 200 as Inf^t was told and either killed or took prisoners the whole of them.— They did not kill the men belonging to the Artillery, keeping them to manage their guns—one officer he heard escaped.—The Army which had marched from Wexford attacked the Rebels, but after losing some of

[1] That is, the troops from Duncannon, Fawcett's advance guard.

their men and a Col. Watson of Le Hunte's corps they retreated into
the Town—one man of the name of Wardeck rode into the town before
the rest and told everywhere that the whole party he had left behind
had been cut off—but he was afterwards taken into custody, as it was
known that he had said this to prevent the people of the town from
making resistance.

Upon the report brought in by Wardeck the Yeomen and Army
who had remained in the town very soon quitted it and went into
vessels and boats, but could not get off as they were aground.—The
Rebels marched into the Town and took possession of the Barracks
and the Quays—soon as they got upon the hill of the Barracks they
hoisted a white flag there upon a pole, and another at the same time
was hoisted on the Bridge, and shortly after all the ships in the harbour
likewise had white flags—at the Barracks they then hoisted a green flag
which was answered by the vessels.

31ST MAY. On Thursday morn^g Inf^t was taken a prisoner by the
Rebels and forced to join them and was stationed as a Centinal at one
of their posts—but on some pretence got a pass to allow him to go
out of the town and in the afternoon of Thursday went to Castlebridge
and was not again in Wexford.—It was on Monday or Tuesday, he
cannot recollect which that the Four prisoners were liberated from the
Gaol—Harvey and Fitzgerald were two of them, but does not recollect
the names of the others.—The Military let them go to prevent the
Rebels from making any attempt to free them—but as soon as the
Army left the town the Gaols were opened and all the prisoners let loose.
—Inf^t is not personally acquainted with any of those four men, but
when he saw them riding at the head of the rebels and enquired who
they were he was told their names—

While Inf^t remained in the Town two men were shot by the Rebels,
one of them a Yeoman who had fought at Enniscorthy—Four houses
were destroyed, Mr. Boyd's, Clifford's and Daniell's—and another—he
heard the people say that things were to be new settled but does not
well know what was meant by this, as he only communicated with the
lower sort of people.

1ST JUNE. On Friday morning the person who had taken Inft. up in
Wexford[1] called upon him at Castlebridge and took him on horseback
behind him to Vinegar Hill, which is just over the town of Enniscorthy.
—There were not at that time more than 150 persons there because in

[1] A carpenter named Kelly.

that morning about 500 had gone from thence to join the party who were to attack Newtownbarry—in the evening about seven o'clock a few men returned from Newtownbarry and reported that the rest who had gone had been killed—they expressed much vexation at this and said that their commander ought to be tried for having brought them to fight where they could not succeed—does not know who this Commander was, but believes he was not one of their chief officers.[1]

2ND JUNE. Inf[t] returned the same night from Vinegar Hill to Castle-bridge where he remained on Saturday, nothing particular that he recollects occurred there on that day.

3RD JUNE. The following morning he was called up to get ready to march for the camp at Gorey and was taken up behind the same person who took him to Vinegar Hill—on getting to Gorey separated from the person and attempted to escape across the Bridge; but no single person was allowed to pass—was joined by a man with whom he went to a house in the neighbourhood and next morning went to the camp which was on the hill above the town.[2]

Never saw so many people together as were there—has seen a Review in the Phoenix Park, but it did not appear that there was half the number at the Review as were in this camp—he heard them say there were 30,000 but thinks the number exaggerated.

He heard that they had Five pieces of cannon; he saw two of them, but was also informed that those which they had taken at Gorey had been render'd useless.—The whole party were armed—every man had either a pike or fire arms, and a great many had firearms.—They had plenty of provisions from about the camp, victuals were sent from a distance by the friends of the persons who had joined the camp.— They had not any salt and complained much for the want of it. —They had not many pots or kettles with them, but mostly dressed the meat in the neighbouring houses.

Roach whose name he believes was Edward was the principal Commander there—he had several officers under him—Mich[l] Sinnott was one and John Rossiter and others whom he cannot recollect—there were likewise several Priests in the camp—does not think they were officers, but directed and advised and seemed to be above the officers.

[1] Father Moses (Mogue) Kearns.
[2] Edwards has mixed his dates here. He was apparently at Castlebridge when the action was fought at Tubberneering on the 4th and went to Gorey on that day and not the 3rd as stated.

On Tuesday marched from the camp with a party who were going to Arklow, and from thence Inf[t] made his escape and came to Dublin. June 10th, 1798.[1]

[1]   I.S.P.O.

Appendix III.

THE FOLLOWING references to the camp at Three Rocks are from the statement of Loftus Richards who, with his brother, was sent to negotiate on behalf of the Wexford Garrison.

On entering they were surrounded by many thousand vagabonds of whom they enquired, to whom they should address themselves as their leaders; and they answered 'To Father John Murphy, of Boulavogue or Lord Edward Fitzgerald', as they usually stiled him. They soon after met this reverend gentleman, on horseback and on communicating to him the object of their mission, he said 'He did not know what terms they could expect from the treatment which he had received: for that, by burning his house and property, and obliging him to take shelter in the ditches, he was under the necessity of raising the whole country'. From his savage aspect, they had very great reason to be alarmed for their safety: they therefore advanced from a crowd, who were debating on putting them to death; and sent for Mr. Edward Fitzgerald of Newpark, another rebel chieftain, who came to them, and treated them with more civility and humanity and who dispersed the rabble. . . . They instantly obeyed. He then led them to a miserable hut at the top of the rocks, which seemed to have been appropriated to the double purpose of an hospital and a place of shelter for their leaders; but in the thatch of which there were many holes. Soon after their arrival they were obliged to deliver up their arms and accoutrements. Mr. Robert Carthy who seemed, from the authority which he exercised, to be chief in command, approached and asked them, 'What terms they could expect, when at the moment they were entering into a treaty for surrounding the town, there was an army marching against them from towards Taghmon? and see,' said he pointing to a mob of assassins, 'where I have my men drawn out to attack them'. And they made a most extraordinary appearance being armed with pikes, scythes, hay-knives, scrapers, currying-knives and old rusty bayonets fixed on poles: but a good number of them had muskets. They expostulated with Carthy and told him they had good authority for saying that the thirteenth regiment which advanced as far as Taghmon, had retreated on hearing of the defeat of a detachment of the Meath regiment; but to satisfy them, they proposed that Fitzgerald, his brother and himself should take horses and proceed to meet the regiment if coming, and to tell Colonel Bradshaw who commanded it of the circumstances as they then stood. They advanced within a mile of Taghmon, where they met a large foraging party proceeding to the rebel camp, with from six to eight car loads of provisions, and who declared that the thirteenth had retreated. They then returned speedily to the insurgent camp, and made their report; but Carthy came forward again and said, 'Can these men be sincere? the whole country towards the barony of Forth is in flames!' alluding to the village of Maglass which our retreating army had set fire to, as they had been treacherously fired on by a party of rebels, who lay in ambush there for them. Mr. L. Richards replied if they had any doubts of their sincerity that he would remain as an hostage with them while his brother and Mr. Fitzgerald went to Wexford, to which they assented. He then remained in the hut, with a guard at the door, and, while there, he perceived through a hole in the wall, about a foot square, a great number of men around with the desperate weapons which he before described, incessantly marching except that now and then, they knelt down to pray; and at the end of each prayer, bent their bodies towards the earth, and thrust the forefinger of their right hand into their mouth, as far as the extremity of the knuckle. When he had remained about three hours in that unpleasant situation, Mr. John Hay came to him and said 'that the people had agreed, that he had betrayed Fitzgerald and therefore that he must be put to death!' Mr. Richards insisted on the contrary. Mr. Hay went off, returned in about half-an-hour and declared, it was universally agreed 'That Fitzgerald had either sold them, or that he had betrayed him'. And he swore vehemently that the forces would be marched immediately towards Wexford, which Mr. Richards said 'would be the best thing to prove his sincerity'. In about five minutes after, the whole body of the rebels proceeded towards Wexford; and as they marched, continued to fire muskets, and give the most dreadful yells. They left two sentinals to guard Mr. Richards; who, in the meantime examined the wounds of six unfortunate wretches who lay upon straw in the hut, and who, though badly wounded, did not receive any nourishment or medical assistance. . . .'[1]

[1] See Musgrave. Appendix XXI, 3.

Appendix IIIA.

Colonel Richard Maxwell's report to General Eustace on the evacuation of Wexford:

Sir,

As Major General commanding in this district, I beg leave to inform you that I was ordered (in your absence) by Major General Fawcett to send two Hundred men of the Donegall Regiment and one six pounder to Wexford, with which party I proceeded last Monday evening, and arrived at our destination at four o'clock the next morning without interruption: as soon after as in my power I endeavoured to get the best information of the defences and true state of the place, which I communicated to Capt. Pigot, aid de camp to Gen¹ Fawcett, and sent him express to the General considering that he could make that representation more fully than by any letter of mine circumstanced as I was at the time, but particularly pressing hard for an immediate and strong reinforcement as the only means of preserving the town. That evening (Tuesday) I had the satisfaction of learning from Gen¹ Fawcett that (on the application of the Mayor of Wexford) he would send by daybreak next morning a company of the Meath, two Howitzers and the 13th Regiment but instead of the arrival of this reinforcement we had the mortification to hear at six o'clock that the Meath and the Howitzers had unfortunately fallen into the hands of the Rebels; on which I immediately advanced . . . with my six pounders, two hundred of the Donegall and a Hundred and twenty yeomanry cavalry, in hopes of effecting a junction with the 13th and by our joint efforts to endeavour to retake the artillery; having proceeded between three and four miles, we perceived a considerable Body of the Rebels posted on strong Heights to our left, from whence they fired on us with one of the Howitzers and a small Field piece, as well as by an irregular fire of musquetry from behind the ditches; which we returned for some time; but on seeing no prospect of the 13th Regt. and fearing we might be cut off from Wexford (not being fully supported) I returned to the Town with my six pounders and Donegall party, having two men missing, one or two wounded, and one of the artillery Horse killed; this failure of the assistance expected and so anxiously wished for, greatly dispirited the troops, who were in general much fatigued, as well as cast a gloom on the principal gentlemen in Military Command, several of whom, and others also, requested I would hold a consultation to determine what was best to be done; and under the Circumstances of the place being considered untenable, from the want of assistance and provisions, without any sudden prospect of relief in either case, the Rebels being in Considerable Force, and in possession of great part of the adjacent country; added to all the Loyal Inhabitants quitting the Town and those only remaining, spies and Friends of the Rebel cause, the general opinion was that the State of the place became so critical, that nothing could be done but to evacuate it, or devote the Troops to destruction; notwithstanding this unfavourable situation of the Garrison, I could not prevail on myself to acquiesce in the opinion of the meeting, and ordered all the troops to their respective stations for the defence of the place; when these arrangements were regulated, I visited the different Barriers and to my astonishment and concern, I found that two Yeomanry corps had quitted their posts; in one instance where I had every reason to expect 60 or 70, I found but *three* privates; and in another, nearly a like number, not a single individual, where there became in a retired part of the Town an open and safe approach for the Rebels; in addition to this Defection or timidity, I recd information that the men of the North Cork Regiment refused to obey their officers, or to take any further part against the Rebels; the state of the place then became in my own opinion so truly alarming, that I could not reconcile to myself further opposing its evacuation; unwilling to take on my own responsibility the consequence of subjecting the Loyal part of the Garrison to the resentment of a numerous and sanguinary Rabble; and with the final advise [sic] of a few of the most respectable gentlemen, I reluctantly called in the outposts, and commenced a retreat from the Town, on Wednesday, the 30th, about eleven o'clock in the forenoon, with part of the North Cork Regt. and Captains Ogle, Boyd, Richards, Grogan, &c., &c., corps of yeoman Cavalry and Infantry, and the Donegall detachment, the whole arriving at Duncannon Fort and Geneva, without any interruption from the Rebels worth noticing; but with excessive fatigue to the troops, from the circuitous route we were unavoidably obliged to pursue. . . .[1]

[1] I.S.P.O.
    It will be noted that there is no reference in this account to the dispatch of the two envoys from the town to the insurgent camp. It is possible that this mission was only undertaken after the departure of the troops,

Appendix IV.

THE OFFICIAL ACCOUNT of the battle of Tubberneering is contained in a dispatch from Loftus to Lake, written at Carnew and dated Tuesday, June 5th, 1798:

It is with inconceivable concern that I have to state to you the events of a business which took place yesterday by which I understand that Colonel Walpole has lost his cannon and was driven back into Gorey and which place by every report is in the hands of the enemy. I have tried in vain to ascertain it to a certainty. I had directed Col. Walpole to meet me at Gorey on Sunday morning. His answer was that he had received certain intelligence that the Rebels were on Ballymore Hill within five miles of Gorey and that this was the place to move from with the best effect, but wishing to talk the business over with him I wrote a more decided letter to him desiring he would join me at Gorey that night, Sunday, which he did leaving one hundred of his men to co-operate with him in his proposed attack.

When he arrived at Gorey I told him that I could get no intelligence to be depended upon respecting the actual situation and Force of the enemy.—He said he knew their situation and that he had a force equal to anything they could do.

In consequence of his great earnestness to attack the Rebels at Ballymore the following arrangement was made.

Col. L'Estrange was to move from N. Town Barry by Scarawalsh Bridge to Ferns whom he was [to] aid and wait for Col. Walpole.

The two Lt. companies making 100 men was [sic] to march from Carnew to Camolin and wait Col. Walpole's further orders.

Col. Walpole himself was to move from Gorey by Clough to look at Ballymore and to halt at Ferns—and I gave him 150 of the Antrim Militia as a support.

237

Lt. Col. Scott was to cover his left flank by moving through Bally-canoe to Ballymore. All these movements took place at ten o'clock and upwards of two hundred Yeomanry and a party of the North Cork and Antrim Regts. were left to take care of the town.

I accompanied Col. Scott and we had passed Ballycanoe when I heard a firing on my Rt. and directly sent to the Antrims detachment to support Col. Walpole [myself] moving on with Col. Scott round Ballymore.

It seems that the affair was very short, at least the firing did not continue ten minutes and I had the mortification to find that the Rebels had defeated Col. Walpole and securing his cannon had taken post on the hills above Gorey—in such force and so very advantageously posted that it would have been madness to have attacked them with two hundred men. After examining their situation for some time and finding it impossible to get into Gorey—and not knowing the fate of that place—I with the opinion of Col. Scott moved to bring off the detachments ordered to Camolin and Ferns, which I fortunately effected without loss tho' with great fatigue indeed to the Troops I brought them to this place.

I must observe that the two Lt. Companies [were to] wait at Camolin for their orders, but retreated to New Town Barry and marched on here this mom^t, accompanied by Lord Bective and part of the Meath Regt. and Donegall.

I find the enemy so very strong not only at Enniscorthy but at Gorey were [sic] I am confident they brought fifteen thousand more yesterday that after consulting with the field Officers and examining into the state of provisions and ammunition—I have determined to move to Tullow where I shall wait further orders, but I beg to press it upon you that in an enclosed country like this where Cavalry cannot act the enemy is very formidable and can only be met by a sufficient force and a well regulated artillery—for every hill and ditch is a post for them. . . .'

Appendix V.

A Minute Description of the
Battle
of
Gorey, Arklow and Vinegar Hill.
Written by
ARCHIBALD M'LAREN
late Sergeant in the Dunbartonshire Highlanders,
who was an Eye-Witness to most of what he relates. . .
Printed in the year MDCCXCVIII[1]

[He states that when the Dunbarton Regiment marched from Dublin, he remained behind as a member of the Commander-in-Chief's guard. What he relates up to the battle of Arklow is, therefore, based on hearsay].

The first night the Regiment arrived at Wicklow and being informed that an Officer and four Privates of the Royal Army had been killed at a place which the soldiers called the Devil's Glen, they next morning (with a detachment of the Ancient Britons and a few Yeomen) went in quest of the Rebels who had committed the murder. When they had entered the Glen they discovered some sculking parties, of whom they killed to the amount of Eighty and then returned to Wicklow; from whence they proceeded to Arklow and from Arklow to Gorey, where they were joined by the Londonderry and Armagh Regiments of Militia, the Tyrone and Suffolk Light Companies, the Ancient Britons,

---

[1] From British Museum Copy. (British Museum Microfilm Service P. 14464). I am indebted to Dr. R. J. Hayes of the National Library, Dublin, for the opportunity of studying this rare document. The writer refers on the title page to six previous publications relating to events in his military career. He does not care for 'Croppies' which is understandable, but his account is obviously genuine and he touches on so many interesting points that no apology is necessary for the following extensive extracts.

and a detachment of the Antrim Militia, all under the command of Gen. Loftus. On the 4th of June this Army moved in two Divisions, having received intelligence that the Rebels were encamped on Carrigrew Hill. The Division under Colonel Walpole kept to the right, and General Loftus with the Dunbarton Highlanders and 5th Dragoon Guards took to the left. The Rebels who had that morning left Carrigrew Hill were advancing to Gorey, when they met a woman who told them that the King's Troops were at hand, upon which they concealed themselves behind the ditches on each side of a narrow Glen through which the Troops must pass. Finding himself thus surprised he [Colonel Walpole] opposed his Cannon and Musketry to the Fire and Pikes of the Enemy; the contest lasted twenty minutes but one of the cannons being dismounted; the Colonel killed; his men overpowered by superior numbers and on the point of being surrounded, were forced to retreat: the Rebels turned their own cannon upon them. General Loftus who had advanced farther on the left, heard the firing and supposed that the enemy had been beat, he therefore turned off to the right, with a design to interrupt them in their reatreat; but when he reached the Scene of Action, the first object that caught his eye was Colonel Walpole lying dead. . . . In an adjacent field our Troops discovered a great number of Saddled Horses a few of which some of our Sergeants (though reluctantly) were obliged to pike lest the Rebels should return and take them. General Loftus seeing no Enemy, moved on for Gorey, which route he suspected the Rebels to have taken. In the course of this march the Soldiers observed a great number of dead Croppies whom their friends had dragged into houses as they past [sic]. As this little Army came opposite to Gorey Hill the Rebels fired a Field-piece, the Bullet fell a little to the right of the Grenadiers. The General who did not think it prudent to attack them in such force marched off for Carnew: Thus ended the Battle of Gorey, in which was lost 25 men and the Rebels 150:[1] Thus ended the Battle of Gorey, which the Soldiers called Gorey Races because each strove to outrun his fellow. The Rebels got possession of Gorey and our Flying Troops retreated to Arklow, which flattered the sons of Rebellion with the fairest prospect of future success.

On Thursday the 7th of June, those of our Regiment who were left behind received orders to hold themselves in readiness to march. Before ten o'clock at night, the Old Custom House Yard was filled

[1] From the nature of the fighting and pursuit it is probable that these figures should be reversed.

with Coaches, Chaises, Jaunting Cars, etc. At nine on Friday morning we moved off. . . . As we passed the Royal Exchange our good friends the Yeomen honoured us with their cheers. . . .

It was past twelve at night ere we arrived at Wicklow and as no beds could be had at that time, we took up our lodgings at a Quaker's Meeting House.

From Wicklow we proceeded to Arklow where we arrived about the middle of the day. . . . Having marched through the town we took up our ground on the left of the Durham Fencibles a few yards beyond the Barracks. Here we had scarce thrown off our Knap-sacks when an alarm was given that the enemy was approaching, owing to the report of a Rebel Deserter; but so little credit was given to his assertions that a Regt. in the Field was making preparations to punish one of their own men, but the arrival of some Yeoman Cavalry who declared that the Rebels were within a mile of us, suspended the opperation [sic]; then all was in a bustle, the Aid-de-Camp, a Brigade Major galloped about and call'd for the General; the soldiers began to examine their Flints; and those who had got their Loaves served out were willing to eat as much as possible lest the bread should fall into the hands of the Croppies, so great an aversion did we bear to those unprincipled gentry, who had even dared to entertain the presumptuous idea of destroying our Glorious King and Constitution. The Inhabitants who had remained in town, fled to their boats which lay ready upon the Beach to receive them. General Needham drew all the Troops out of Town and formed them to the best advantage. The Cavin [sic] Regt. with the Gorey dismounted Cavalry, the Arklow Yeomanry and some detachments from other Corps, under the Command of the brave Colonel Maxwell, extended a line from the centre of the town along the Ditches almost to the Fishermen's Huts on the left near the sea. On the right of the Cavin, the Durham Fencibles were drawn up in front of their encampment with two field pieces.

Detachments of the Armagh and some others occupied the end of the Main Street adjoining the King's Highway on the right of the Durham. The Antrim and some other detachments were stationed in the Barracks on the right of the Armagh near the River in rear of the Town. The 4th Dragoon Guards, the Ancient Britons, and several Corps of Yeoman Cavalry were drawn up on the Dublin road, north side of the Bridge. Those were the different positions of the Army when the Dunbartonshire Highlanders were ordered out about a Quarter of a mile in front of the Army to line the Ditches on each side of the main road where the Enemy was advancing: It was my chance to be of this party.—When the Croppies appeared with their green flags fixed to Pole-heads in imitation of Colours; they fired which compliment was returned. As I did not think my Halbert a proper weapon to annoy the Enemy at a distance, I exchanged it for a Firelock. . . .

I remember to have seen one fellow who stood in the centre of the road, neither advancing nor retreating, but seemingly encouraging others; several shots were fired at him without effect; but at length he was brought to the ground. When we had exchanged about a dozen rounds, an Aid-de-Camp from the General ordered us to retreat and join the Armagh in the Street. This we did in seeming confusion, and the Rebels (no doubt) thinking that we fled, came on with great vaunting, setting up a loud Huzza. One fellow (an Officer) inspired with spirits and Whiskey (of which they had drank very copiously at a village called Coolgreene) galloped in front, having something resembling a stand of colours in his hand, (Sergeant Major Fisher of the Dunbarton has it in his possession) and Waving his Hat, called out 'Blood and wounds my Boys, come on, the Town is ours'. But ere the foolhardy Hero was aware he turned the corner of a House which brought him almost to the mouth of a Field piece, surrounded by some hundreds of Soldiers ready to fire or receive him on the points of their Bayonets. . . .

A volley of small shot laid his Horse sprawling in the dust and broke his own Thigh; though he fell under his Horse he had cunning enough to lie still and might probably have passed for a dead man had he not . . . raised his head to take a peep round about him: this being observed four or five bayonets were plunged into his body. In the midst of his agony he stretched out his arm to shake hands with one of the soldiers. . . . But the soldier sent a Bullet through his head. . . .

Another Cavalier who came coursing at his heels, having his Horse shot under him, ran into a house, where in the hurry of Battle he might have lain concealed, had he not had the temerity to fire a Pistol at Corporal McDougald. This corporal give him a sleeping dose. . . . Father Murphy . . . as he rode forward encouraging his Troops to advance an unmannerly Grape Shot obtruded itself upon his skull before the good man had time to put forth his Hand to stop it. Some of his followers who saw him fall dragged him into a House. . . . Our troops to deprive them of their sculking places, set fire to one Hut; the flames communicated with others and reached that in which the remains of the Mob-deceiving Father Murphy lay. . . .

Though the Rebels were deprived (as I said) of their sculking places yet they still continued to pour in fresh Troops . . . but a six pounder

which served as a base to the music of the Musketry, made many of
them dance back in quick time.

Having failed in their attempt upon the Main Street, they extended
a long irregular line in front of the Durham and Cavin (as I think)
with a design to turn our left flank, but those two Regiments with the
dismounted Gorey men and Arklow Yeomanry plied them so well
with hard Pills that many a poor Croppy died under the operation.
However, their Musket-men kept up a brisk fire from behind ditches
(which covered them up to the very chin) and sorry I am to say with
too much success, for three brave fellows of the Durham and one of
the Londonderry fell martyrs to their Loyalty. . . . Colonel Maxwell
had his Horse shot under him; he likewise had several Bullets through
his Hat. . . .

Two field pieces taken from the Londonderry at Gorey were played
upon us from an eminence opposite the Durham and Cavin; but as
the chief management of these Pieces was entrusted to a Sergeant of
the Antrim who had been made their prisoner, we sustained no damage
for some time, for at every shot he pointed with so much elevation that
the Balls whistled over our heads; but being observed by one of his
officers, he was so far obliged to rectify this seeming mistake that the
very next Shot struck one of the Durham Field-pieces, and smashed
the Carriage to pieces which pleased the Croppy officer so well that
he cried out 'a Hundred Pounds for a Soldier' meaning I suppose that
one trained Soldier was better than many of his rude followers.

Another shot struck the Halbert out of the hands of a Sergeant of
the Cavins; some forced their way through the Tents, and others struck
the roofs of Houses.

When the Dunbarton Detachment had retreated according to orders,
the enemy advanced on the right of the road in front of the Barracks
(which was well surrounded by a strong wall), but they did not seem
to relish their entertainment, for they turned their back before they
completed their visits. As the General was riding up street, a man of
seeming respectability came and told him that the Rebels were making
full speed for a lane which led (on the right of the Barracks) from the
River to the centre of the Town. To check their progress the General
ordered out a Subaltern, Sergeant and twelve men . . . under the
command of Mr. Douglas. . . .

As we turned down the lane to take possession of our post, we
observed some hundreds of the united gentry advancing towards us;
but we sent so many leaden messengers to forbid their visit, that
many of them (to speak in a military stile) fell back. . . .

When their design of forcing the lane had miscarried, they attempted to ford the water, but in this they were also disappointed. However, that it might not be said that they came on a Fool's Errant [sic] they retreated across a Field to a Protestant Clergyman's house which they burnt, destroyed and drank all the Liquor in the cellar; and set up such a hallooing and hooping as might be mistaken for the music of Savages at an Indian sacrifice . . . in a few minutes thereafter I was ordered up the street to observe how matters went on. As I passed though the Lane an old woman popt. her head out of a Cabin door 'Holy Jesus' (said she) 'the sound of the guns shakes the cabin. . . .'

The Firing still continued at the south of the Town and I was tempted to make towards it. . . . When I reached the scene of Action, I found the Troops firing away behind a ditch, a good way to the front of the spot where the Battle had begun; some Croppies had by this time entered the Street by the end of the Bridge under cover of the Smoke, but this post was so well defended by some detachments from different Regiments that their scheme proved abortive; for Colonel Sir Watkin Wynne with some of the 4th and 5th Dragoons, a part of his own Regiment and some Yeoman Cavalry, made a charge which they attempted to resist with their Pikes; however it was but an attempt for they were obliged to fly; though Capt. Knox lost his life in the contest. The Foot on the right ceased firing while the charge lasted; but when the pursuit dropt they commenced again. By this time the Sun was almost set, and the Rebels began to retreat in every direction.

I remember we took a tall fellow prisoner; he protested his innocence, and showed us a protection he had from Dublin, but the soldiers were for dispatching him; however I did what I could to save his life and succeeded so well that a Sergeant of the Tyrone or Londonderry took him to the General, tho' next morning I saw him lying dead in a brook below the Barracks and some of the Arklow Yeomanry swore that he had been Tarr'd a few days before. . . .

I returned to my post and stood all night (as did the rest of the Troops) under arms. Though many of the most headstrong of the Rebels were for renewing the attack at night, some of the more moderate dissuaded them from their purpose; which was perhaps no difficult task. . . . I took an opportunity of surveying the road and adjacent fields. I confess I was shocked by seeing such a number of miserable wretches brought by their own folly to an untimely end; some were shot through the head, several through the breast; others had half their faces torn away by the Cannon Balls; some were stript quite naked by the Soldiers while others were suffered to lie in their rags, because they

were not worth the taking. I remember to have heard two wounded
Rebels in a ditch, consulting how to make their escape, but two
Yeomen with their Swords put an end to their consultations. Dead
men and Horses were lying in heaps in the Fields, on the Road, and
in the Ditches.

As I was returning to the Barrack my Nose was accosted with a
disagreeable Smell, upon enquiry I found it to proceed from the body of
Father Murphy, whose Leg and Thigh were burnt into the very bone.
. . . I could eat no meat for some days. His Head was fixed upon the
wall of a Burnt Cabin. . . . On the Monday after the Battle, a Yeoman
found an old servant of his own wounded in a ditch, and while he was
bringing him to the General, had it not been for the interposition of
an officer, the soldiers would have killed him. On the same afternoon
two men were found among straw, in one of the Fishermen's Huts.
Tuesday forenoon a Courtmartial sat, and in the afternoon the three
were hanged upon three trees in the centre of the Town. The Yeoman's
servant said he would die by the Green; and strange to say, yet true it is,
that as he hung a small piece of a green branch fell into his bosom
by way of a posie. Every day the Picquets and Foraging parties
discovered some dead bodies in the fields or ditches; and indeed the
stench was intolerable, for two days had elapsed before the slain were
buried, nor were their funeral obsequies attended with much ceremony;
some being dragged by the heels, others, with cord about their necks
were drawn into the burnt huts and the walls knocked down upon
them. I saw Father Murphy's head, three days after the Battle, lying in a
ditch before the Tents.

. . . . , ...

On the 19th of June we left Arklow and after marching a few miles
we halted by the way side . . . after two or three hours halt we resumed
our march, in the course of which the Horsemen killed about fourteen
or fifteen fellows whom they found sculking behind ditches with arms
in their hands. We entered Gorey without the least opposition, the
Rebels having abandoned it with precipitation a few hours before our
arrival. The afternoon brought on a deluge of rain—The Troops
quartered themselves the best way they could in the Houses, most of
which were dispoiled of their furniture. We found a Howitzer which
was ordered to be spiked: Books, Papers, etc., were scattered about the
streets, and great quantities of Pork, Beef and Mutton lay stinking in many
of the Houses which the Croppies had occupied. Some Yeoman Cavalry

discovered an emaciated wretch concealed below a parcel of hay; they brought him to the General, his arm was tyed in a handkerchief with a piece of red tape, and his shirt sleeve bloody, being asked when he received his wounds he answered in a whining tone 'At Arklow'. The General ordered them to let him go; but another fellow taken near the same place was not so lucky; as he was found with a Pike in his hand, some kicked him, others struck him, and two Yeomen with swords knocked him down and clove his skull, Captain Hardy of the Durhams with one stroke of his sword severed his head almost from his body.

On the 20th some light troops marched through the Town, we followed them and arrived at Oulart where we encamped; here Major Lambert with a hundred and twenty-six of the North Cork were cut off by the Rebels. . . .

We had not been above an hour at Oulart when an Express arrived from General Lake to General Needham in consequence of which we were ordered to strike our tents and begin our march in the dusk of the Evening with positive injunctions to observe the most profound silence. The occasion of this movement was, that the Commander-in-Chief had designed to collect as many troops as he thought expedient to surround Vinegar Hill the reduction of that place being so necessary for carrying on his operations against Wexford, the headquarters of the Rebels—Generals Johnson and Eustace with a column from Ross (where they had lately gained a most signal victory over the sons of rebellion) were already arrived in the neighbourhood of Enniscorthy. Lieutenant General Dundas, Major Generals Sir James Duff and Loftus had also brought their columns close to the scene of action where they lay impatient for daylight. In order to co-operate with these troops we marched all night and arrived about daybreak within a mile and a half of the hill[1] on the left, where we lay for about an hour, rolled up in our Blankets in the ditches by the road's side. I was just beginning to dose when I heard some of our men cry out that they had a fair view of Vinegar-hill from a piece of rising ground a little to the right of us. I instantly started up and repaired to the place above mentioned, from which I could easily discern the Rebel flag and tree of liberty displayed from an old windmill near the summit of the hill (but the hill is by no means so high as some people imagine) it is said that upon this and an adjacent height they had 30,000 men (including those at Enniscorthy)

[1] The writer does not explain why Needham's force required from dusk to daybreak on a June night (say six hours) to travel not more than seven miles. See pages 159 and 160

but I am doubtful if they could muster quite so strong; for though the day previous to the attack many were employed in casting musket bullets to the amount of 6,000 and in making other necessary preparations for a vigorous defence, yet I am told that hundreds slunk away and took a french leave of their fellow rebels.

When our men (General Needham's army) saw the rebel flag they showed the most eager desire to begin the attack, but it was near six o'clock before we were put in motion and even then, instead of marching straight forward we were ordered to take a circuit of at least five or six miles, which made it impossible for us to be up in time. This we much dreaded because ere we had marched two miles from our last ground we heard the cannonading from General Johnson's column who began the attack upon the town of Enniscorthy near the Foot and a little to the right of Vinegar-Hill. Lieutenant General Dundas commanded the other column supported upon the right by Major Generals Sir James Duff and Loftus.

All the field pieces attached to the different Regiments which composed these columns, commenced firing by pouring out thick showers of grapeshot among their enemies. The night before the attack the Croppies had planted a field piece at the foot of the hill with which they no doubt promised to perform wonders, but the day of the battle it was dragged up to the top where it was made to contribute its part (in concert with some other field pieces) to vomit forth the thunder of rebellion against his Majesty's liege subjects. The Croppies' musket men lined a ditch that ran along the foot of the hill and kept up a very smart fire which did some damage to our troops.

Alexander Hatterick of the Dunbartonshire Highlanders, who was taken at Gorey[1] told me that they had the impudence to entertain some hopes of a victory. Several of them asked his opinion and when he gave his advice to retreat he narrowly escaped being Piked; however the thunder of the Royal Artillery had a wonderful effect in making them change their tone, a large party of them attempted to force their way on the left of the hill, but the Light Brigade under Colonel Campbell who occupied that post saluted them with a shower of hail stones something harder than boiled peas, drove them back and pursued them up the hill. In their retreat they were severely galled by the grape shot which flew from the field pieces belonging to the Dunbartonshire Regiment, under the command of Lieutenant Dougald M'Dougald.— General Needham's army (of which I made one) was by this time advanced on the left almost to the foot of the hill, when we were

[1] Tubberneering.

commanded to order arms and stand at ease. I jumped upon the top of a ditch whence I could observe the confusion among the Croppies. I remarked in particular one fellow galloping up and down upon a white horse[1] in apparent disorder and though I am told the Gentleman was a Commanding Officer I am apt to believe he would willingly have given his commission to be out of the reach of the unmannerly bullets which threw up the dust about his horse's heels.

As soon as the Light Brigade had gained the summit of the hill, a general footrace commenced among the Croppies and happy was the man who could sit down some miles hence and thank his legs for carrying him so far out of the reach of danger. When the enemy retreated the cavalry pursued and made great havock among them, though some of them had the impudence (when they got on the inside of a ditch) to turn about and fire on their pursuers.

It was thought by some of the soldiers (who are perhaps none of the greatest politicians) that General Needham had orders to let the Croppies escape as Government might be unwilling to cut off so many deluded wretches in the very midst of their sins. The reason they assign for this opinion is, that had the General advanced a little sooner and drawn a line from the left of General Dundas's column to the river, it would be impossible for the rebels to escape to Wexford, but this is but mere conjecture and very immaterial to us whose sole business was to obey.

The King's County and 89th Regiment ran up the hill with great impetuosity, every man firing as he thought proper, and so eager were they to get at the enemy that the swiftest man was the foremost regardless of any order. Colonel Scott marched up his Regiment in line and took possession of a great quantity of ammunition, etc., left by the rebels. He received the thanks of General Dundas for not suffering his men to break their ranks. . . .

I am told that some of the soldiers found a great quantity of plate and other valuable articles which the rebels had collected in their marauding excursions through the country.

In this battle two subalterns, two sergeants and sixteen privates were killed, two field officers, two subalterns, one sergeant and sixty-two privates wounded. After the battle we saw a young woman with a hat and green band lying dead by the wayside. Another who came to visit her husband had the mortification to see him killed before her face and in addition to her misery, her daughter a girl of eleven years of age had her arm shot away almost at the shoulder. . . .

[1] From the description, this was probably Father Thomas Clinch of Enniscorthy.

As we passed we saw a woman wounded in a ditch, surrounded by three or four children. She told the General and other Officers a piteous tale, how her husband had been forced to join the rebels and how she herself had been wounded. She begged the soldiers to shoot her, but they would not contaminate their arms with a woman's blood. She asked for a drink of water and they gave her grog which revived her drooping spirits for a little. The General took the children and sent them to Dublin to be taken care of, and Death took the Mother. . . .

General Needham's army after receiving a little refreshment of Bread and Whiskey took the route for Wexford, in pursuit of the flying enemy: the road for a mile or more was strewed with dead bodies. That evening we arrived at Mr. Hay's mansion[1] where we encamped all night.

Several prisoners were brought in, one of them was shot near the Park Gate, others were set at liberty by the General's orders. . . . In the morning we continued our march for Wexford; some miles to the westward we saw a great dust ascending from the road, but Colonel Skerret who had recourse to his perspective glass told us it proceeded from our own troops who were making to Wexford by the Carrick-ferry road.

Having passed Castlebridge we halted and Lieutenant Colonel Bainbridge with some horse and foot returned to Mr. Dixon's house, where he found a hat with a green cockade and band. When we halted it was reported that Wexford Bridge had been burnt by the rebels, in consequence of which a light horse man was detached off who returned with orders for us from General Lake (who was arrived in town) to return to Owlart [sic] Camp. On our retreat I saw Mr. Dixon's house (from which I suppose the hat had been taken) all in flames. A few miles from Castlebridge we set fire to a Malt House belonging to the Arch-Rebel Fitzgerald.

In the evening we encamped at Owlart. Next morning I saw a large pit where some of the brave but unfortunate North Cork were buried; Their legs and arms were bare and a few of their fingers and toes were eaten by the pigs, but we covered them decently with earth.

[1] Ballinkeele.

Appendix VI.

READERS MAY BE interested in the following extracts from *Holinshed's Chronicles* (1586), Vol. II, and also the references to the use of the Irish language in County Wexford at a much later period.

Rosse, an hauen towne in Mounster not far from Waterford, which seemeth to have been in ancient time a towne of great port. Whereof sundrie and probable coniectures are given, as well by the old ditches that are now a mile distant from the wals of Rosse, betweene which wals and ditches the reliks of the ancient wals, gates, and towers, placed betweene both are yet to be seen. The towne is built in a barren soile, and planted among a crue of naughtie and prolling neighbours. And in old time when it flourished, albeit the towne were sufficiently peopled, yet as long as it was not compassed with wals, they were formed with watch and ward, to keep it from the greedie snatching of the Irish enimies. . . . It hath three gorgeous gates, Bishop his gate, on the East side: Algate, on the east south east side: and South Gate, on the south part. This towne was no more famoused for these wals, than for a notable woodden bridge that stretched from the towne unto the other side of the water, which must have beene by reasonable suruete twelve score [feet] if not more. Diuerse of the pooles, logs, and stakes, sticke to this daie in the water.   (PAGE 25).

The inhabitants of the English pale have beene in old time so much addicted to their civilitie and so far sequestered from barbarous savagenesse, as their onelie toong was English, And trulie as long as these impaled dwellers did sunder themselves as well in land as in language from the Irish: rudenesse was daie by daie in the countrie supplanted, civilitie ingraffed, good lawes established, loialtie observed, rebellion suppressed, and in fine the coine of a young England was

like to shoot in Ireland. But when their posteritie became not altogether
so warie in keeping, as their ancestors were valiant in conquering, the
Irish language was free dennized in the English pale: this canker tooke
such deepe root, as the bodie that before was whole and sound, was
by little and little festered, and in a manner wholie putrified, and not
onlie this parcell of Ireland grew to that civilitie, but also Ulster and
the greater part of Mounster, as by the sequele of the Irish historie shall
plainlie appeare. But of all other places, Weisford with the territorie
baied and purclosed within the river called the Pill, was so quite
estranged from Irishrie, as if a Traveller of the Irish (which was rare
in those daies) had pitcht his foot within the Pill and spoken Irish, the
Weisfordians would commend him forthwith to turne the other end of
his toong and speake English, or else bring his Trouchman with him.
But in our daies they have so acquainted themselves with the Irish,
as they have made a mingle mangle or gallimaufreie of both the
languages, and have in such medleie or checkerwise so crabbedlie
jumbled them both together, as Commonlie the inhabitants of the
meaner sort speake neither good Englishe nor good Irishe. (PAGES 10
and 11).

Father Patrick F. Kavanagh, referring to County Wexford in 1798
states that 'in a sense it was more English and less Irish than any other
part of Ireland. The Irish language had long ceased to be spoken.' This
was no doubt true of his own part of the county, which was the
neighbourhood of Castlebridge, but it was certainly not true of many
other parts. Irish was sufficiently widely understood at or near that time
in the diocese of Ferns for sermons to be preached in it. James Alexander[1]
states that most of the Wexfordmen he heard speaking during the
battle of New Ross spoke in Irish, as was the case also in the neighbouring
County Waterford village of Glenmore. As late as 1814 the Protestant
rector of Adamstown and Newbawn reported that 'the people are
very sagacious, industrious and obliging. They are also sober and
honest. During my constant residence there for the last ten years the
Irish Language which was generally spoken is getting rapidly out of
use and the civilization of the country is happily supplying its place.'[2]
About the same time the Rev. James Gordon, the historian, who was
then rector of Killegny near Clonroche, wrote: 'The poorer classes are
industrious and quiet in general, not, however, averse to insurrection if
opportunity should occur; they are in extreme subjection to the

[1]   *A Succinct Narrative.*
[2]   Quoted by W. Shaw Mason: *Statistical Account,* Vol. I, page 5.

priests . . . the language among the peasants, except the Protestants, in their discourse with one another is mostly Irish, but they all speak English. The only man who could not speak English died a few years ago.'[1]

[1] Ibid—page 456.

Appendix VII.

'. . . on the 4th of June we found Ross in a state of siege. A body of
rebels amounting to between fifteen and eighteen thousand men were
said and believed to be collected at Castlehill and the adjacent heights
within a mile or two of Ross. On the night of the 4th of June some
thousands of the above body were reported to have deserted that post.
. . . At four o'clock in the morning of the 5th of June, the rebels were
observed to be preparing for irruption; previous to which a young
man in black, a Lieutenant Furlong, on entering our lines with an
intent to summon the town was shot; as was another who rode after
him. They were well mounted. . . . Shortly after, the rebels in large
bodies issued from Corbet hill and rushed headlong (driving before them
a quantity of cattle) upon the outposts who, after a short resistance,
were driven into the town. The rebels did not give *quarter* to *some*
who in the first *shock* were willing, 'tis said, to receive it. Such a scene
of confusion perhaps never before happened in any country. Cavalry,
infantry—men, women and children, like a torrent running toward
the bridge: and pike men and musqueteers shouting after them.

'Having dismounted early in the engagement and near the scene of it,
to relieve a soldier that was wounded, I could not recover my horse
—he was carried onward and I was obliged to take the same route
until I fell near to the Barrack-gate, from which dangerous situation
I was helped, and brought into the barrack by General Johnson's
servant: There were remaining in it seven or eight dragoons and an
assistant surgeon. The barrack gate was shut, after a few shots were
fired on the rebels who were running down the street by the barrack
gate. The barrack commands a view of the great part of the town.
I saw plainly most of our little army retreat over the bridge to the
County of Kilkenny; and turn to the left towards Waterford. Between

six and seven o'clock it was supposed there were three thousand rebels in the town, the upper part of which was set on fire by them. The flames extended almost to the barrack, from which, with others I passed through a door that opened into a street which led to the market house[1] at which there was a Donegall post and two small pieces of artillery which did great execution. While I was in the barrack I did not perceive that it was attacked. The rebels were dispersed throughout the town and in the greatest confusion looking for *one another*. Of this circumstance General Johnson availed himself. . . .'

(The writer mentions a second and third attempt on the part of the insurgents before they withdrew.)

'The remaining part of the evening was spent in searching for and shooting the insurgents, whose loss in killed was estimated at two thousand, eight hundred and six men.'[2]

---

[1] Bakehouse Lane.

[2] Jordan Roche, L.R.C.S.: *A Statement and Observation*, &c. (1799).
   (Late surgeon to the 4th Brigade and 89th Regt.)
   This statement of an eye-witness contains several points of interest not mentioned elsewhere. (Library of Royal Irish Academy).

Appendix VIII.

LETTER FROM Henry Lambart Bayly of Lambarton to his father, describing the battle of Arklow:

. . . Thus prepared, about 4 o'clock all of us at our posts I first saw in a moment thousands appear on the top of ditches, forming one great and regular circular line from the Gorey Road through the fields quite round to the Sand Banks near the sea as thick as they could stand. They all put their hats on their pikes and gave most dreadful yells. I could clearly distinguish their leaders riding through their ranks with flags flying. One of our guns was placed in the road above the Barrack, two in the fields to the left, opposite the little Rock. This last first opened on the Rebel line, and I had a fair opportunity of seeing the effect of grape shot, as I was within 10 yards of the Cannon. It tumbled them by twenties—I could see large gaps made which were as quickly filled up. This awakened them from the seeming astonishment into which our appearance had thrown them for a few moments—not having expected to find us prepared. They then rushed on like madmen, and their cannon began to play—two in the front of our line and a third more to the Southward which advanced very near us. They fired them quick, but two of their gunners (privates of the Antrim whom they forced to serve the Cannon) fired rather high by which means many lives were saved—but our cannon was fired by a rascal who had deserted from the Antrim and was determined to do mischief. He planted it for half an hour opposite our line of cavalry and how we all escaped unhurt, Providence alone can tell—the balls went through our ranks and close over our heads for a great time. At last the General seeing that we were the object ordered us about a hundred yards to the rear: there we were more covered—but we heard them over our heads as clear as possible—they struck several houses and the Barracks during the Cannonade; they also kept up a very brisk fire of musquetry from all quarters, and the Pike men who were the most numerous rushed forwards on all sides to take the town—skulking along the ditches. At first our troops from too great eagerness fired at random and at a great distance. Latterly they reserved their fire until they came within one hundred yards and then every shot told.

The North Arklow and our dismounted cavalry made a most gallant defence and fired as briskly as the line and even pursued them—their attacks were well concerted and most desperate—they rushed on in every quarter from the Chapel quite round to the river above the town—they forced in the Fishery which they immediately set on fire—however they were driven from thence by the Ancient Britons and poor Knox's corps who charged them out and dashed up the lane after them: poor Knox from his eagerness went too far and getting into our line of shot a six pound ball killed him and two of his men. At the Upper Town the rebels rushed down in the very mouths of three cannons which opened upon them with grape and soon cleared the road of men and horses—for the leader Father Murphy, rode at their head with a fine standard in his hand and on it a cross with *Liberty or Death.* He made them kneel several times between Gorey and Arklow to pray for success and told them he would catch the bullets in his hands—which they firmly believed, but I suppose he only vouched for musket balls for a six pound ball struck him, taking off his head.

They made their last charge about half past seven to cover the retreat of cannon having spent all their Ammunition. Had we one hour's light the cavalry would have cut thousands off, but at night when they retreated it was quite dark. They carried off nine cartloads of Dead, which with those we found here and the numbers we hear are dead of wounds in the woods and ditches cannot amount to less on the whole than 1,000 men. . . . During the Action numbers remained at the House of Lamberton praying for success—had they conquered it would have been safe, but for revenge they burnt it. The House is a melancholy sight—most of the offices have escaped. . . .[1]

[1] From the *Bayly Papers—Ainsworth Transcriptions.* National Library, Dublin.

Appendix IX.

THIS IS A description of the battle of Arklow, as related to Luke Cullen by a participant on the insurgent side:

They were met by the advance of the Royal Troops near a place called the Charter School and shortly after they came to a skirmish. Mr. Byrne and the officer leading this party of the Royal Troops had now come within pistol shot of each other and both of them fired but without effect. The popular army now pressed forward and Mr. Byrne and this officer came on to measure swords, but the latter fell and his division being without a Commander thought it prudent to fall back on the garrison. . . .

Mr. Byrne had but very few gunsmen in his division but under the cover of these few he made one attempt to bring his Pikemen up to Col. Skerrett's Durham fencible regiment which were at this time entrenched behind very high and close hedges. In his attempt to carry this point he had to [cross] the open fields exposed to the heavy fire of this well disciplined regiment which arrived there on that day fresh and free from fatigue having been conveyed there in the best travelling vehicles that could be pressed for that purpose in Dublin: but it was in consequence of their scanty supply of ammunition that they had to relinquish this enterprise.

There were, I think, three guns planted at the South end of the barrack yard and their fire was directed along the road that led from Coolgreany and those guns constantly kept a stream of grape and round shot pouring along that road. Father Michael Murphy, in order to silence those guns . . . led on a division of his Wexford men to capture them. Mr. Byrne seeing this bold attempt was rapidly advancing to his assistance. He was here assailed by a shower of musketry, many of his men fell, himself narrowly escaped . . . he led on his Pikemen to the aid of that intrepid party. They had now advanced within nine perches of the guns when a discharge from one of them killed the leader and some others. The attacking party staggered . . . and fell back.

Mr. Byrne still rallying his men met some of the gunsmen from the front rank retiring. He endeavoured to force them back and asked them if they were going to quit the field on the point of victory. They replied that they had fired their last round and could get no more. . . .

Richard Monks, a Wexford Captain, observed this havoc by the enemies' guns and requested Esmond Kyan to direct a shot from their own artillery on that point. The military gunners that had been taken beyond Wexford were now put from the guns whilst Monks and a few other intrepid fellows served the guns for Col. Kyan. The first shot he fired passed through an ammunition cart . . . and the next struck one of the royal guns and broke its carriage in pieces, killing thirteen of the men that attended them. Some years since the police sergeant then stationed in the old barrack showed me where they were interred. . . . Mr. Byrne . . . was in the thickest and hottest parts of it, cheering, encouraging and rallying the men.

The ammunition of the insurgents (having) been completely expended they drew off with a sulky reluctance carrying off every one of their wounded that they possibly could get.[1]

---

[1] In view of the frequent references to Garrett Byrne, it is a reasonable guess that Luke Cullen's informant on this occasion was a member of the Wicklow contingent.

Appendix X.

LUKE CULLEN indicts General Needham for his conduct in Oulart on the morning of the 20th of June, when he and his force arrived from Gorey and made McAuley's Hotel his headquarters. His authority is Daniel McAuley, the proprietor of the hotel.

The latter states that Needham and some of his officers among other paltry acts, actually scrambled for the contents of the till like thieving children! A scout named Patrick Doyle sent out from Vinegar Hill to locate these troops saw them from Boleyboy Hill. The scout was seen and a party was sent out in his direction who in their march up the hill found some old men hidden in the whins and shot them. Two of them were Michael Prendergast and John Grimes.

General Needham 'left Arklow at 3 o'clock on the 19th of June and marched to Gorey—nine miles—where he halted. . . . Next morning he arrived in Oulard—nine miles more. On the same evening he marched from Oulard to Solsborough instead of marching to take up the position assigned to him by Gen. Lake. His march from Oulard to Solsborough was exactly six miles. The original position assigned to him was on the east side of the Slaney near Mr. Beal's brewery and to the south of Vinegar Hill. This would be placing him exactly between Wexford and Vinegar Hill, a spot that it is said he showed a great reluctance to occupy. . . . This thing I know myself from the nature of the ground, that it was impossible for any man to be in Gen. Needham's elevated position and not to see Gen. Ed. Roach rapidly advancing over a plain level country at the head of his Shelmaliers until he reached Darby's Gap within two miles of Enniscorthy and from that place for about three miles Gen. Ed. Roach acted in the most cool and military manner in repelling the charges of the pursuing cavalry and covering the retreat.

The popular army had now got into Wexford and Gen. Needham got to Ballinkeele, a distance of 3 or 4 miles to the mansion of Mr. Hay where he was time enough to dine that evening and to illuminate the neighbourhood in commemoration of the victory with the blaze of the Catholic chapel of Ballymurren standing in the Ballinkeele domain. The night of the 21st and next day was one woeful scene of violating, plunder and burning.

Appendix XI.

LETTER FROM A. Brownrigg (a magistrate) to Colonel Blaquiere—
written from Gorey, 17th January, 1799:

. . . a very false statement of Transactions that Happened at the Fair of
Ballycanew, 30 Novr. last having appeared in the Publick Papers,
I beg leave to Represent that great Abuse was given there to several
Country people without any Provocation by the yeomanry, viz. By
Part of Ballaghkeen Cavalry and Hunter Gowan yeomen, who Burned
about 9 houses that night, the above Transactions passing without
Proper Notice gave I suppose encouragement for the most wanton
Barbarity (which might make the Rebels rise again) and took place on
Wednesday Night 16 inst. from about 7 o'clock till half past 12 two
Chapels one Priest's House and 9 others consumed; the Priest's House
being Plundered of Silver Chalices etc and servant girl killed before
it was burned, as also the other Houses Plundered; another of the Houses
a Shoemakers the man was shot and afterwards thrown into the Slaney
this Conflagration extended the Length of 6 miles from the first House;
this originated (as I am informed) from a Recruit who had been in the
Rebellion that ran into Capt. Sparks House (he is a very loyal man and
a Half Pay Officer) in the Absence of the Family at service Hour on
Sunday 13 to save himself from some Cavalry who were searching
for Robbers the Sd. man Fired at and Killed Sergt. Johnson Ballaghkeen
Troop and wounded another that were searching the House for Arms,
so the Captain of the Troop ordered the House to be set on Fire and
the man was Burned in the House which Being a good sleat one was
consumed with every sort of office thereto Belonging and 2 of the
Servants shot on Wednesday 16 inst a great many yeomen being
assembled at the burial of Sd. Sergt. from Ballaghkeen Troop and

Wingfield Yeomen Hunter Gowan and Gorey Troop and others a party out of them committed Sd Flagrant Acts on night of the 16 inst endangering the Peace of the County and the Lives of us several Loyal Inhabitants now living at our Places of Abode. I went to look at the Body of the Girl, and destroy'd Places and a great number of People was there Quite Peaceable most not having a stick in their Hand. . . . I hear John Redmond, and Willm Porter, both of Ballaghkeen Troop knows every man concerned and were with them some time about 10 Horsemen were concerned 3 of whom it is said were the Godkins of Gorey Troop—the People will not go to Gorey to Prosecute. . . . . I Request my name to be secret as a Gentleman of this Neighbourhood has been and is yet in continual fear of his Life for Forwarding a Prosecution against a yeoman for Night murder. . . .[1]

In January, 1799, Father Nicholas Redmond of Donoughmore, memorialised the Lord Lieutenant stating that he had been in the same parish since 1777 and never did anything contrary to his oath of allegiance to King George III 'or was he out with Rebels, or in the smallest way engaged in the late Rebellion'.

He mentioned that on the 13th of January, 1799, the chapel of Monamolin was burned and that on Tuesday night (the 15th of January) his own house and chapel of Ballygarrett were set on fire by horsemen unknown to him. He claimed £137.4.5½d. damages.[2]

At the end of the same month (January, 1799), James Murphy of the Glebe, Monamolin, was murdered at his own house by Edward Stacy ('Stacy the Brogue'). A ballad said to have been sung by the young widow, ended with the lines:

> And for the man I loved I'll live and die his bride;
> Leave me in Castle Ellis down by James Murphy's side.[3]

[1] I.S.P.O.
[2] Fraser MSS. Public Record Office, Dublin.
[3] I.S.P.O.

Appendix   XII.

PHILIP HAY of Ballinkeele was a Captain in the 18th Light Dragoons. He was the youngest son, but his father, who died in 1796, left him the principal part of his estate. His elder brother disputed the will and took possession of the property. Philip returned home and instituted proceedings against his brother. The action ended in April, 1798, in favour of Philip.

It was stated later in the court of the King's Bench that he joined Richards' Corps as a volunteer and fought with him against the insurgents in Enniscorthy and was also in action against the insurgents at Three Rocks on the 30th of May; that he was made prisoner on board ship in Wexford with Richards and that he was forced to join when 'a spit was put to his throat by some of the rebels whilst others of them girt a sword upon his side'. He was probably in the insurgent ranks at Tubberneering. Eleven days after his capture he escaped through the insurgent outposts to Carlow and thence to Dublin where he reported to Castlereagh and Marsden at the Castle.[1] Lake told him his conduct was above suspicion, but on representations of 'certain magistrates and others of the county of Wexford' he was brought before a Courtmartial on the 27th of July (President, Col. Ancram) who honourably acquitted him on the grounds that 'the prisoner's conduct proceeded from arbitrary compulsion'.

Philip Hay afterwards applied for and received compensation as 'a suffering loyalist'. The Earl of Kingston (formerly Lord Kingsborough) having made some slighting and other references to Hay, the latter accompanied by two friends, challenged him to a duel.

---

[1] Castlereagh wrote to Elliott (15th June): 'I understand from Captain Hay of the third foot who has been in their hands for some days and has just made his escape, that they have little ammunition and still continue, though in immense numbers, in a very irregular and undisciplined state'.

The noble earl refused to fight stating 'I do not consider you a fit person for me to meet, as you have evaded appearing before a jury of your countrymen to take your trial for the swindling transaction you have been guilty of in obtaining compensation as a suffering loyalist when you were in fact a rebel and I most certainly will not meet you. . . !'

This discreditable episode did not deter the Earl of Kingston from publishing a *Narration . . . in the case of Captain Philip Hay*, undated, but about 1807.

Appendix XIII.

IN 1798 there were two priests named Dixon living in the neighbourhood of Castlebridge. Father James Dixon was Parish Priest and the other Father Dixon was presumably a curate. They were both relatives of the Thomas Dixon mentioned in the text.

The second named was sentenced to transportation and sent to Duncannon Fort the day before the insurrection.[1] He had been charged with having attempted to induce one Francis Murphy to become a United Irishman and he was informed against by Murphy who paid the penalty with his life in the Bull Ring, Wexford, in the early days of June.

Father James Dixon was arrested much later and confined to Waterford Gaol awaiting transportation when Lord Cornwallis was approached on his behalf by the Protestant Rector of Ardcolm as follows:

'Petition of Revd. Frederick Draffen, Incumbent of Ardcolm near Wexford in behalf of Revd. James Dixon, late P.P. of said parish at present a prisoner in Waterford Gaol.

'Had full opportunity of observing the conduct of Revd. James Dixon he did consider him to be very averse to any rising of the people for the disturbance of Publick Tranquillity. Confirmed in conversation on forenoon of 27th August. Petitioner escaped to Wales on evening of 27th May and some days after Mr. Dixon arrived at Milford with the wife and daughter of his neighbour Col. le Hunte of Artramont.

'Father Dixon was afterwards courtmartialled on a charge of being present at the battle of Gorey[2] but Mr. Draffen questioned some Protestants who had been compelled to be present at that engagement, but found no confirmation and is fully convinced of Fr. Dixon's innocence.'[3]

[1] Hay.
[2] Tubberneering.
[3] Frazer MSS. Public Record Office, Dublin.

He was sentenced to transportation for life.

It may be that Mr. Draffen was made to suffer for his kindly effort on behalf of his friend and neighbour, His modest claim for £107 to cover the loss of 'furniture, books, a mare, clothes and gun' was disallowed by Government.

Father James Dixon is stated to have returned from Australia after some years and to have been appointed to the parish of Crossabeg in 1819. It is pleasant to record that, according to local tradition, he attended the funeral of Mr. Draffen. He himself died in 1840.

Appendix XIV.

THE FOLLOWING are extracts from *Reminiscences of a fugitive loyalist in 1798.* The author, a clergyman and magistrate, lived in Enniscorthy at that time and was a newcomer there. The entire publication will be found in *The English Historical Review*, Vol. I, (1886), pp. 536-544.

About 23 May 'Luke Byrne, a brewer of Enniscorthy . . . called on me and with much hesitation said he understood that he, with the Roman Catholics of the town, were to be slaughtered during the night by the Orangemen, of whom I believe, there were scarcely ten persons in the town, and almost all of them men of the North Cork Militia.[1] . . . I desired him to keep quiet, in which case I pledged myself for his security, but added that if, as I suspected, this was adopted as a pretext for arming and rising by the Roman Catholics, the Protestants were prepared and would inflict a dreadful punishment for the first aggression. . . . Hardly had he left me when Thomas Cloney, of whose treason I had proof, demanded an interview. As it was dark I did not grant it to him in my own house, but took him to the market-house in which was the main guard. He whispered intelligence and apprehension of the same purport as Byrne. . . .'

'I was present at the execution of William Beaghan who was hanged on 28 March 1801 for the murder of the Rev. Francis Turner. He walked to the place of execution without shoes, a common practice at the time and which, it was said, intimated that no information had been given against his accomplices. He advanced to the fatal spot with a steady step, reading a small book of devotions . . . and seeing the gallows over his head, he deliberately and without emotion turned down the leaf of the book, which he placed in his bosom saying: "Here I am

---

[1] There were, however, ninety-one officers and men of the North Cork Militia and two hundred and forty yeomanry actually in the town at that time.

at last arrived at my journey's end. Now I call heaven and earth to witness that I die innocent; that hand, art or part I had not in the death of Mr. Turner; and now I am ready". This delusion of innocence was very common with dying culprits, however numerous and credible the witnesses against them; almost all of them died with a firmness and serenity worthy of the most meritorious cause, some even uttering effusions of their native humour.'

'In justice I must allow that the rebels often displayed humanity and generosity deserving of praise and admiration.'

'Father Sinnot in Enniscorthy sheltered Mr. Nunn, the Protestant clergyman and Father James Doyle of Whitechurch screened as many of that faith as he could.'

The writer mentions Dudley Murphy and Murtagh Murphy, both of whom fought in the attack on Enniscorthy. Dudley was afterwards killed in Wexford and Murtagh was sold to the King of Prussia.

Appendix XV.

MS DEALING with the life in County Wexford of Charles Lett
(1773-1853), in possession of Mrs. John Ainsworth (formerly Lett).
The following extracts are of special interest:

'In 1833 Charles Lett removed from Seafield to Tincurry, a farm . . .
pleasantly situated on the river Slaney near the church and village of
Ballycarney, between Enniscorthy and Newtownbarry. The first
house that was burned in the rebellion of 1798 by the King's Army
was that of Priest Murphy in Tincurry, it was done as a reprisal for
the murder of Lieut. Bookey near the Harrow.'

Referring to William Lett (of Kilgibbon) the MS. states:

'On the retreat from Wexford the rebels being encamped at the
Three Rocks on the Forth Mountain, it was necessary to give them as
wide a berth as possible. On arriving at the Scar of Barristown which
they expected to ford, the tide was found to be full in and that was
impracticable. Some accused him of treachery in thus bringing them
where they were cut off from escaping should the rebels, who were
much the stronger party, attack them and for a time William Lett was
in extreme peril of death. Had it not been that his brother Richard
Lett of Balloughton was there, and invited the officers to take some
refreshments at his house, William Lett would have had a speedy death.
They did not wait for the fall of the tide, but marched round by Goff's
Bridge. It is said that on this occasion a considerable quantity of
valuables was hidden by the soldiers who buried it, expecting to be able
to return and take it up, which in many cases they never did and the
money and plate remain there still about Barristown House.'

INDEX

Adams, Mrs. Jane, 44 (note).
Alexander, James, 36.
Ancram, Col. Lord, 177.
Armstrong, Capt. J. W., 96.
Asgill, Sir Charles, 171 et seq.

Ballynabola, 110.
Barker, William, 78, 89, 162, 206 et seq.
Barrington, Sir Jonah, 165.
Bayly, Rev. H. L., 41 (note).
Bayly, Henry Lambart, 255 et seq.
Beaghan, William, 267.
Beale's Barn, 77, 156, 163.
Bellamont, Lord, 13.
'Black Mob', 12.
Bookey, Lieut., 54, 56.
Boxwell, John, 109.
Boyd, James, 87, 88, 126.
Boyne, John, 53, 55.
Brownrigg, Mrs., 18, 91.
Burrowes, Rev. Robert, 57 et seq.
Byrne, Garrett of Ballymanus, 132, 138, 152.
Byrne, Luke, 77, 152 (note), 267.
Byrne, Miles, 18, 22, 43, 93, 133, 166, 203 et seq.
Byrne, Morgan, 152.

Carrickbyrne, 109 et seq.

Carrigrew Hill, 99.
Carty, Robert, 81.
Castlecomer, 171.
Castlemore, 173.
Catherine de Medici, 4.
Catholic Committee, 15, 16.
Catholic Relief Act, 15, 16.
Caulfield, Bishop, 17, 52 (note), 152.
Clements, Henry, 26.
Clinch, Father Thomas, 24, 164.
Cloney, Thomas, 30, 75, 111, 143, 154, 158, 198 et seq.
Colclough, John Henry, 79, 111, 143, 166.
Corish, Father, 149.
Cornwallis, Lord, 14, 172.
Crawford, Lt.-Col. Robert, 115.
Crumlin Gap, 168.
Curran, Father, 152.
Cushinstown, 110.

Daniel, Major, 145, 146.
Darby's Gap, 154, 163, 165, 166.
Dawson of Fortchester, 43, 67.
Defenders, 9, 10, 150.
Devereux, John, 109, 170.
Devereux, Walter, 109, 120, 170.
Diamond, Battle of, 26.
Dixon, Father James, 265.
Dixon, Thomas, 151 et seq.

271

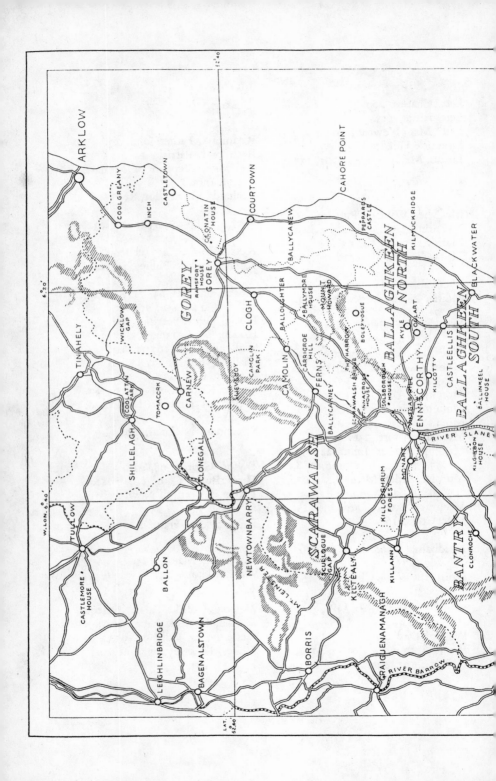

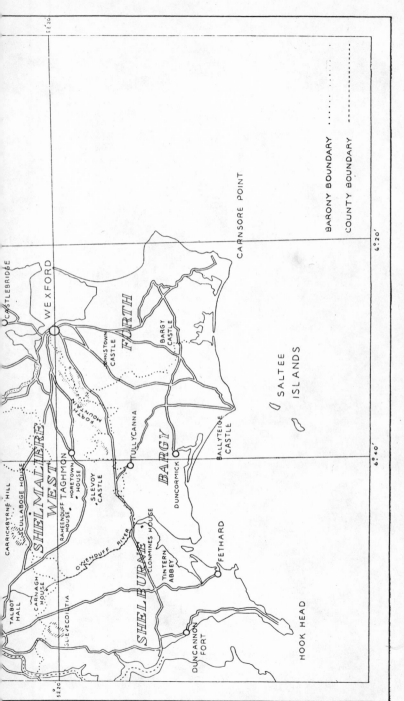

SCALE IN MILES

Based on the Ordnance Survey by permission of the Minister for Finance.